The Mafia at
Apalachin, 1957

D1568475

The Mafia at Apalachin, 1957

MICHAEL NEWTON

McFarland & Company, Inc., Publishers
Jefferson, North Carolina, and London

LIBRARY OF CONGRESS CATALOGUING-IN-PUBLICATION DATA

Newton, Michael, 1951–
    The mafia at Apalachin, 1957 / Michael Newton.
        p.   cm.
    Includes bibliographical references and index.

    ISBN 978-0-7864-6640-5
    softcover : acid free paper ∞

    1. Criminals—United States—History.   2. Mafia—United
States—History.   3. Law enforcement—United States—
History.   I. Title.
HV6789.N494 2012
364.1060974'09045—dc23   2012010699

BRITISH LIBRARY CATALOGUING DATA ARE AVAILABLE

On the cover: (top, left to right) Rosario "Russell" Bufalino
(National Archives), Albert Anastasia, Meyer Lansky (Library
of Congress) and Francesco "Frankie Yale" Ioele (National
Archives); (inset) The main street of Apalachin, New York, 1957
(National Archives)

Front cover design by Rob Russell

Manufactured in the United States of America

McFarland & Company, Inc., Publishers
  Box 611, Jefferson, North Carolina 28640
  www.mcfarlandpub.com

For Hank Messick

Contents

Preface

On November 14, 1957, New York State Troopers raided an estate in Apalachin (pronounced App-a-*lay*-kin), arresting 59 affluent men. Nearly as many more escaped on foot, through the surrounding woods, and managed to elude police. The next morning's headlines hailed the gathering as a summit meeting of organized crime — or, more specifically, the Mafia.

The very name had the power to enthrall and terrify. Since 1891, reports of Mafia activity in the United States had fueled investigations and indictments, editorials and lynching parties. Leaders of the nation's highest-ranking law enforcement agencies quarreled bitterly, and very publicly, over the Mafia's existence. Finally, it seemed, the proof was evident for anyone to see.

Or was it?

For the next two years, a series of investigations at the state and federal levels probed the Apalachin meeting, grilled participants, imprisoned some, then saw them all released by various appellate courts. None of the charges stuck, and in the wake of their dismissal came more published claims that there had never been a Mafia in the United States— or, some claimed, anywhere on Earth.

The truth is more complex than any simple "Yes" or "No." Perhaps the most surprising aspect of the Apalachin conference is that no author in the past half-century has taken time to study it in detail. Often mentioned as a footnote, rarely understood, the gathering remains a pivotal event in both the history of syndicated crime and of the government's response. That meeting literally changed the course of history: inspiring federal legislation to crack down on labor racketeering; forcing drastic policy revisions within the U.S. Department of Justice; and prompting charges of criminal fraud in one of America's most heatedly contested presidential elections. Some scholars maintain that it also paved the way for America's covert war against Cuba and the assassination of two Kennedys.

I owe special thanks to David Frasier, friend of many years and researcher *par excellence* at Indiana University's Lilly Library, for his assistance on this project. Without him, several hundred articles pertaining to events of 1957 through 1960 would doubtless have eluded me, and *The Mafia at Apalachin, 1957*, might have died as one more notion on the drawing board. Thanks also to the gang at Gangsterologists.com — Jeffrey Gusfield, John DuMond, and Richard Warner. Finally, I wish to thank my wife, Heather, for her support during the research and writing of the work in hand.

The Mafia at Apalachin, 1957, aims to close a gap in scholarship concerning both the Cosa Nostra and the broader, more diverse network of organized crime in America. Events appear as they occurred. All dialogue is drawn from published articles, transcripts or interviews, sourced in the book's endnotes. Any opinions offered, if not credited to a specific outside source, remain my own.

· 1 ·

"Our Thing"

Myth surrounds the Mafia as rancid fog once filled the streets of London — or as smoke envelops fire, obscuring its origin, its size, even the damage it has caused. Apologists maintain that no such thing as "Mafia" exists, or ever has. No one has ever sworn an oath to it, or broken any law on its behalf. Of course, there have been murders, woundings, mutilations, but they have been private acts of "honor," carried out as retribution for some injury. No boss directed them for profit, much less any "Boss of Bosses" powerful enough to dominate multiple "families" of crime.

All false.

The Mafia exists. It has been actively involved in criminal conspiracies — has murdered thousands, likely tens of thousands — over some 150 years in Italy, in the United States, and all around the world.

What is the origin of that conspiracy? For all that has been written of the Mafia, is it as powerful as some critics maintain? To what extent has its influence been exaggerated for sensational effect?

The answers to those questions are obscured by time and distance, but the truth is known.

Honored Societies

For decades, crime historians asserted that the Mafia was born spontaneously on March 30, 1282, when oppressed residents of Palermo, Sicily, rose in armed revolt against French/Angevin King Charles I to win independence. Their battle cry, supposedly, was *"Morte alla Francia, Italia anela!"* — "Death to France, Italy cries!" — which yields the acronym "Mafia." Mafiosi were, therefore, simply a group of noble patriots. Some authors still promote that romanticized tale, but most rightly dismiss it as a fable.[1]

In fact, the dreaded name did not appear in print for the first time until 1863, when Siclian playwright Giuseppe Rizzuto staged his drama *I mafiusi di la Vicaria "The Mafiosi of the Vicaria."* Set in Palermo's Vicaria Prison, the play depicts a gang of inmates who extort cash and favors from other convicts at the direction of their boss. However, since *mafiusi* only appears in the title, and never in dialogue, scholars were left to ponder its meaning. The first official mention of a Mafia — spelled "Maffia" — appeared in a report written by Filippo Antonio Gualterio, prefect of Palermo, in April 1865. Gualterio described the "so-called Maffia or criminal associations" as organized extortionists and murderers. In 1868, the term made its first appearance in a Sicilian dictionary.[2]

Despite its formal naming in the 1860s, few Sicilian gangsters referred to their organization as "Mafia." Oath-bound members preferred to call it the "Honored Society" or *La Cosa Nostra* — "Our Thing." A police report from 1876 offers the first description of the Mafia's bloodletting initiation rites.[3]

In fact, we know today that factions of the Mafia existed throughout Sicily for 20 years or more before their crimes were publicized, preying on farmers who exported lemons by the ton to Britain and America. Beginning in the 1840s, if not sooner, Mafia bosses forced wealthy farmers to employ their men and pay a portion of their profits for "protection." Those who refused were murdered, sparking vendettas that decimated some villages. By 1860, the Cosa Nostra had a stranglehold on the Sicilian citrus industry.[4]

There was, also, an older criminal society in Italy. Called "Camorra," it was known by name from 1735, when a royal decree authorized operation of eight gambling casinos in Naples. The term supposedly derives from a combination of *capo* (boss) and *morra*, a popular — but illegal — Neapolitan street game. Some historians, however, claim that the Camorra is an offshoot of the Spanish *Garduña,* a prison gang founded in 1417, later exported to Italy by wandering members. First official mention of the syndicate came in 1820, when police records described a Camorra disciplinary meeting. In 1842, documents exposed a support fund established for imprisoned Camorra members.[5]

As with Cosa Nostra, the Camorra was — and is today — a network of local "families" or "clans," sometimes collaborating, sometimes locked in mortal combat with each other. Its members — known as camorristi — sometimes work in concert with the Mafia; at other times, the two societies wage war for turf with no holds barred.

Invading America

Members of both the Mafia and the Camorra found their way to the United States before the Civil War. The first confirmed mafiosi to land on

American soil, brothers Joseph and Raffaele Agnello, were established in New Orleans by 1860. Natives of Palermo, they recruited other *Palermitani* for their clan, and were opposed in turn by immigrants from Messina, led by Joseph Macheca. Born in New Orleans to Sicilian parents, Macheca had prospered as a blockade-runner during the Civil War, then founded a steamship company while doubling as leader of the *Innocenti* (Innocents), a gang allied with the local Democratic Party.[6]

Conflict between the Agnello and Macheca factions came to a head during the 1868 presidential election. On October 28, following a Democratic rally at the Orleans Ballroom, *Innocenti* member Litero Barba died in a shotgun ambush. His kinsmen blamed Raffaele Agnello, who in turn accused black Republicans. Racist riots ensued, but tension remained between the Palermo and Messina clans, while a third Mafia faction — the *Stoppaglieri*, made up of immigrants from Monreale, Sicily — stayed on the sidelines, uncommitted. In December 1868, Joseph Agnello convened a peace conference at his Royal Street home, but mayhem erupted, leaving Agnello lieutenant Alphonse Mateo and Messinian mafioso Joseph Banano wounded by gunshots.[7]

Mafia violence escalated in 1869. Joseph Agnello led a raid against the Messinians on February 15, wounding Joseph Banano and four others. On April 1, Macheca gunman Joseph Florada killed Raffaele Agnello on Toulouse Street, then was slain himself by Agnello's bodyguard. Joseph Agnello and Salvador Rosa finally killed Joseph Banano, with Pedro Allucho, near the French Market on July 22. Around that time, Salvatore Matranga's *Stoppaglieri* clan joined Macheca's faction to suppress the *Palermitani*. Still, Joseph Agnello continued resistance until he was slain by triggerman Joseph Maressa on April 19, 1872.[8]

Even then, the Matranga-Macheca clan was not supreme among New Orleans mafiosi. Sicilian fugitive Giuseppe Esposito arrived in spring 1879, using the alias "Vincenzo Rebello," and carved out a niche for himself on the local waterfront, supported by second in command Giuseppe Provenzano. Their faction, known as the *Giardinieri,* soon dominated racketeering on the docks and among local produce dealers. An informer, one Tony Labruzzo, tipped New Orleans police to Esposito's true identity in 1881, prompting his arrest by detective—cousins David and Michael Hennessey on July 5. Deported to Italy on September 21 for trial on murder charges, Esposito received a life sentence. Giuseppe Provenzano blamed the Matranga-Macheca clan for Esposito's arrest, a view perhaps confirmed when the Matrangas moved against the *Giardinieri*. Both sides imported reinforcements from their native villages in Sicily, with open hostilities flaring in 1888.[9]

By that time, David Hennessy had been appointed to serve as chief of police in New Orleans, his rise unhampered by his trial in 1882 on charges

A mob storms the New Orleans jail to lynch acquitted mafiosi in 1891 (Library of Congress).

of murdering Chief of Detectives Thomas Devereaux. Jurors found that Hennessy had fired his gun in self-defense against Devereaux, a rival for the chief's position, and while Hennessy briefly left the police department, he returned to accept appointment as chief in 1888. He soon cultivated a relationship with the Provenzano clan, either for profit or, as some historians contend, to gain their covert support in prosecuting rivals now led by Charles "Millionaire Charlie" Matranga.[10]

Giuseppe Provenzano tried to negotiate peace with the Matranga clan, but gave up after emissary Vincenzo Ottumvo was hacked to death with an axe on January 24, 1889. Sixteen months later, on April 6, 1890, Provenzano gunmen killed two Matranga loyalists at the corner of Claiborne and Esplanade Streets. Police arrested several members of the gang, whereupon Matranga mafiosi breached the code of silence to provide the state with evidence. The defendants were convicted of murder in July 1890, but a friendly judge voided the jury's verdict and scheduled a new trial for October 17. Chief Hennessy announced that he would testify for the defense, while exposing the Matranga clan in court.[11]

Late on the night of October 15, gunmen ambushed Hennessy near the corner of Girod and Basin streets, leaving him mortally wounded. Before expiring the next morning, Hennessy blamed "the dagoes." Police detained 250 Italians, 19 of whom were indicted for Hennessy's murder on December 13. The defendants included Charles Matranga and Joseph Macheca, with four known gang members, plus 13 men who had no police records. Nine faced trial on February 16, 1891, but key police witnesses—including Hennessy's personal bodyguard—refused to testify. As a result, six defendants were acquitted, while Judge Joshua Baker declared a mistrial for three others. Enraged by that result and charging bribery of jurors, a lynch mob stormed the jail and killed 11 of the original 19 defendants, including Joseph Macheca. Charles Matranga, spared for reasons still unclear, emerged as the city's dominant mafioso and squeezed the Provenzanos out by 1900, retaining power until his retirement in 1922.[12]

Beyond the Big Easy

While New Orleans mafiosi dominated U.S. headlines, *La Cosa Nostra* set up shop in other cities nationwide. Fugitive Sicilian murderer Rosario Meli and several cohorts deserted Joseph Macheca's family in 1875 to try their luck in San Francisco, California. Three years later, Meli faced new murder charges, but a subordinate confessed to the slaying and called it a "matter of honor." Prosecutors dropped that case, subsequently indicting the whole gang for robbery. Immigration agents deported Meli on September 8, 1880, and while he reportedly boarded a ship bound for Sicily, it appears that he never arrived. On January 1, 1892, alleged mafiosi Joseph Battomaco and Angelo Nasta were jailed for firing shots at policemen, but the outcome of that case is lost to history. Without Meli's guiding hand, the local Mafia languished until a belated revival during Prohibition.[13]

St. Louis, Missouri, got a taste of Mafia fever on November 11, 1890, when two affluent Italian merchants received letters postmarked from New Orleans. One, addressed to Antonio Capestro, informed him that "By order of the Mafia," his brother-in-law, Joseph Gazzolo, "has been tried and he has been found guilty." Gazzolo, the letter said, "has already been notified and will receive another warning, which will be the last." Capestro was urged to have his kinsman "do what is just to prevent the execution of his sentence." Oddly, the letter received by Gazzolo himself, that same day, was headed "Notice of Condemnation" and said, "You will receive no further warning." Both men pled ignorance of any motive for the threat, though Gazzolo recalled "some kind of a business transaction with a Sicilian" several years earlier, when he owned a saloon. Capestro acknowledged the presence of a Mafia clan in St. Louis, adding, "Get the Mafia after you once and your life won't be worth a cent." The threat was not carried out, but six months later, on May 3, 1891, St. Louis resident Tony Pandolfin blamed the Mafia for a barroom stabbing that left him wounded. His offense: "I upheld the action of the New Orleans mob and made use of the remark that every one of the damn 'dagos' got no more than he deserved." A month after that, on June 20, 32 Italian workers fled from a local labor camp after a stabbing climaxed a "reign of terror" employing "Mafia tactics."[14]

New England logged its first known Mafia murder on November 21, 1889, when victim Edward Cunningham was slain in Dedham, Massachusetts. Jurors convicted mafioso Giuseppe DeLucca of that crime on January 1, 1890, despite reports that a key state witness was threatened with death. On January 9, 1894, Boston police blamed "a branch of the Mafia or the Camorra" for the razor-slashing murder of Pasquale Sacco, still officially unsolved. Two months later, on March 8, gangsters Dante Regali and Augusto Ferrari stood trial for beating and robbing banker John Caproni in Providence, Rhode Island. On June 21, 1895, Boston barber Gioacchino Cocchiara shot and killed a friend, Antonio Armblissa, afterward telling police that he feared Armblissa was plotting against him with imprisoned mafioso Giuseppe DeLucca. Witnesses in Springfield, Massachusetts, developed convenient amnesia after watching mafioso Natale Giuliano murder Pietro Fazzio in broad daylight, on June 13, 1898. Despite those outbursts, the New England Mafia lacked coherence and a strong leader until the First World War.[15]

While Massachusetts suffered its disturbances, police blamed the Mafia for a shooting in Savannah, Georgia. The victim in that March 5, 1893, incident was reputed mafioso Catello Coumo, shot by local resident Tony Esposito. Though expected to die, Coumo survived and escaped from his hospital room on March 31, then attempted to kill Esposito and another Sicilian at their homes before fleeing the city. *The New York Times* reported that "a posse of constables and Italians is on his trail," ranking Coumo as a menace whose escape "causes terror and excitement in Italian quarters." He apparently eluded man-hunters, since no follow-up reports appeared.[16]

On the morning of June 19, 1893, police found Italian immigrant Ignazio Camparito slain in Tampa, Florida, with his throat slashed from ear to ear, his torso and arms ripped by 25 knife wounds. The cash and watch found on his body ruled out robbery, while a hat dropped near the corpse apparently belonged to Camparito's assailant. Authorities detained an unidentified Italian for questioning, while rumors blamed the killing on "the Mafia Society," but no Sicilian boss would be identified in Tampa until 1925.[17]

Chicago had no shortage of corruption in the 19th century, but it remained primarily the province of WASP and Irish gangsters until 1895, when Calabrian native Giacomo "Big Jim" Colosimo arrived from Italy at age 17, soon muscling his way to control of a thriving prostitution empire, operated in collaboration with First Ward aldermen John Coughlin and Michael "Hinky Dink" Kenna. That

Giacomo "Big Jim" Colosimo with fiancée Dale Winter (Library of Congress).

same year witnessed the incorporation of the Unione Siciliana, founded by Sicilian-American entrepreneurs as a fraternal association licensed to sell insurance. While never a part of the Mafia per se, the Unione would be co-opted by Illinois mobsters during Prohibition, and to a lesser extent in neighboring states.[18]

Carving Up the Big Apple

Prior to 1880, Italian immigrants reached the United States in relatively small numbers, most arriving from the nation's northern sector. That profile changed dramatically in 1880, with a shift toward southern Italy and vastly increased numbers. By 1900, some 960,000 Italians—two-thirds of them men—arrived in America. Another 3.2 million entered the United States between 1900 and 1920.[19]

Among those new arrivals, tens of thousands landed in New York and

Camorra members in nineteenth-century New York City (Library of Congress).

never left, flocking together in the squalid tenements of lower Manhattan's "Little Italy." As in other cities, some were fugitives and felons, members of the Mafia and the Camorra. The first known crime associated with Italy's "honored societies" occurred on July 21, 1857, when bookbinder and "noted member of the Mafia" Michaele Cancemi shot and killed Patrolman Eugene Anderson during a holdup. Sentenced to 20 years for the slaying, Cancemi served his time and then returned to Italy, where "some say that he bore a title when he died."[20]

New York's next known Mafia murder occurred on October 14, 1888, when a quarrel erupted among several Sicilians gambling at Manhattan's La Trinicria restaurant, owned by Giuseppe Canizzaro and Natale Sabatino. Brothers Carlo and Vincenzo Quarteraro attacked grocer Antonio Flaccomio, inflicting fatal wounds. Investigating officers claimed that all three combatants were mafiosi, suggesting that the gambling squabble was a ruse. In fact, they said, Flaccomio's murder resulted from dissension within a Sicilian counterfeiting ring, and was somehow linked to another slaying — that of victim Camillo Farach in April 1884. Carlo Quarteraro fled the country, leaving brother Vincenzo to face trial alone on March 26, 1889. His subsequent acquittal disgusted police, prompting one detective to say that Manhattan's Italian immigrants had won approval to kill one another.[21]

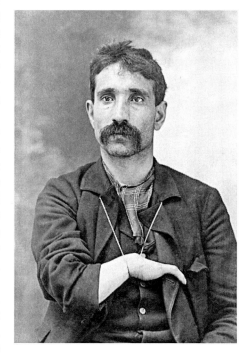

On April 19, 1891, Ferdinando Lagrano stabbed Charles Mauro to death outside Mauro's home, on East 104th Street. Captured near the crime scene, Lagrano was charged with murder but no record of his trial survives today. Manhattan's coroner declared that the apparently unprovoked stabbing "looks like a Mafia murder."[22]

Whatever Lagrano's theoretical link to Sicilian organized crime, at least one Mafia family did exist in Manhattan by 1892. Its boss was Giuseppe "The Clutch Hand" Morello, a native of Corleone, Sicily, who immigrated with his family and set-

Police photo of Giuseppe Morello, revealing his deformed "clutch hand" (National Archives).

tled in East Harlem, quickly rising to dominance in the neighborhood with three half-brothers from his widowed mother's second marriage: Ciro, Nicola and Vincenzo "Tiger" Terranova. While building up their local fiefdom, leaders of the Morello-Terranova clan visited and corresponded with mafiosi in Chicago and New Orleans, cementing alliances for mutual profit. Expansion into Brooklyn's dockyards placed the *Corleonesi* in conflict with a Camorra family led by Francesco Meli, described in press reports as a "one-armed organ grinder." Giuseppe Morello killed Meli on December 4, 1892, thereby settling the feud, but new battles between mafiosi and camorristi would erupt in the next century.[23]

May of 1893 brought a spate of Mafia news to readers of *The New York Times,* with three separate exposés published on May 16 alone. The first, headlined "Mafia's Code in New York," decried the criminal activities of "aliens who place but slight value on human life," citing the April shooting of mechanic John Brennan by Italian laborer Filipo Vetro. While the incident arose from a love triangle, the *Times* blamed Vetro's actions on "impulses dominated by the tradition of the Mafia." An unnamed city official of northern Italian heritage complained that "these southern Italians have monopolized many disagreeable callings." A second story — "Mafia Methods in New York" — bemoaned the fact that Italian defendants in court somehow managed to produce "twice as many witnesses for the prisoner as for the people." As a result, the *Times* proclaimed, "at least 200 murderers, whose crimes were typical of the Mafia and Camorra," had escaped execution in capital cases. The third piece, headlined "Ready with Knife or Pistol," warned that recent murders and assaults committed "by so-called Italians" in New York proved that mafiosi had not learned the lesson offered by New Orleans vigilantes two years earlier. This time, at least, there were specifics: a list of seven murders and 47 aggravated assaults by "hot-blooded aliens" between August 1892 and April 1893.[24]

Despite that grim tally, former Assistant District Attorney John Goff assured New Yorkers on May 22 that no "Mafite tribunal" had ever existed in their city. Claiming that the Mafia "was originally a patriotic organization founded by young patricians," Goff asserted that the society's name translated as "the man with the hat." Affirming the contempt of "decent" — that is, northern — Italians for their southern compatriots, Goff predicted that "the Italian in New York will ere long cut a conspicuous figure in politics. He has a natural aptitude for it. He is beginning to appreciate very keenly the power of the ballot, and he will make his influence felt."[25]

Goff's words were prophetic, though not in the sense he intended. Democratic leaders of New York's Tammany Hall had long since learned the value of alliances with street gangs such as the Jewish clique led by Edward "Monk"

Eastman and the mostly–Italian Five Points Gang bossed by counterfeit Irish-man Paolo "Paul Kelly" Vaccarelli. The Five-Pointers were not mafiosi per se — though Vaccarelli was Sicilian by birth — but many later would be. In the meantime, the Morello-Terranova Family was happy to cooperate with Tammany and gain police protection by occasionally herding fellow kinsmen to the polls.[26]

A year after *The New York Times* trumpeted alarms over the Mafia's infes-tation of Manhattan, readers learned of the society's first alleged slaying in New Jersey. Anthony Prisco, described as an "Italian padrone and New York politician," had been found on April 26, 1894, mangled on railroad tracks outside New Brunswick. On May 22 a coroner's jury ruled his death murder by persons unknown, accepting testimony from an Italian witness that a "rose-shaped carving" found on a tree outside Prisco's home was "a signal of the Mafia."[27] The case remains officially unsolved.

Two months later, after being stabbed at an Italian festival in Hoboken, New Jersey, victim Vincenzo Muchio told police that Antonio Carapine and Vincenzo Valino attacked him "in pursuance of an order by the Mafia." At trial, on December 20, police testified that they saw Carapine holding Muchio down, while Valino stabbed him with a stiletto. Nonetheless, jurors acquitted Carapine, while convicting Valino of assault.[28]

New York mafiosi avoided further headlines until January 1896, when agents of the U.S. Secret Service raided a nest of Sicilian counterfeiters in Steinway, Long Island. The agents seized $20,000 in fake two- and five-dollar bills, while arresting 14 suspects. Named as the gang's ringleader was Cande-lara Bettini, with Joseph Giordano charged as his right-hand man. The others detained included fruit vendors, peddlers, a barber and a liquor salesman, charged with passing the counterfeit currency. Bettini had served a prior prison term for counterfeiting in 1888, as had accomplice Rino Vengenzo in 1890. Secret Service Chief William Hazen publicly branded the ring a Mafia operation.[29]

Five months later, the Mafia's name was invoked once again, after Gio-vanni Monia shot and wounded fellow longshoreman Frank Sabella. *The New York Times* reported statements indicating that the shooting "was the result of the work of the Mafia," but granted that "nothing could be discovered to indicate that such was the case." In custody, Monia "pretended" that he did not speak English, while victim Sabella told police, "I no say anything 'bout it."[30]

Another supposed Mafia assault occurred at Ballston Spa, outside Saratoga, New York, in January 1898. Police detained suspect Carlo Piazzi for attempted murder, but victim Carlo Ferrona lost his memory after receiving $200 in hush money from "the Mafia Society." The case, again, went nowhere.[31]

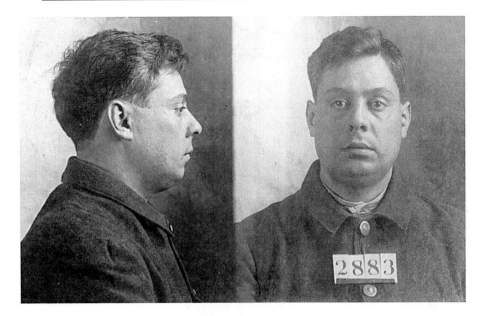

Ignazio Lupo (National Archives).

A new arrival on the New York scene, Ignacio "The Wolf" Lupo, arrived from Corleone to join the Morello-Terranova Family in 1899. Age 22, Lupo had killed a man named Salvatore Morello—no relation to his new employers—back in Sicily, and found it wise to emigrate. He married Giueseppe Morello's half-sister, served initially as an enforcer for the gang, and bought a Harlem stable said to be the scene of many homicides before moving to a stylish home in Brooklyn. There, he shared turf with Giuseppe "Battista" Balsamo, a senior mafioso who entered the U.S. in 1895 and dominated rackets in Brooklyn's Red Hook neighborhood.[32]

As the century turned, New York mafiosi stood ready to confront new challenges and reap new rewards. Ambitious as they were, however, none could visualize the wealth that lay in store for them.

· 2 ·

Black Hands

The Mafia's first enterprise in Sicily had been extortion — a variation on what Americans would later call the protection racket — and so it remained when the society was transplanted to the United States. Its members preyed on fellow immigrants, demanding tribute in return for peace of mind: freedom to live, to raise a family, to pursue a trade without the risk of being bombed, burned out, kidnapped, or murdered. Immigrating felons who were not sworn members of the Mafia observed the trend and soon went into business for themselves. Collectively, those operators became known as the "Black Hand" — *La Mano Nera* in Italian — for the inked-palm symbol used to sign their written threats.[1]

There was never any single Black Hand syndicate, much less a national network, though mafiosi might collaborate with their *fratelli* from associated families. Some of the terrorists were solitary operators. Others threatened rival gangsters, sparking battles over turf. Most victims were of modest means, but wealth alone was no defense against extortion. Famed operatic tenor Enrico Caruso paid $2,000 for peace of mind on receipt of his first Black Hand threat, then notified police when the extortionists demanded $15,000 more. Officers nabbed two suspects at the second drop, later convicting Antonio Cincotta. When an appellate court overturned Cincotta's conviction, mobsters friendly to

Black Hand victim Enrico Caruso (**Library of Congress**).

15

Caruso imposed rough justice of their own, gunning him down in Brooklyn's Little Italy.[2]

Whose Hand?

Throughout the Black Hand's reign of terror, reporters speculated over the origins of the supposed "mysterious secret society." Edwin Bjorkman was first off the blocks, in January 1905, telling readers of *The New York Times* that *La Mano Nera* had its roots in Spain, concocted by an unnamed police chief in 1881, to intimidate Andalusia's 60,000-member Federation of Laborers. Where warnings failed to cow the union, violence followed, but the Black Hand itself was "a myth," Bjorkman said.[3]

Three years later, the *Times* reversed itself, declaring methods of the "ubiquitous" Black Hand "so similar ... to those of the Sicilian brigands that there cannot be the slightest doubt of the model which the American organ-

Black Hand suspects arrested in West Virginia, early 1900s (Library of Congress).

ization has used." Said brigands, sadly, were no longer the "romantic figures" of the early 19th century who victimized only the wealthy, à la Robin Hood, but now preyed on their fellow countrymen of meager means.[4]

In July 1909 the *Times* inquired, "Is there a Mafia?" Police spokesmen denied it, and the newspaper agreed that "[a]s an organization, with any defined government, any real chief, the Mafia, it is conceded, does not exist." Still, the paper saw a "significant parallel" between Sicily's honored society and the case of Staten Island barber Carlo Maresse, facing trial for the murder of alleged extortionist Giuseppe Vena, branded by the *Times* as "one of the Mafia's blackest men."[5]

In fact, as we have seen, the Mafia *did* exist in New York City and across the nation, composed of families sometimes related by blood or marriage, collaborating on various crimes or offering shelter to fugitives, at other times engaged in fratricidal warfare. Most, if not all, engaged in Black Hand racketeering, fattening their coffers with money extorted from the 655,888 Italian immigrants who entered the United States between 1890 and 1900. Neighborhood banks, run by and for immigrants, were irresistible targets. One such institution, Manhattan's Pasquale Pati & Son, defied black-handers—and Salvatore Pati killed one who tried to rob the bank at gunpoint—but the institution lost $400,000 in deposits and went bankrupt after it was bombed in January 1908.[6]

Fake Hands

As many Black Hand racketeers were independent of the old-line Mafia, others were neither Italian nor gangsters, per se. Sensational publicity surrounding Black Hand crimes inspired a host of imitators, including the following:

• Ignatz Wenzler, an ironworker in Lebanon, Pennsylvania, arrested by U.S. Secret Service agents in January 1905, after he sent a "Black Hand" letter to Hungarian Premier Count von Tisza, demanding $2,000.[7]

• Thomas French, a youth from East Orange, New Jersey, jailed for sending threats to a secretary of the Prudential Insurance Company in Newark, in September 1905. Police found bomb components at his mother's home, subsequently adding charges of arson and burglary to French's rap sheet.[8]

• Nellie Nussbaum, a Manhattan teenager charged in September 1905 with sending Black Hand letters to her father and various neighbors, "for fun."[9]

• A Bronx teenager, unnamed in press reports from November 1905, who tormented her neighbors with letters demanding sums between $1,000 and $200,000.[10]

• Boston residents Ralph Brosnan and Raymand Lombard, arrested in

March 1906 for mailing Black Hand threats to Charles Steele, in Springfield, Massachusetts.[11]

• Edward Schanel, a teenage employee of the Chicago Northwestern Railroad, who ironically used extortion to raise dues for the Young Men's Christian Association in November 1906.[12]

• Antoinette Barris, a teenager fined in December 1907 for forging checks and sending Black Hand threats to neighbors in Newark, New Jersey.[13]

• Brooklyn janitor Pietro Pino, who falsely blamed Black Hand arsonists for a March 1908 fire at the building he supervised.[14]

• Frank Galler, a miner in Bessemer, Michigan, who joined his wife to extort cash from local businessmen with Black Hand notes, in summer 1908. Police jailed Frank without a fight, but traded gunfire with his spouse at a money drop before they captured her, on September 9.[15]

• Annie Gergely, a Manhattan seamstress who mailed Black Hand threats to herself in May 1909, hoping that her handsome bachelor employer would "protect" her.[16]

• Mrs. Charles McDonald, a discontented housewife on Long Island, who likewise mailed herself threatening notes in November 1909, hoping that her husband would take their family home to Scotland.[17]

• Dairyman William Beall of Manhattan, convicted on blackmail charges in December 1910, for demanding $10,000 from business rival Marker Dadirri-ari under threat of death.[18]

• Charles Franklin and Gilbert Perkins, two private detectives in Pennsylvania, indicted in July 1911 for sending letters signed "Black Hand's Death" to victim Charles Strong, demanding $50,000 to avert assassination. At trial, Franklin and Perkins blamed the boss of a rival detective agency for sending the threats.[19]

• A group of unnamed girls, residing at a California boarding school, who amused themselves by papering the office windows of Santa Monica attorney Delphin Delmas with Black Hand threats in July 1915.[20]

Such cases made it easy to dismiss the Black Hand as a myth, but those disclaimers missed the point. During the first two decades of the twentieth century, the Mafia, Camorra, and a host of unaffiliated gangs were all alive and well from coast to coast.

Black Hand Nationwide

In New Orleans, where the U.S. Mafia first planted roots, lynch-mob survivor Charles Matranga kept his grip on local rackets but could not suppress the Black Hand operations of competitors who envied his position. In the circumstances, troubled immigrants were sometimes left to help themselves—as when affluent wine merchant Pietro Gioacona shot and killed three would-be extortionists on June 17, 1908. A year later, Josephine Manzella gunned down the black-hander who had slain her father moments earlier. Bombers still managed to inflict $1,000 damage on historic St. Louis Cathedral in April 1909, while others threatened to kill private detective Benjamin Gallin unless he dropped his investigation of Black Hand racketeers.[21]

Chicago's Big Jim Colosimo was not a mafioso, but he certainly behaved like one, rising to dominate vice in the Tenderloin district by 1908, for a conservative estimate of $50,000 personal profit per year ($1.2 million today). Meanwhile, the nearest things to Old World mafiosi in the Windy City were the Genna brothers, six in all, who built a network based on the Unione Siciliana in the "Bloody Nineteenth" Ward. They left Colosimo alone and corrupted police on their own behalf, as required.[22]

Chicago newspapers reported Black Hand activity from 1904 onward,

Five of Chicago's six Genna brothers, with their wives. From left are Sam, Angelo, Peter, Tony and Jim (National Archives).

with the crime wave peaking between 1910 and 1915. A total of 161 murders were attributed to black-handers during those five years, along with countless bombings and assaults, but some — if not most — of the killings may have resulted from gang warfare, rather than traditional Black Hand extortion. So many victims were slain at the intersection of Oak and Milton Streets, in Little Sicily, that the site became known as "Death's Corner." Newspaper headlines indiscriminately blamed the Mafia and the Camorra for those crimes, while laying nearly a dozen to the credit of a still-unidentified "Shotgun Man."[23]

The mayhem quickly lowered property values in Little Sicily, prompting formation of a vigilante White Hand Society in 1907, which in turn was quickly targeted for Black Hand threats and violence. Jim Colosimo drew attention from the gang run by racketeer "Sunny Jim" Cosmano and paid up on their initial demand for $5,000, then balked at forking over five times that amount. Instead, he summoned nephew Johnny Torrio from Brooklyn, an alumnus of the Five Points Gang and future architect of America's national crime syndicate. Torrio arrived in 1911, met with three of Cosmano's men, and quickly agreed to their terms. At the drop, they met gunmen instead of a bagman, however, and all three were killed.[24]

Elsewhere in the Midwest, extortion target James Sorreullo shot Frauno Abolpo, said to be "a member of the Black Hand Society" in Gary, Indiana, on June 19, 1909. The same year saw Detroit black-hander Sam Lafata convicted of extortion, handed a sentence of seven and a half to 15 years in prison. By then, Vito Adamo was in charge of Motor City's first recognized Mafia family, holding the post until his murder in November 1913. Antonio Gianolla succeeded Adamo, but soon clashed with the rival faction led by Giovanni Vitale. Open war broke out in 1918, climaxed with the slaying of Antonio Gianolla in January 1919 and his brother Sam nine months later. Vitale would rule the local family for less than a year, until a blizzard of bullets deposed him in 1920.[25]

Near the turn of the twentieth century, two groups of brothers emigrated from the sulfur mines of Licata, Sicily, and put down roots in Cleveland, Ohio. Ostensibly, the four Lonardos and seven Porellos were all legitimate businessmen, but in fact they formed the hard core of Cleveland's first Mafia family. Known publicly as barbers, grocers, and restaurateurs, soon dominating the corn sugar trade, the Lonardos and Porellos — allies on arrival, later deadly enemies — pursued covert sidelines in robbery, vice and Black Hand extortion.[26]

They were not Ohio's sole practitioners, however. On June 8, 1909, agents of the U.S. Post Office arrested ten Italian immigrants in Marion, Dennison, Cleveland and Columbus, proclaiming Samuel Lima the boss of a Black Hand syndicate spanning the Midwest, sending an average $3,000 per month to confederates in Italy. On June 15, Postal Inspector E.F. Hutches told reporters "the Black Hand situation [was] more serious than was at first thought"—and as if to prove it, black-handers firebombed the home of Bellefontaine mayor William Niven the same day. On June 17, federal agents jailed 12 more suspects in Cincinnati. Those raids allegedly prompted Cincinnati racketeers to change their collective name, from the "Society of the Banana" to the "Society of Brothers in Law"—a secret move that somehow found itself reported in *The New York Times*. Facing trial in Toledo on January 19, 1910, 14 defendants were convicted 10 days later, receiving prison terms that ranged from 2 to 16 years.[27]

Postal inspectors congratulated themselves on that victory, basking in a proclamation from *The New York Times* that they represented "the best detective corps in the world," but Black Hand threats and violence continued. Eight weeks after the Toledo verdicts, the Rev. Adolph Cascianelli resigned from his parish in Canton, Ohio, to lead a Vatican investigation of Black Hand rackets nationwide. While the results were never published, Cincinnati police raided another Society of the Banana stronghold in August 1912, seizing nine men with an arsenal of handguns, ice picks, and "twined nooses ... like those used by the Paris Apaches." Black Hand extortionist Giuseppe Pomaro mailed his last letter from Youngstown in June 1913, demanding $5,000 from President Woodrow Wilson. Undeterred by Pomaro's arrest, James Spano of Youngstown sent another threatening letter to Wilson in January 1915.[28]

Missouri harbored independent Mafia families in St. Louis and Kansas City. The first reports of Black Hand violence in St. Louis hail from 1876, perpetrated by "The Green Ones"—a gang whose members named their clique after the green fields of their native villages in Sicily. Leaders included Alphonse Palizzola and the Giannola brothers, John and Vito. All were affiliated with the Mafia's *Stoppaglieri* faction, financing their passage to America with robberies at home. Under their supervision, black-handers plied a lucrative trade in the Gateway City, extorting $5,000 from Illinois mine owner Louis Lumaghi in December 1909, murdering police informant Peter Cordone at gang headquarters in April 1910, and prompting local manufacturer Russell Gardner (brother-in-law of Tennessee's governor) to flee in terror, eight months later. Another blackmail target—John Holmes, Grand Keeper of Records and Seals of the Knights of Pythias—died "of worry" after a series of threats and home break-ins during April 1914, while his wife was reported "in a dying condition."[29]

The *Kansas City Star* introduced its readers to the local Mafia in an article published on November 24, 1897. Over the next decade, unsolved Black Hand murders and bombings prompted formation of a special police squad led by

Officer Joseph Raimo in 1909. Raimo had barely two years on the job when he died in a still-unsolved shotgun ambush on March 28, 1911. Soon afterward, Joseph "Scarface" DiGiovanni emerged as the leader of the KC Mafia, supported by his three brothers. Disfigured by a fire he set as part of an insurance scheme, DiGiovanni would maintain at least nominal control of the local family until the mid–1920s.[30]

On the East Coast, Baltimore police jailed five New Yorkers in August 1906 for sending extortion letters signed "The Mafia Association." In January 1908, five black-handers faced charges of bombing a home occupied by Joseph di Giorgio, the "Banana King of Baltimore." In March 1909, officers in Cumberland, Maryland, bagged three Italians on charges of threatening a Frostburg fruit dealer and a Catholic priest in Morgantown. These and other Black Hand crimes occurred in Maryland with no apparent Mafia family in residence.[31]

New England's Mafia-Black Hand scene remained largely disorganized until Prohibition's advent in 1920. Most of the century's early Black Hand activity was reported from Connecticut, where Greenwich blackmail victims pulled guns on their tormentors in August 1904, and Rockville grocer William Baumeister fired at an extortionist in November 1905. Waterbury shoemaker John Nolan offered "gunpowder stew" to black-handers who threatened him in February 1908. New Haven police arrested "Black Hand King" Vincenzo Sabbataro in June 1909; two months later he received a 28-year prison term for robbery. Hartford authorities blamed mafiosi for the December 1911 murder of police informant Antonio Pietrolino, but they named no suspects. In May 1914, police in Henniker, New Hampshire, found a Black Hand letter near the corpse of murdered toymaker Howard Peaslee.[32]

Rumors aside, New England showed no signs of organized Mafia activity until World War I. Two families emerged in 1916, one led by Gaspare Messina in Boston, the other by Frank "Butsey" Morelli and his brothers in Providence, Rhode Island. By the mid–1920s, both factions would swear allegiance to Boston-based godfather Filippo Buccola.[33]

Pennsylvania seethed with Black Hand activity during the 1900s, and saw three Mafia families established by 1919. Tomasso Petto fled Manhattan to avoid prosecution for the 1903 "barrel murder" of Black Hand victim Benedetto Madonia, and landed in Scranton, where he founded the state's first crime family and was himself slain during 1905. By 1908, immigrant coal miner Santo "King of the Night" Volpe, collaborating with brother-in-law Stefano LaTorre, led a family with headquarters located in West Pittston through the early 1930s.[34]

Philadelphia's first godfather, Salvatore Sabella, committed his first murder in Sicily at age 14, in 1905. After serving a lenient three-year sentence for that crime, he emigrated to Brooklyn, then to Philadelphia in 1914. New York mafioso Salvatore "Toto" D'Aquila supported his bid for power in the City of Brotherly Love, establishing Sabella as Philly's undisputed godfather by 1919.[35]

Pittsburgh's premiere Mafia family was established in 1910, competing for turf with Neapolitan camorristi. Sicilian visitor Nicola Gentile found Gregorio Conti in charge of the local Mafia by 1915, running the family with nephew Peppino Cusumano from their wholesale liquor dealership, while Ferdinand Mauro led the Camorra. Natural enemies, the two factions bombed one another sporadically through the Prohibition era, although Conti had retired by 1920, ceding power to John LaRocca.[36]

Independent black-handers went their own way, in the meantime. A dozen witnesses rallied against Philadelphia practitioner Demetrio Alanto at

his arrest, in January 1905. Four months later, dynamite wrecked the store of a defiant blackmail target in Monessan. State militiamen rounded up 140 black-handers at Monongahela in January 1906, one month before McKeesport's former mayor received a demand for $3,000. Eleven defendants drew prison terms for Black Hand crimes at Wilkes-Barre in May 1907, while 14 more were charged at Allentown that August. Western Pennsylvania suffered a three-year reign of Black Hand terror, climaxing with the hanging of convicted murderers Giovanna Graziano and Georgia Quagenti on August 8, 1907, but gangsters retaliated two weeks later, bombing Vincenzo Paiumbo's home and store in Monessan. Arrests continued, but did not prevent three Black Hand murders in Pittsburgh on September 22. As in Chicago, Pittsburgh's "reputable" Italians formed a White Hand Society, waging a fierce pistol battle with black-handers at the local railroad yards, leaving two men gravely wounded on December 9, 1907. Mayhem continued for years afterward, with Pittsburgh's police station rocked by a bomb in January 1908, a church bombed at Export the following

Mafioso Nicola Gentile during one of his many arrests (National Archives).

month, a Scranton factory dynamited in January 1909, and two brothers murdered at Wilkes-Barre in April 1910.[37]

New York mafiosi viewed New Jersey as their private satrapy in 1900, and for long years afterward. Black Hand activities first made headlines in August 1904, when terrorists bombed a barber shop in Passaic. A dispute between black-handers left two Paterson residents wounded by gunfire in April 1906, while an extortionist's bomb killed Justice of the Peace Robert Cortese in the same town on February 8, 1907. Frank Amazzo confessed in that case and named his cohorts, but mayhem continued, including the mutilation-slayings of two Mesino brothers at Midland Park, in May 1908. The same month saw barns torched at New Brunswick, while successive arrests did little or nothing to solve the problem.[38]

Stealing the Big Apple

Police and press denials notwithstanding, both the Mafia and the Camorra had infested New York City by the turn of the twentieth century.

Sicilian godfather Vito Cascioferro emigrated to New York in 1901 (National Archives).

The Cosa Nostra's bulwark in Manhattan was the Morello-Terranova Family, supported by Ignazio Lupo and other experienced killers. Brothers Fortunato and Gaetano LoMonte supervised operations in East Harlem. Sicilian godfather Vito Cascioferro found the family running smoothly when he visited New York in September 1901, with vice and robbery proceeds supplemented by Black Hand extortion.[39]

One case that riled New Yorkers was the murder of Brooklyn grocer Joe Catania, crammed into a potato sack with his throat slashed and bones crushed in July 1902. Reports differed as to whether Catania was a Black Hand victim or a Lupo-Morello accomplice in counterfeiting, and the case remains officially unsolved. (Twenty-nine years later, Catania's son died in a Mafia ambush in the Bronx.) A year later, mafioso Benedetto Madonia arrived in Manhattan from Buffalo, and tried to muscle in on Morello turf. Police found him at 11th Street and Avenue D on April 14, 1903, punctured by a dozen stab wounds before he was packed in a barrel of sawdust. Police arrested Lupo, Giuseppe Morello, Vito Cascioferro and others on suspicion of killing Madonia, but none went to trial.[40]

The official response to Black Hand terrorism was creation of a special Italian Squad within the New York City Police Department. Various sources date the squad's beginning to anywhere from 1903 to 1905, and while *The New York Times* publicized a six-man, all–Italian squad in October 1905, Police Commissioner Theodore Bingham was still requesting approval of a "secret service squad" to hunt black-handers in December 1906. He repeated that plea in January 1908, long after the Italian Squad was visibly active.[41]

Whatever its startup date, the squad was led by Giuseppe "Joe" Petrosino, a native of Salerno, born in 1860, who emigrated at 14 and joined the NYPD

Giuseppe Petrosino (left) escorts Mafia hit man Tomasso Petto (in white hat) to jail in 1903, accompanied by NYPD Inspectors Carey and McCafferty (Library of Congress).

in 1883. Assigned to track Italian felons by 1890, Petrosino earned his first press notice two years later and was promoted to the rank of detective sergeant in 1895. In 1905 he called for Washington to move against immigrant gangsters, saying, "Unless the federal government comes to our aid New York will awaken some morning to one of the greatest catastrophes in history. You may think I am foolish making this statement, but these Black Hand blackmailers are growing bolder every day."[42]

As boss of the Italian Squad, elevated to lieutenant in December 1908, Petrosino made life miserable for mafiosi and camorristi. He arrested black-handers at every opportunity, sending some to the electric chair and more to prison, arranging for deportation of others as undesirable aliens. By 1908, Petrosino had compiled a list of 742 deportable immigrant felons and had opened negotiations with the Italian government to receive them. Vito Cascioferro, worried enough on his own behalf to flee America, paused in transit to discuss the "Petrosino problem" with Ignazio Lupo before he returned to Sicily.[43]

Petrosino sailed from New York on February 19, 1909, bearing a list of immigrant gangsters including the names of Lupo and Giuseppe Morello. Today, we know two mafiosi were aboard the ship, maintaining telegraphic contact with Morello. Commissioner Bingham, meanwhile, showed a remarkable lack of discretion. When reporters inquired about Petrosino's whereabouts on February 20, Bingham told the world, "Why, he may be on the ocean bound for Europe for all I know."[44]

Petrosino disembarked in Rome on February 21 and reached Sicily seven days later. On the night of March 12, while walking alone through Palermo, he was fatally shot by by two men outside a restaurant. Palermo's police commissioner named five local suspects, including a brother-in-law of Giuseppe Morello, but the list did not end there. Back in the states, various theorists blamed immigrant gangsters in Manhattan, Chicago, and Ohio; one report even fingered Italian anarchists based in London. Finally, no one could decide if Petrosino had been slain by the Cosa Nostra, the Camorra, or through a collaborative effort of both. William Bishop, American consul in Palermo, predicted accurately that the slaying would remain unsolved because "Sicilian lips are sealed." A sinister touch was added to the mystery in August 1913, when *The New York Times* reported that police had destroyed Petrosino's list of 742 deportable gangsters. Authorities "found" the misplaced dossier three weeks later, when the statute of limitations on deportation had lapsed.[45]

Petrosino's successor on the Italian Squad, Lt. Antonio Vachris, was billed as a "terror of Italian criminals," but that reputation did not spare him from a rash of personal Black Hand threats. Passage of a new law tripling the prison sentence for extortion, from five to 15 years, failed to put a dent in the crime wave. Murder victims—16 in 1911 alone—were shot, stabbed, and dismembered; some simply disappeared. Two arson incidents, in October 1913 and November 1914, killed 10 tenement dwellers and left scores homeless. Some immigrants fought back, killing black-handers, but most paid up and suffered in silence. Police spokesmen declared "bomb terror" at an end in October 1913, but their confident pronouncement failed to stem the bloodshed.[46]

While Black Hand operators kept police and journalists occupied, the Mafia founded its first cohesive family in Buffalo, New York, in 1910. Boss Angelo "Buffalo Bill" Palmieri ruled the gang until 1916, when he retired to *consigliere* (counselor) status, ceding power to underboss Giuseppe DiCarlo. Generally overlooked in those years, Buffalo's family bided its time, then prospered during the Prohibition gold rush.[47]

Back in New York City, the Morello-Terranova-Lupo gang suffered through trials and tribulations. Lupo and Giuseppe Morello, with 10 associates, dodged prosecution for the February 1903 "barrel murder" of victim Pietro Inzerillo, while U.S. Secret Service agents threatened them with counterfeiting charges. Three years later, police detained Lupo on suspicion of kidnapping a banker's son, then released him once more. Lupo fled his bankrupt produce dealership in November 1908, leaving $700,000 in debts, then returned a year later, claiming that Black Hand predators had ruined his business. Four days after his return—on November 15, 1909—Secret Service agents jailed Giuseppe Morello, Nicola Terranova and 11 cohorts for counterfeiting. Lupo joined the list on November 23, while free on bond from an extortion charge. At trial, in February 1910, jurors convicted Lupo, Morello, and six codefendants, resulting in cumulative sentences of 150 years. *The New York Times* proclaimed the Black Hand "manacled at last," then recanted in 1911 as black-hand crimes doubled in number.[48]

The More Things Change...

One mafioso who escaped the Secret Service dragnet was Giuseppe Masseria, a native of Marsala, Sicily, who reached New York in 1903, at age 16. Four years later, he received a suspended sentence on conviction of burglary and extortion. By 1910, Masseria was among the ambitious mobsters primed to fill the Morello-Lupo power vacuum in Manhattan. A second burglary conviction, in June 1913, sent Masseria to prison with a 54-month sentence, but he emerged in time for service in a new turf war that left him well-positioned for his future role as "Joe the Boss."[49]

That struggle was primarily between the Cosa Nostra, headquartered on East 107th Street, and a gang of camorristi led by Giosue Gallucci from East

109th. Police files labeled Gallucci the "mayor of Little Italy," noting his strict control over the local "policy" or "numbers" gambling racket. Hostilities began within the Neapolitan camp when rival camorristo Aniello Prisco killed Gallucci's bodyguard, in September 1912. Prisco was slain in turn three months later, and *The New York Times* counted 33 "feud" murders in East Harlem by May 1914.[50]

Such violence could not be contained within a single faction. As the First World War erupted in Europe, five major Italian gangs claimed turf in New York City. Sicilian cliques included remnants of the Morello-Terranova Family and another led by Toto D'Aquila, both based in Harlem; a smaller Harlem faction led by Alfredo "Al Mineo" Manfredi; and another in Brooklyn, composed of Castellammarese immigrants led by Nicola Schiro. Camorristi were divided between Pelligrino Moran's clan on Coney Island, and the Navy Street Gang, jointly led by Leopoldo Lauritano and Allesandro Vollero. According to Secret Service informant Salvatore Clementi, the Morello, Manfredi and Schiro gangs collaborated in various rackets, while D'Aquila's group stood opposed to all three. The Lomonte brothers, previously mentioned, worked in concert both with the Morello Family and Giosue Gallucci's Neapolitans.[51]

Mayhem resumed within the Mafia on May 23, 1914, with the murder

Giuseppe "Joe the Boss" Masseria (National Archives).

of Fortunato Lomonte. Nicola Gentile named Umberto Valenti as one of the killers, acting on orders from Toto D'Aquila. Gaetano Lomonte survived until October 13, 1915, when he was slain on suspicion of turning informer. Nicola Terranova met with leaders of the Navy Street and Coney Island camorristi on June 24, 1916, to discuss collaboration in eliminating rival Joe DeMarco and dividing his rackets in lower Manhattan. Ciro Terranova led a hit team that gunned down DeMarco on July 25, but the camorristi then devised a plot to wipe out the Morello Family and claim all Harlem's rackets for themselves. They launched the new offensive on September 7, 1916, killing Nicola Terranova and bodyguard Eugene Urbiaco en route to a scheduled meeting with Navy Street Gang leaders.[52]

Thus ended any hope of peace between the Cosa Nostra and Camorra. *The New York Times* counted 23 dead by November

1917, when murder suspect Raffaelo "Ralph the Barber" Daniello turned informant. Prosecutors indicted 21 defendants that month, with trials continuing through 1923. The net result was a disaster for the camorristi, effectively dismantling the Navy Street Gang, while recalcitrant witnesses spared the Morello Family from any serious damage. One surprise catch was NYPD Detective Michael Mealli, exposed in courtroom testimony as a hired Camorra ally. He avoided prosecution and retained his job, but was demoted to the rank of patrolman.[53]

As 1919 dawned, the Cosa Nostra stood supreme within New York's Italian underworld, but it was still far from united. Providence and Congress lent a hand within a year to change that situation, and to make neighborhood mobsters rich beyond their wildest dreams.

Ciro Terranova (National Archives).

· 3 ·

Liquid Gold

Organized crime exists, in large part, to supply forbidden goods and services. Whenever anything is banned or rationed, criminals immediately fill the void. Prior to 1920, gambling and prostitution, coupled with extortion, were the underworld's chief money-makers. Gangs were localized, most limited to ethnic neighborhoods, clearly defined. Even the Cosa Nostra and Camorra, with their rituals and bonds of blood, rarely cooperated between major cities or across state lines. All that would change with the advent of Prohibition's "noble experiment."

America Goes "Dry"

Liquor has always been a problem in the United States. Alexander Hamilton's attempt to tax it sparked the first armed rebellion against America's new government, in 1791, and efforts to regulate the sale of alcoholic beverages have been a headache ever since. Thirty-five years later, residents of Boston formed the American Temperance Society to lobby for alcohol's abolition, expanding to claim 8,000 chapters with 1.5 million members by 1836. John Russell of Michigan founded the Prohibition Party in 1869, followed in turn by the Woman's Christian Temperance Union in 1874, and the Anti-Saloon League in 1893. All campaigned for a dry America, from town halls to Washington, with mixed results.[1]

By 1909, ten states had outlawed liquor, though the first to dry up — Maine, in 1851—changed its mind five years later. In the early twentieth century, resurgent nativism and anti-Catholicism fueled the temperance movement, as mostly-rural Protestants declared an early culture war on urban, "wet" minorities. Congress helped out with the Webb-Kenyon Law of February 1913, banning liquor shipments into dry states, buttressed two years later by the "bone-dry" Reed Amendment, barring alcoholic cargos from states that permitted importation, while punishing manufacture and sale. America's entry into World War

I, with its federal rationing and propaganda campaigns against all things German (including established brewers), added the Food Control Law of 1917, forbidding manufacture of distilled spirits from foodstuff such as grain. That act closed U.S. distilleries in August 1917, followed by breweries in September 1918. Congress then approved a blanket wartime prohibition, though the law did not take effect until July 1919, seven months after the end of hostilities.[2]

Nine more states passed dry laws between 1914 and 1918, while gangs in each took up the slack, importing alcohol from "wet" jurisdictions or producing it themselves in covert breweries and distilleries. Gangsters were therefore not upset when Congress passed the 18th Amendment to the U.S. Constitution in December 1917, imposing a nationwide ban on the manufacture, sale, transportation or importation of intoxicating liquors. Thirty-six states ratified the amendment by January 16, 1919, whereupon it was scheduled to take effect one year from that date. Since the amendment had no teeth, in terms of punishment, Congress also passed a National Prohibition Act, drafted by attorney Wayne Wheeler of the Anti-Saloon League and commonly called by the name of its congressional sponsor, Representative Andrew Volstead of Minnesota.[3]

Ban? What Ban?

Prohibition's advocates expected it to cure most of the nation's ills, both physical and spiritual. Among the benefits proclaimed — still championed, by some — were declining rates of public drunkenness, domestic violence, school truancy and worker absenteeism. Celebrity author Charles Hanson Towne painted a very different picture, however, when he surveyed 30 major U.S. cities in 1921. He found that crime rates had increased by 24 percent, including a 9 percent rise in burglary, 12.7 percent rise in homicide, 13 percent increase in assault, and a stunning 44.6 percent increase in drug addiction. Not surprisingly, the cost of law enforcement also had increased, by 11.4 percent. An additional problem, the higher potency of illicit alcoholic beverages, occurred because high-octane booze was more profitable for smugglers. The Volstead Act also permitted continued production of industrial alcohol, but its diversion by bootleggers prompted Treasury Department agents to render it unpotable by adding toxic chemicals. Gangsters forged ahead, regardless, and by Prohibition's end the federal tampering had claimed at least 10,000 lives.[4]

In hindsight, we may say that Prohibition was doomed to fail from its inception. Congress could have seen the future easily enough, by looking at those states where alcohol was banned before 1920, but crusading moralistic zeal carried the day. In fact, the Volstead Act proved unenforceable. In 1920, a total of 4,550 Customs and Prohibition agents were assigned to guard 18,700 miles of border and coastline, while simultaneously hunting violators in 48 states. By 1933, nearly one-fourth of the Prohibition Bureau's personnel — 1,600 agents in all — had been fired for various crimes including bribery, extortion, forgery and perjury. Between 1920 and 1932, another 512 federal agents were killed on duty, while civilians killed by agents totaled 2,089. No tally exists for local police or mobsters slain in liquor wars (though the Chicago Crime Commission counted 664 gangland murders between 1920 and 1933).[5]

Intoxicants, meanwhile, were readily available in "dry" America. In the first four years of Prohibition, licensed distillers turned out 130 million gallons of medicinal alcohol, 24 million gallons of sacramental wine, eight million gallons of brandy (used in food and medicine), and seven million gallons of rum (for tobacco products), while legal breweries produced one billion gallons of "near-beer." The U.S. Commerce Department claimed that $90 million worth of Canadian booze crossed the border illegally from 1921 to 1923, while Customs called that tally too conservative.[6] Aside from smuggling and diversion of stockpiled liquor, outlaw breweries and stills deluged the nation.

It was simply too good to resist, and the Cosa Nostra didn't even try.

Hitting the Jackpot

Overnight, in every major city, mafiosi rode the cresting wave of alcohol to fortune, infamy — and sometimes, gruesome ends. New Orleans, where the Mafia first garnered headlines, was run by Charles Matranga until 1922, when he retired and ceded power to Sylvestro "Silver Dollar Sam" Carolla. Arrested several times during the "dry" years, Carolla drew an 8-to-15-year sentence on narcotics charges in 1933, as Prohibition waned, but friendly Governor Oscar Allen commuted that term to 12 months.[7]

New Orleans mafiosi had a tendency to wind up in Los Angeles. Charles Matranga surfaced there in 1925, colluding (or competing, sto-

Ignazio "Jack" Dragna (Library of Congress).

ries differ) with Joseph Ardizzone. Future boss Ignazio "Jack" Dragna arrived from Sicily, via Chicago, in 1930, trailing a record that included four years served in prison for a 1916 extortion conviction. He helped steer the family into operation of gambling ships moored outside the 12-mile limit, a source of income that survived until the eve of World War II.[8]

In Cleveland, Big Joe Lonardo ruled the Mafia roost, supported by Toto D'Aquila in New York, until Porello Family rivals executed him and brother John on October 13, 1927. Fourteen months later, Angelo Porello hosted a meeting of Mafia bosses at the Hotel Statler, to confirm his title as local boss of bosses, but someone tipped police, resulting in two dozen arrests. Embarrassed on his home turf, Porello planned a move to Buffalo, New York, but he was too slow leaving. On July 5, 1930, Porello and bodyguard Sam Tilocco were murdered at rival Frank Milano's restaurant. Drive-by gunmen killed Vincente Porello on July 26,

Cleveland mafioso Big Joe Lonardo (**Library of Congress**).

and bombers leveled brother Raymond's house on August 15. Frank Milano thus assumed command of Cleveland's Cosa Nostra, aided by Alfred Polizzi and pseudo-brother/cousin Charles (né Leo Berkowitz). Charles Polizzi, in turn, bridged the gap to Cleveland's Jewish syndicate led by Moe Dalitz, while Tom McGinty's Irish mob joined the combination in a rare display of multicultural solidarity.[9]

By 1920, Kansas City politics—and much of Missouri's at large—was firmly controlled by Thomas Pendergast's Jackson County Democratic Club. When "Boss Tom" needed dirty work performed, he often turned to local mafiosi led, successively, by James Balestrere, Frank DeMayo and Giovanni Lazia. Regarded as a wide-open town, K.C. thumbed its nose at Prohibition and the law in general until June 1933, when an ill-conceived attempt to liberate fugitive Frank Nash from federal custody left Nash and four lawmen dead outside Union Station, producing intense heat that hampered operations until autumn 1934.[10]

Detroit, next door to Canada, smuggled vast amounts of whiskey and produced even more, dubbed "a city upon a still" by one local observer.

Kansas City's Union Station massacre, June 17, 1933 (National Archives).

Guglielmo "Black Bill" Tocco (National Archives).

Detroit's assistant prohibition director called it "the wettest city I have been assigned to," and while police seized 3,000 outlaw stills during Prohibition, they missed many more. The local Cosa Nostra, frequently at odds with members of the Jewish Purple Gang, took orders from Gaspare Milazzo until he was murdered in May 1930, on orders from rival Cesare "Chester" Lamare. Lamare was slain in turn on February 7, 1931, and replaced by partners Guglielmo "Black Bill" Tocco and Giuseppe Zerilli. When their Jewish rivals were eradicated in the early 1930s, some reporters started calling Motor City's Mafia the Purple Gang. The name was just too colorful to die.[11]

Jewish mobster Charles "King" Solomon and partner Dan Carroll, based in Boston, were New England's most successful bootleggers, but mafiosi soldiered on, accumulating fortunes of their own. Gaspare Messina ran the Boston family until 1924, when he retired in favor of Filippo Buccola, lately arrived from Palermo. Joe Lombardo had a separate clan, operating from Springfield, Massachusetts, where he skirmished with Irish rivals from Frankie Wallace's tough Gustin Gang. The link between Buccola and Lombardo is obscure, but mafiosi disposed of Wallace in December 1931, and persons unknown assassinated King Solomon in January 1933.[12]

Pennsylvania continued to harbor multiple Mafia families during Prohibition. Pittsburgh boss Salvatore Calderone retired peaceably in 1925, but successors Stefano Monastero and Giuseppe Siragusa were murdered in May 1927 and August 1929, respectively. John Balzzano tried to survive the dry era by killing rivals Arthur, James, and John Volpe at Balzzano's coffee shop on July 29, 1932, but his own luck ran out eight days later, when he was ventilated with ice picks, his body dumped in Brooklyn. Successor Vincenzo Capizzi finally secured a measure of national respect for the Pittsburgh crime family. Santo Volpe — Scranton's top mafioso, unrelated to the murdered Pittsburgh brothers — prospered during Prohibition by collaborating with New York mobsters, then retired in 1933, ceding authority to Giovanni Sciandra.[13]

In Philadelphia, Salvatore Sabella ran his bootleg fiefdom from behind the cover of a soda fountain and a company importing cheese and olive oil. Turf wars with rival Mafia factions sparked the murders of Leo Lanzetti in August 1925 and the drive-by slaying of Vincent Cocozza and Joseph Zanghi in May 1927. Retiring at age 40, in 1931, Sabella passed the reins to hand-picked heir John Avena, but echoes of the liquor wars came back to haunt him when Lanzetti loyalists gunned down Avena in 1936, leaving Joseph "Bruno" Dovi in charge of the local Cosa Nostra.[14]

New Jersey, meanwhile, was a happy hunting ground for mob-

Abner "Longy" Zwillman (Library of Congress).

sters from New York, including Buffalo's future godfather, Stefano Magaddino. Arrested in 1921 for the murder of Camillo Caizzo—who allegedly
killed Magaddino's brother five years earlier—Magaddino avoided prosecution and subsequently moved upstate to a healthier climate. With his depar-
ture, bootlegging in the Garden State was dominated by Jewish gangsters
Abner "Longy" Zwillman and Irving "Waxey Gordon" Wexler in Newark,
while Enoch "Nucky" Johnson ran Atlantic City. Near the end of Prohibition,
Guarino "Willie" Moretti teamed with Zwillman to represent the Mafia's
interests in New Jersey.[15]

Windy City Wars

No American city was more notorious than Chicago for free-flowing
liquor or mayhem during the "dry" era. Control of Little Sicily, on the Near
North Side, was contested between the Aiello clan, from Bagheria di Palermo,
and the Gennas, from Marsala. While they grappled for control of the Unione
Siciliana, both families commissioned others to produce liquor at home. Some
15,000 home-brewers supplied the Gennas, for a yearly income of $5 million
($63 million today).[16]

New York mafioso Francesco "Frankie
Yale" Ioele (National Archives).

Mainland Italians Jim Colosimo
and Johnny Torrio were ineligible for
Mafia membership, but the wealth
they gained from gambling and prostitution made them power players in
Chicago's underworld. For reasons
yet unclear, Colosimo resisted the
move into bootlegging, and that ret-
icence cost him his life. An unidentified gunman—believed to be New
Yorker Francesco "Frankie Yale" Ioele
(or Uale)—killed Colosimo at his
café on May 11, 1920, whereupon Torrio assumed command of the gang,
backed by Brooklyn-born protégé
Alphonse "Scarface" Capone. Torrio's organization, dubbed "The
Outfit," was a true melting pot, with
a Jewish paymaster (Jake "Greasy
Thumb" Guzik), a Welsh political
fixer (Llewelyn "Murray the Camel"

Humphreys), and soldiers of diverse ethnic backgrounds. As they plunged full-bore into bootlegging, Torrio and Capone faced their main opposition from Irish mobsters: Dean O'Banion's North Side gang, Myles O'Donnell's West Side gang, and the unrelated South Side faction led by Edward "Spike" O'Donnell.[17]

After Colosimo's murder, Torrio negotiated a division of turf with his Chicago competition, moving on to meet with other mobsters around the Midwest and

Alphonse "Scarface" Capone (in straw hat) with attorney Abe Teitelbaum (Library of Congress).

along the East Coast during summer 1920. The talks reduced bloodshed, but never truly ended it, either in Illinois or elsewhere. Ethnic antipathy still sparked violence, as did politics. Periodic "aldermen's wars" left Chicago's Nineteenth Ward littered with corpses, and Frank Capone (brother of Al) was killed by police during a wave of terrorism surrounding a Democratic primary election in April 1924. Torrio's truce unraveled a month later, after Dean O'Banion pulled a "joke" that left Torrio jailed on Volstead charges. Frankie Yale paid another visit to Chicago on November 8, 1924, join-

Johnny Torrio fled Chicago in 1925 but remained active in Mob affairs (National Archives).

ing mafiosi Albert Anselmi and John Scalise — borrowed from the Gennas — to slay O'Banion in his flower shop.[18]

Thus ended any hope of peace in Chicago. O'Banion successor Earl "Hymie" Weiss tried to kill Al Capone on January 12, 1925, and left Torrio gravely wounded 12 days later. By the time Torrio was able to travel in June, leaving Chicago to Capone, three of the six Genna brothers were dead, the remainder in hiding. Capone's allies introduced the Tommy gun to gangland warfare in September 1925, and used one to kill Hymie Weiss, with two

Top: George "Bugs" Moran, a leader of Chicago's North Side gang against Capone (National Archives). *Bottom:* The St. Valentine's Day massacre of 1929 killed seven members of Moran's gang (Library of Congress).

companions, in October 1926. George "Bugs" Moran then rose to lead the North Side gang through an accelerating cycle of strikes and counter-strikes, continuing until machine-gunners slaughtered seven of his men on February 14, 1929.[19]

Meanwhile, a secondary war erupted in Chicago. With the rival Gennas defeated, Giuseppe Aiello launched a camaign to wrest control of the Unione Siciliana from officers promoted by non–Sicilian Al Capone. Aiello imported gunmen, but each in turn was slain soon after his arrival in Chicago. When Aiello bribed a chef to poison Capone, the frightened cook informed Scarface. Capone, suspecting Frankie Yale of supporting Aiello, sent men to kill Yale in New York on July 1, 1928. Three weeks later, hit men slew Aiello's uncle in Chicago. When gunmen Anselmi and Scalise plotted with Aiello to depose Capone in May 1929, they were invited to a banquet and beaten to death for dessert. Aiello lived "on the lam" until October 1930, when he emerged from hiding to flee Chicago—and died in a machine-gun ambush that left him with 59 wounds.[20] So was Chicago pacified, after a fashion, with Capone more or less in control.

Manhattan Melodrama

New York City was no less "wet" than Chicago. It had claimed 15,000 legal saloons in 1919, increased to 23,000 by December 1920, and estimates topped 100,000 by the end of Prohibition. Jewish gambler and racketeer Arnold "The Brain" Rothstein, fixer of the 1919 World Series, pioneered liquor smuggling in New York with aid from ex-stevedore William "Big Bill" Dwyer and Wall Street manipulator Joseph Kennedy, Sr., still 18 years away from his appointment as U.S. ambassador to England. In the process of becoming fabulously rich, Rothstein employed and educated scores of mobsters—including four who would reshape the image of organized crime in America.[21]

That quarter included Sicilian Salvatore Lucania, alias Charles "Lucky" Luciano; Calabrian Francesco "Frank Costello" Castiglia; Russian-born Meyer Suchowljanski, better know as "Lansky"; and native Brooklynite Benjamin Siegelbaum, commonly known (behind his back) as Bugsy Siegel. Together, those four and various allies planned to realize Rothstein's vision of a bootleg syndicate spanning the nation, with its tentacles outstretched to Europe, Canada, and the Caribbean. With Rothstein's still-unsolved murder in November 1928, they were prepared to start—but first, they had to overhaul the Mafia.[22]

The Cosa Nostra, in those days, was led by old-school bosses whom the

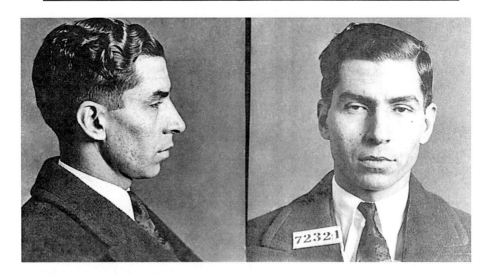

An early mug shot of Salvatore Lucania, a.k.a. "Lucky Luciano" (National Archives).

younger breed privately branded "Mustache Petes." One such hardliner, Toto D'Aquila, was slain in Brooklyn by three gunmen on October 10, 1928. Suspicion for that murder fell on Joe Masseria, whose rise to power in Manhattan's Mafia began with the murder of Salvatore Mauro on December 29, 1920. Mauro was a bootlegging partner of Umberto Valenti, who retaliated by killing Masseria ally Vincent Terranova on May 8, 1922. Masseria retaliated the same day, with an ambush that missed Valenti but killed associate Silva

Giuseppe "Joe Bananas" Bonanno (left), seen with attorney Albert Krieger, supported Salvatore Maranzano in the Castellammarese War (National Archives).

Tagliagamba and wounded five bystanders. Arrested near the shooting scene, Masseria was charged with that slaying but never faced trial. Valenti tried to kill Masseria on August 4, and again on August 11, but the second shootout left Valenti dead, with two civilians injured. Found by police with two bullet holes in his fedora, Joe the Boss basked in his new reputation as a man who could cheat death.[23]

A new rival prepared to test that premise in 1925. Freshly arrived on U.S. soil at age 39, Salvatore Maranzano established his reputation as a mafioso before he fled Fascist persecution in Castellammare del Golfo, Sicily. His allies from the same vicinity included Giuseppe "Joe Bananas" Bonanno in Manhattan, Nicola Schiro in Brooklyn, Stefano Magaddino in Buffalo, and Giuseppe Aiello in Chicago. As Aiello despised Al Capone, so Maranzano's Castellammarese faction chafed at the dictates of Joe the Boss Masseria.[24] While they plotted war, however, the underworld was changing.

From Mob to Syndicate

As mobsters fought for bootleg turf from coast to coast, the cooler heads among them realized that war was bad for business. Moe Dalitz and his partners pioneered ethnic cooperation in Cleveland, and sometime during 1927 and 1928 their example inspired creation of the Seven Group — also called the "Big Seven" or "The Combine" — among East Coast gangsters. Participants included the "Bug and Meyer Mob" led by Lansky and Siegel; Charles Luciano, allied with "retired" Johnny Torrio; a Brooklyn gang led by Giuseppe "Joe Adonis" Doto; Nucky Johnson's network in Atlantic City; Longy Zwillman and Willie Moretti in northern New Jersey; the Philadelphia syndicate led by Waxey Gordon, Harry "Nig" Stromberg, and Irving "Bitsy" Bitz; and King Solomon's gang in Boston.[25]

"Seven Group" member Giuseppe "Joe Adonis" Doto (National Archives).

Before year's end, the Seven Group outgrew its name and Eastern Seaboard limitations, as it forged or strengthened existing alliances with New York labor racketeers Louis "Lepke" Buchalter and Jacob "Gurrah" Shapiro, Arthur "Dutch Schultz" Flegenheimer in the Bronx, the Cleveland syndicate, Detroit's Purple Gang, the Chicago Outfit, Joe Kennedy in Boston, and Daniel Walsh in Providence, Rhode Island, among others. Luciano and his non–Sicilian partners recognized the Mafia's ability to sabotage their efforts and began to scrutinize solutions. Mafia historian Giuseppe Selvaggi asserts that Luciano called a meeting of his closest friends on Christmas Day 1928, to plot removal of the Mustache Petes.[26] Before that happened, though, agreements with their allies had to be confirmed.

On May 13, 1929, gangsters from various cities rallied in Atlantic City, New Jersey, ostensibly to celebrate Meyer Lansky's recent marriage. Their true reason for gathering was the foundation of a national crime syndicate, expanding on the Seven Group's foundation. Nucky Johnson hosted the event, resolving an initial upset when his first choice of hotels refused rooms to the Jewish and Italian delegates. Once that hurdle was cleared and flaring tempers

Enoch "Nucky" Johnson (in straw hat) with Al Capone (third from right) and unidentified companions on the Atlantic City Boardwalk, 1929 (National Archives).

cooled, the delegates spent three days drawing boundaries for respective territories, settling their various disputes, plotting eradication of rogue hijackers, and looking forward to the eventual repeal of Prohibition. Between sessions, the mobsters partied and strolled on the Boardwalk, observed by reporters.[27]

New York sent the most delegates, including Luciano and Torrio, Lansky and Siegel, Lepke and Shapiro, Costello and Adonis, Vito Genovese, Albert Anastasia, Francesco Scalice, Vincent Mangano, Carlo Gambino, Gaetano Lucchese, Dutch Schultz, Owen "Owney the Killer" Madden, and Rothstein gambling heir Frank Erickson. From New Jersey, in addition to their host, came Zwillman and Moretti. Al Capone came from Chicago, with Jake Guzik, Francesco "Frank the Enforcer" Nitti, Franklin Rio, and alcoholic gunman Frank McErlane. Philadelphia contributed Waxey Gordon, Nig Rosen, Bitsy Bitz, Charles Schwartz, Samuel Lazar, and Max "Boo Boo" Hoff. Moe Dalitz represented Cleveland, with partners Louis Rothkopf and Jewish mafioso "Charles Polizzi." Brothers Abraham and Joseph Bernstein sat in for the Purple Gang, while King Solomon and Frank "The Cheeseman" Cucchiara spoke for Boston. Frank "Butsey" Morelli came from Providence, Rhode Island, and Giovanni Lazia represented the Pendergast machine. Some accounts add Sylvestro Carolla of New Orleans and Tampa's Santo Trafficante, Sr., to the guest list. Notable for their absence were Joe Masseria, Salvatore Maranzano, and most of America's top Irish gangsters.[28]

Al Capone suffered a scolding from the other delegates for rampant mayhem in Chicago, dubbed "a goddamn crazy place" by Luciano. Atlantic City's police declared him *persona non grata* on May 16, but by the time they went looking for Al he was already gone, entrained for Philadelphia, where he and Frank Rio were jailed and sentenced to one-year terms for carrying concealed pistols. Most historians today regard that sentence as Capone's enforced penance for the St. Valentine's Day massacre, demanded in Atlantic City as the price of his survival. Beyond that disciplinary action, the delegates agreed to live in peace, eliminate renegades with a minimum of fuss, and pave the way to other rackets after Prohibition was repealed. A second meeting, headlined in Detroit's *Free Press* on June 13, created "a giant combine of Great Lakes rum-runners" to outwit dry agents.[29] Formation of a national crime syndicate was underway.

Cleaning House

Maranzano and Masseria certainly knew of the Atlantic City conference. Indeed, Masseria may have felt he had been represented, since Luciano, Costello, Joe Adonis and Vito Genovese had all joined Masseria's family in

1922, thereby safeguarding their speakeasies and casinos from attack. Maranzano, frozen out of the meeting, added that slight to the list insults that fueled his hatred for Joe the Boss. Battle lines were drawn for a war that would leave one man or the other in charge of the Cosa Nostra.[30]

Luciano himself was nearly the first casualty. Kidnapped on October 17, 1929, he was beaten, slashed with knives and left for dead, but he survived to earn his "Lucky" nickname. Maranzano's soldiers were presumed responsible, though some accounts claim Masseria ordered the near-one-way ride after Luciano refused to betray his Jewish partners. Around the same time, Maranzano rallied his supporters nationwide. Salvatore Sabella led nine soldiers from Philadelphia to aid the Castellammarese. Masseria responded by naming recently-paroled Giuseppe Morello as boss of bosses and arbiter of Mafia disputes, while serving as the new appointee's puppeteer.[31]

Masseria kicked off the war by killing one of his own lieutenants, Gaetano Reina, who planned a defection to Maranzano. Several Reina loyalists, including Gaetano Gagliano and Gaetano Lucchese — both called "Tommy"— promptly switched families. Three months later, on May 31, gunmen killed Maranzano ally Gaspare Milazzo and bodyguard Sasa Parrina in Detroit. Marazano scored on August 15, with the murder of Giuseppe Morello, then executed Reina's successor, Bonaventura "Fat Joe" Pinzolo on September 5. Al Capone eliminated Maranzano ally Joe Aiello on October 23. On November 5, Marazano's men killed Masseria ally Alfredo Manfredi — successor to Toto D'Aquila — and his lieutenant, Stefano Ferrigno. By February 1931, with six murders recorded in a single week, New York police announced a crackdown on bootlegging gangs to end the violence.[32]

Lucky Luciano had a better idea. After secret meetings with Maranzano, he invited Masseria to a Coney Island restaurant for lunch and a game of cards, on April 15,

Albert Anastasia, a member of the firing squad that executed Joe the Boss (Library of Congress).

1931. Midway through their meeting, Luciano excused himself to use the lavatory. In his absence, four gunmen — believed to be Albert Anastasia, Vito Genovese, Joe Adonis and Ben Siegel — entered and killed Joe the Boss, thus ending the Castellammarese War.[33]

Maranzano soon convened a meeting to annoint himself as boss of bosses. At the same time, he created five New York Mafia families that remain in place today, although diminished by successful prosecutions. The bosses, serving Maranzano as lieutenants, were Luciano, Giuseppe "Joe" Profaci, Joe Bonanno, Vincent Mangano, and Gaetano Gagliano. As a sop to the Chicago Outfit, non–Sicilian Al Capone was named an honorary *caporegime* (captain). Nationwide, other existing families remained in place with bosses who survived the war and paid tribute to Maranzano.[34]

Some of Marazano's "reforms" pleased Luciano, but Lucky still despised him as the ultimate Mustache Pete. Maranzano, meanwhile, remembered Luciano's betrayal of Masseria and fumed over Lucky's continued alliance with Jewish mobsters. Planning to eliminate Luciano, Maranzano scheduled a meeting between them for September 10, then hired Irish rogue Vincent "Mad Dog" Coll to kill Lucky on arrival. Tipped to the plot, Luciano sent a team of Lepke Buchalter's gunmen in his place. They warned off Coll, then finished Maranzano with pistols and knives.[35]

Luciano, triumphant, left New York's five families intact, but abolished the boss of bosses position. In its place, he created a corporate-style commission with New York's five bosses plus two more — Philadelphia's Angelo Bruno and Detroit's Giuseppe Zerilli — empowered to vote on national Mafia issues and settle territorial disputes. More importantly, Lucky and his non–Italian allies forged ahead with a series of meetings that confirmed and expanded the work begun in Atlantic City, establishing a national crime syndicate from coast to coast. The Mafia would have its place within that network, but it would not rule the roost.[36]

As Lucky and his partners knew, there was enough to go around.

· 4 ·

Gangbusters

Fine-tuning of the Cosa Nostra and the larger syndicate was not complete with the removal of selected Mustache Petes. Organizational meetings convened between autumn 1931 and summer 1934 in Chicago, Kansas City, Nova Scotia, Arkansas, and New York City, where Lucky Luciano presided as "Charles Ross" at the Waldorf Towers. Chicago police detained Luciano and Meyer Lansky after one gathering in April 1932, with Outfit leaders Paul Ricca and Rocco Fischetti, but all were soon released.[1]

While no minutes were kept of those discussions, testimony by informers and the evidence of various investigations gives us some idea of their agenda. Territories were defined, and rules established for the use of deadly force, exempting journalists and law enforcement officers except on rare occasions. When murder was required, significant killings were delegated to Lepke Buchalter's Brooklyn-based team of professionals. On a more profitable note, with Prohibition's end in sight, focus shifted to illegal gambling, labor racketeering, and the infiltration of the entertainment industry.[2]

Despite the best intentions, violence could not be totally eradicated. Rogue outsiders had to be eliminated, and the Mafia was not alone in suffering a bloody overhaul. Between 1931 and 1933, Dutch Schultz, Waxey

Chicago Outfit member Paul Ricca participated in meetings that formed America's national crime syndicate (National Archives).

46

Irving "Waxey Gordon" Wexler fought a bloody war with rival Jewish mobsters Meyer Lansky and Dutch Schultz (National Archives).

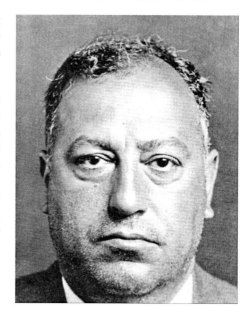

Gordon, Meyer Lansky and Ben Siegel fought a bloody "War of the Jews" in New York and New Jersey. Unlike the Castellammarese War, all of the principal leaders survived, with hostilities ended by Gordon's conviction on tax-evasion charges. Farther west, Lepke's gunmen eliminated holdout members of Detroit's Purple Gang, claiming their last victim in 1937.[3]

New Deals

While the Great Depression's onset virtually guaranteed election of a Democratic president in 1932, following 12 years of corruption, scandal, and laissez-faire handling of Wall Street by three successive Republican administrations, the syndicate still had to choose a candidate. Both Democratic frontrunners were past or present New York governors. Catholic Alfred Smith, Jr., a product of Manhattan's Lower East Side and a personal friend of high-ranking mobsters, held office from 1923 to 1928, when the Ku Klux Klan led successful opposition to his first White House bid on sectarian grounds. Successor Franklin Roosevelt came from old money but opposed the Tammany machine and had appointed the Seabury Commission to investigate municipal corruption in 1930, driving Mob-friendly Mayor Jimmy Walker from office in 1932. While both candidates favored repeal of Prohibition, Smith was the syndicate's logical choice.[4]

When the Democratic National Convention began in Chicago on June 27, 1932, delegates found liquor flowing freely at hospitality suites run by Luciano, Lansky, Frank Costello, Moe Dalitz, Frank Nitti and Longy Zwillman. From that meeting grew collaboration with Louisiana "Kingfish" Huey Long and Roosevelt himself, who promised to relent on federal prosecutions in return for syndicate support. It proved to be a ruse, but gangland's leaders only learned of their mistake in retrospect. Despite a tearful meeting with Al Smith, who warned that Roosevelt would break his promises, the Mob backed

FDR. On November 8 he crushed incumbent Herbert Hoover, claiming 89 percent of the popular vote.[5]

One promise kept by Roosevelt was Prohibition's repeal. Twelve days before FDR's inauguration, Congress passed the 21st Amendment, repealing the 18th. Thirty-six states ratified the amendment by December 5, when it took effect and legalized the sale of alcoholic beverages. Some mobsters quickly "went legit" as partners in new liquor franchises, while others stuck with bootlegging despite repeal, preferring the profits from untaxed liquor. One such operation, dubbed Molaska Corporation, was a joint project of the Cleveland and New York syndicates, chartered on November 25, 1933. Molaska ran huge outlaw distilleries in Ohio and New Jersey, closing shop only after Treasury agents struck two of the plants in January 1935.[6] By then, it was clear that FDR had reneged on his campaign promise, but the federal assault was disjointed at best.

A House Divided

While many mobsters had paid fines or served short jail terms for Volstead violations since 1920, the first serious federal campaign against organized crime began 10 years later, led by the Treasury Department's Bureau of Internal Revenue. Ratification of the 16th Amendment in 1913 had created America's first federal income tax, and subsequent court rulings held that the law applied equally to criminal sources of revenue. Frustrated in their efforts to dry up the country or jail gangland killers, the feds thus turned to prosecuting Mob leaders for cheating Uncle Sam.[7]

Wide-open Chicago was the first proving ground, with Cook County's assessor the first defendant imprisoned. Frank Nitti was convicted in December 1930, followed by Ralph Capone in March 1931. Jurors convicted brother Al in October 1931, with a stunning 11-year sentence resulting. By January 1933, another 102 gangsters and politicians faced similar charges. Murray Humphreys joined the list in June, and was subsequently imprisoned.[8]

In New York and environs, where Treasury agents announced their campaign in November 1930, targets included NYPD vice officer James Quinlivan, Harlem "policy kings" Wilfred Brunder and Jose Miro, Bronx mafioso Gaetano Gagliano, New York State Federation of Labor Vice President Patrick Commerford, and "artichoke king" Joseph Castaldo. It was no accident that the gunmen sent to kill Salvatore Maranzano in September 1931 came disguised as Treasury auditors.[9]

While revenue agents were busy gang-busting, the Federal Bureau of Investigation was curiously apathetic toward organized crime. The reason for

J. Edgar Hoover (left) and an unnamed FBI agent pose on the bureau's firing range. Hoover's gun is unloaded (Library of Congress).

that strange blind spot remains a topic of debate among historians, and contradictions still persist within the FBI itself. Director John Edgar Hoover — appointed in 1924, commanding until his death in 1972 — publicly denied the Mafia's existence until 1963. Meanwhile, the bureau's website to this day insists that "the legal tools given to the FBI by Congress [in 1934], as well as Bureau initiatives to upgrade its own professionalism and that of law enforcement, resulted in the arrest or demise of all the major gangsters by 1936."[10]

Hoover was not entirely blind from the beginning of his tenure. FBI agents arrested Al Capone on a contempt charge in 1929, later suggesting (falsely) that the bureau was responsible for his imprisonment. In the 1930s, Hoover established a Hoodlum Squad in Miami, Florida, to identify visiting mobsters, but took no action against them. In 1935 he called Dutch Schultz "public enemy number one," and in 1937 Hoover led raids against Mafia-owned brothels in Baltimore. Internal memos from that campaign claimed that Hoover "was interested in the big racketeers and the tide of dirty money that flowed from the houses to the racketeers and through them filtered out to local protectors, police, small-time politicians and even ultimately into the coffers of state political machines." Hoover personally vowed that he would continue that crusade "until Baltimore is completely cleaned up."[11]

But he did not, and it never was. Instead, something changed at FBI headquarters. Hoover forgot about the Mafia in 1938, adopting the line that "hoodlums" only ran in local gangs, and were "not of a foreign county, but of American stock with a highly patriotic American name. The names are monotonously of a type that we have come to classify as American, against the Latin or north of Europe foreigners."[12] So much for Luciano, Lansky, Anastasia and the rest.

What caused that change of heart? Clearly, we cannot credit claims by Cartha Deloach, the FBI's third-in-command, that the bureau lacked "sufficient proof to say that there was such a thing as the Cosa Nostra — a national crime syndicate" prior to the Apalachin conference of 1957. And, in any case, Hoover *still* labeled any mention of the Mafia "baloney" for another five years afterward.[13]

The most charitable view of Hoover's blind spot on organized crime suggests that he feared corruption of his agents if they tangled with the Mob, and that he worried that the low conviction rate in Mafia-related cases might subvert the bureau's image as a law enforcement agency that "always got its man." More to the point, perhaps, was recognition of the ties between the underworld and some of Hoover's wealthy friends—including politicians who controlled the FBI's annual budget. At the opposite extreme lie tales of blackmail, claiming that the Mob held photographs of Hoover dressed as a woman, engaged in homosexual acts.[14]

Meyer Lansky (right), escorted by an unidentified detective, allegedly blackmailed J. Edgar Hoover with incriminating photographs (Library of Congress).

In fact, Hoover himself apparently had friends among high-ranking mafiosi. Next to the FBI, Hoover's great passion was horse-racing. His annual "inspection tours" of FBI field offices invariably led to Mob-owned racetracks and resorts, where he and constant companion Clyde Tolson were "comped" across the board. Hoover bet heavily on races, helped by inside tips, and also profited from stocks recommended by Mob-allied friends. Columnist Walter Winchell and others reportedly introduced Hoover to high-ranking mobsters including Frank Costello, Meyer Lansky, Santo Trafficante, Jr., Salvatore Giancana, and John Rosselli—who told friends, "I knew Hoover. I'd buy him drinks and we'd talk. It was fun to be with the director of the FBI like that." Many witnesses describe Hoover's cordial relationship with Frank Costello, although one—political operative and longtime Hoover friend George Edward Allen—recalled a hostile exchange between Hoover and Costello at Manhattan's Waldorf Astoria, where both kept apartments. On that occasion, Costello approached Hoover but allegedly was rebuffed, Hoover telling him, "You stay out of my bailiwick and I'll stay out of yours."[15]

Allen's presence may have prompted Hoover's curt response, staged for the benefit of witnesses. In any case, the comment fairly summarized FBI actions from 1938 onward. Despite surveillance and collection of fat dossiers on various mobsters, the bureau made no moves against them until the 1960s.

Meanwhile, another federal agency took the opposite view. Formed in August 1930 and led for three decades by Director Harry Anslinger, the Treasury Department's Federal Bureau of Narcotics trumpeted the news of Mafia involvement in drug trafficking and other crimes. Hoover despised Anslinger for publicly contradicting him, and for "copying" the FBI's initials—although Hoover's bureau did not take its present name until July 1935. Anslinger's agents were the antithesis of Hoover's "G-men," operating undercover, trailing mobsters abroad, compiling a Black Book of 800 mafiosi with full criminal records. Hoover declined the offer of a copy for his records, and never missed a chance to denigrate Anslinger or the FBN. In 1939, after Walter Winchell arranged fugitive Lepke Buchalter's surrender to Hoover on narcotics charges, Hoover blocked Anslinger's access to Lepke for two days of fruitless questioning. That pointless rivalry continued until Anslinger retired, in 1962—a year before Hoover "discovered" *La Cosa Nostra*.[16]

Taking Hollywood

Since Prohibition, mobsters have enjoyed associating with celebrities. Most of the era's entertainers got their starts at nightclubs and resorts owned

by the syndicate. In 1933 the Mob took aim at Hollywood directly, through the International Alliance of Theatrical and Stage Employees, demanding tribute from theater chains and staging strikes if the cash was not delivered. At the IATSE's convention in July 1934, members elected syndicate front man George Browne as their president, while Meyer Lansky, Ben Siegel, Frank Nitti, Longy Zwillman and Cleveland's Al Polizzi watched from the sidelines. Next came wholesale extortion from Hollywood's top studios, but Chicago operative Willie Bioff overstepped his bounds in 1937, when he tried to muscle the Screen Actors Guild. SAG president Robert Montgomery launched a private investigation of Bioff, leading to Willie's indictment for tax evasion in 1939.[17]

En route to prison three years later, Bioff cut a deal. While mobsters from New York and Cleveland went unscathed, his testimony produced

Mobster-turned-informer Willie Bioff (Library of Congress).

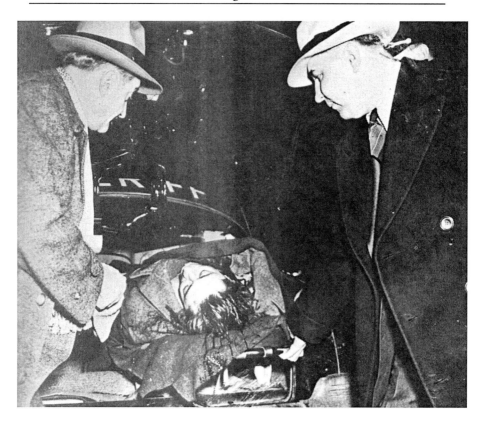

Alleged suicide victim Frank "The Enforcer" Nitti (**National Archives**).

indictments of seven Chicago Outfit leaders in March 1943, on federal extortion charges. Defendant Frank Nitti allegedly killed himself prior to trial, though a witness saw him in the custody of Chicago detectives the night he died. The surviving defendants—Paul Ricca, Philip D'Andrea, Louis "Little New York" Campagna, Charles "Cherry Nose" Gioe, John Rosselli, and Francis "Frank Diamond" Maritote, plus Louis Kaufman of New Jersey—were convicted in December 1943. The six Chicago hoods got 10-year prison terms, while Kaufman received seven years.[18]

On top of Nitti's death, it was a stunning blow to the Outfit—but behind the scenes, the fix was in. In August 1947, surprise early paroles were granted to Campagna, D'Andrea, Gioe, Ricca and Rosselli. Mayor Edward Kelly warned the newly-freed convicts to stay out of Chicago, while the *Chicago Tribune* asked, "Who Fixed This One?" The answer: U.S. Attorney General Thomas Clark. In Chicago, mafioso Antonio Accardo told acquaintances that Clark was "100 percent doing favors" in exchange for "a lot of cash" funneled through "high-powered influential lawyers." When congressional investigators held hearings on the controversial paroles, Clark sealed his files with a claim of executive privilege. Congress finally pronounced the paroles "improvidently granted," but proof of Clark's corruption did not reach FBI headquarters until 1964, by which time Clark was in his 15th year as an associate justice of the U.S. Supreme Court. Hoover kept the information to himself.[19]

Dewey's Crusade

Thomas Edmund Dewey graduated from Columbia University's law school in 1925, then entered private practice while campaigning for political reform. March 1931 saw him appointed as a federal prosecutor in charge of prosecuting Waxey Gordon for tax evasion. Meyer Lansky's brother Jake furnished incriminating evidence against Gordon, seeking to end New York's "War of the Jews," but murdered witnesses and other setbacks stalled Gordon's conviction until December 1933.[20] As Gordon shuffled off to serve a 10-year sentence, Dewey fixed his sights on Dutch Schultz.

Indicted for tax evasion in January 1933, Schultz fled into hiding, remaining at large until November 1934. Represented by ex–Capone attorney James Noonan, Dutch won dismissal of seven felony counts, then escaped conviction when his jury deadlocked in April 1935. Dewey suspected jury-tampering and moved the second trial upstate to Malone, New York, where Schultz impressed the locals with his generosity. Jurors acquitted him on August 1, 1935, and earned a scolding from the judge, while Mayor Fiorello La Guardia forbade his return to New York City. When Dewey — now Manhattan's special prosecutor — filed new tax charges in Syracuse, five days later, Schultz went berserk.[21]

His plan, addressed to the syndicate's board of directors, was simple: Dewey must die. Albert Anastasia and Gurrah Shapiro supported the scheme, but Lucky Luciano led the negative majority, whereupon Schultz vowed to proceed on his own. Shooters from Lepke's private army scotched the plot on October 23, 1935, assassinating Schultz and three of his aides at Newark's Palace Chop House.[22]

Luciano soon had cause to regret saving Dewey. On April 2, 1936, Dewey charged him with leading a $12 million vice ring that enslaved prostitutes. Lucky fled to Hot Springs, Arkansas, where Manhattan expatriate Owney Madden sheltered fugitives from justice, but detectives found him and his extradition fight proved fruitless. Three of his indicted cohorts testified for the state, naming Luciano as the "czar" of white slavery, while various madams joined the chorus. Convicted with eight codefendants on 62 counts, Luciano

Dutch Schultz, fatally wounded at Newark's Palace Chop House (Library of Congress).

Police escort Lepke Buchalter (in plaid tie) to his trial on racketeering charges (Library of Congress).

received a sentence of 30 to 50 years on June 18, 1936. At the time, Lucky claimed he was framed — an assertion supported when several prosecution witnesses later recanted their statements.[23]

Guilty or not, Luciano was on his way to prison at Dannemora, known as "New York's Siberia," when Dewey convened a grand jury to investigate industrial racketeering. Defendants Lepke and Gurrah received two-year terms in November 1936, for terrorizing members of the fur-dressing trade, then posted appeal bonds and vanished. Pursuers ranged from Manhattan to Poland, all in vain, until Shapiro surrendered in April 1938. Lepke remained at large, now facing narcotics charges filed by Harry Anslinger, until Walter Winchell arranged for J. Edgar Hoover to "capture" Buchalter in August 1939. Convicted of drug trafficking with cohort Max Schmukler, Lepke received a 14-year sentence in January 1940. Fuming over his pre-emption by the feds, Dewey convicted Buchalter and two accomplices on further racketeering charges in March 1940, producing another sentence of 30 years to life.[24]

And still, Lepke's problems were not behind him.

"Murder, Inc."

In February 1940 prosecutors indicted Brooklyn mobsters Martin "Buggsy" Goldstein, Anthony "Duke" Maffetore and Abraham "Kid Twist" Reles for a murder committed 17 years earlier. All were members of Buchalter's organization, soon dubbed "Murder Incorporated" by journalists, and Reles was the first to squeal for leniency. First naming other gunmen from the crew, he fingered Lepke as their boss in April, with specific details of a homicide from 1936. By September, Reles had confessed to 11 slayings and furnished details of 57 more.[25]

Next in line to "sing" was gunman Harry "Pittsburgh Phil" Strauss, joined by Vito "Chicken Head" Gurino after ex-friends tried to silence him preemptively. Gurino confessed to three murders to escape execution, while Strauss reneged, feigned insanity, and wound up on death row. He would not be alone: with Reles as the state's star witness, death awaited Buggsy Goldstein, Frank "The Dasher" Abbandando, Harry "Happy" Maione, Emmanuel "Mendy"

Contract killer-turned-informer Abe "Kid Twist" Reles (left) with codefendant Martin "Buggsy" Goldstein (National Archives).

Weiss and Louis Capone (no relation to Al). Charles "Bug" Workman got life for killing Dutch Schultz, while Vito Gurino received 80 years. Irving "Knadles" Nitzberg was twice sentenced to die, but appellate courts voided both verdicts. Jacob Drucker received 25 years and died in prison. Lepke himself was convicted in November 1940, and died in Sing Sing's electric chair on March 4, 1944. He remains the only syndicate leader executed in American history.[26]

Abe Reles did not survive to witness Lepke's death, or to testify against an even bigger target. Murder Inc. witness Harry Greenberg had run to California in 1939, where he was murdered. Reles fingered Bugsy Siegel and mafioso Paolo "Frankie" Carbo for the hit, resulting in their September 1941 indictment. Seven weeks later, on November 12, Reles plummeted from the sixth-floor window of his room at Coney Island's Half-Moon Hotel, where

Police surround the corpse of Abe Reles following his plunge from a window at Coney Island's Half-Moon Hotel (National Archives).

he lived under police protection. Knotted sheets found beside the corpse suggested an escape attempt, oddly revised in some accounts to a "practical joke" planned by Reles. Police Commissioner Lewis Valentine demoted five officers for "laxity," but their commander, Captain Frank Bals, was subsequently promoted to deputy commissioner when ex–district attorney William O'Dwyer—a friend of Frank Costello—became New York's mayor in 1946. Meanwhile, Frankie Carbo was acquitted of the Greenberg murder in Los Angeles, and Siegel's charges were dismissed. Mob insiders later claimed the guards received $100,000 to kill Reles before he could testify against Siegel or implicate Albert Anastasia.[27]

Operation Underworld

America's belated entry into World War II sparked widespread concern about "enemy aliens," including Italians. Those fears were realized on February 9, 1942, when fire ravaged the troop carrier USS *Lafayette*—formerly the French luxury liner SS *Normandie*—at its berth on the Hudson River. The blaze was accidental, but it aggravated fears of Axis sabotage on New York's waterfront.[28]

The Office of Naval Intelligence soon determined that said waterfront was controlled, in effect, by the International Longshoreman's Association — and the union, in turn, was owned by brothers Albert Anastasia and Anthony "Tough Tony" Anastasio. District Attorney Frank Hogan suggested that ONI spokesmen approach the Mob through Joseph "Socks" Lanza, Mafia boss of Lower Manhattan's Fulton Fish Market, and so began the curious episode known as Operation Underworld. In simple terms, the ONI wanted gangsters to police the waterfront for spies and saboteurs. Lanza, facing extortion charges and embarrassed by expulsion of his United Seafood Workers Union from the American Federation of Labor, met with ONI Lieutenant Commander Charles Haffenden to arrange a deal. Lanza's first condition was a bid for leniency. Beyond that, he explained, any aid to the war effort would depend on Lucky Luciano.[29]

Lucky, caged at Dannemora, was not in a helpful mood. More meetings followed, between Haffenden, Luciano attorney Moses Polakoff, and Meyer Lansky. Finally, the ONI persuaded state authorities to transfer Luciano from Siberia to Sing Sing, and from there to Great Meadow Correctional Facility at Comstock, north of Albany, the thousand-acre country club of New York's penal system. From his new, more comfortable digs, Luciano issued orders to his troops. The New York waterfront suffered no sabotage, and some accounts suggest that Lucky also paved the way for the Allied conquest of

Sicily in 1943, with messages sent to his Mafia brethren back home. Lanza was the operation's loser: jailed without bond in November 1942, he pled guilty to extortion two months later and received a term of seven and a half to fifteen years.[30]

While Lucky Luciano helped the ONI, his fellow mafiosi earned a fortune from the war, peddling stolen or counterfeit ration stamps, along with rationed products themselves. Gasoline and auto tires were top sellers, and Carlo Gambino organized Brooklyn's butchers in a thriving black-market meat trade. Nationwide, mobsters bought hundreds of gas stations that never felt the pinch of government restrictions.[31]

One mafioso who missed the Manhattan bonanza was Vito Genovese. Indicted in 1937 for the 1934 murder of racketeer Ferdinand "The Shadow" Boccia, Genovese fled to Italy and befriended Benito Mussolini, despite the dictator's legendary hatred of mafiosi. In January 1943, Genovese arranged the Manhattan murder of Carlo Tresca, an Italian anti-fascist whose essays outraged Mussolini. Awarded Italy's highest civilian medal, the Order of St. Maurice, Genovese nonetheless switched sides when Allied forces liberated the country, attaching himself to the American Military Government of Occupied Territories as an interpreter and all-around fixer. He ran a lucrative black market on the side, until word of his outstanding murder warrant reached Italy. Returned to New York for trial in November 1944, Genovese denied the charge and secured its dismissal in June 1946.[32]

Vito Genovese fled from New York to Italy, avoiding murder charges (National Archives).

In exchange for Lucky Luciano's service to the nation, whatever it was, New York's parole board recommended commutation of his sentence on December 3, 1945. Thomas Dewey, now the governor, granted that plea on condition that Lucky be deported to Italy. On February 8, 1946, guards moved him to the SS *Laura Keene*, bound for Genoa from Brooklyn's Bush Terminal. Before it sailed on February 10, Luciano enjoyed a lavish going-away party with America's top gangsters, guarded by Albert Anastasia's stevedores. Charles Haffenden, meanwhile, became New York's Commissioner of Marine and Aviation on January 1, 1946, controlling both the city's waterfront and airports. In months to come, he would be seen golfing with Frank Costello.[33]

On May 17, 1946, J. Edgar Hoover received a memorandum outlining the terms of Luciano's parole. While still allegedly convinced the Mafia did not exist, he wrote across the page, "This is an amazing and fantastic case. We should get all the facts for it looks rotten to me from several angles ... a shocking example of misuse of Naval authority in the interests of a hoodlum. It surprises me that they didn't give Luciano the Navy Cross."[34]

In other home-front news, William O'Dwyer won election as New York City's mayor on November 6, 1945. One week earlier, a grand jury convened by D.A.–successor George Beldock had accused O'Dwyer of scuttling a "perfect" murder case against Albert Anastasia. O'Dwyer denied the charge and sought to refute it in marathon testimony, but a presentment issued on December 20 charged him with "negligence, incompetence and flagrant irresponsibility whereby Anastasia was permitted to escape prosecution for ... murder and for a number of other vicious crimes." Beldock pledged an Anastasia hunt that ultimately came to nothing, while Judge Franklin Taylor voided the grand jury's charges in February 1946. Two months later, Governor Dewey refused to permit a second probe of O'Dwyer's behavior in office. Elected to a second term in 1949, O'Dwyer faced a police corruption scandal revealed by Kings County District Attorney Miles McDonald. Claiming poor health, O'Dwyer resigned in August 1950.[35]

Winning the Peace

Luciano had no intention of staying in Italy. In October 1946 he sailed to Caracas, Venezuela, flew from there to Mexico City, then moved on to Havana, where Meyer Lansky waited with a luxurious suite at the Hotel Nacional. He registered under his birth name and was protected by dictator Fulgencio Batista. Lansky offered Lucky a share of the hotel-casino for $150,000, but Luciano declined to front the money himself. Instead, he planned to deduct it from "welcome-home" tribute supplied by fellow mafiosi he had summoned to a meeting in Havana, scheduled to convene on December 22.[36]

Vito Genovese arrived early, urging Luciano to retire and name Genovese as his successor. They should also kill Albert Anastasia, Genovese said, because Anastasia planned to assassinate FBN Director Harry Anslinger. Luciano angrily rebuffed Genovese, reminding him that Don Vito trafficked narcotics while Anastasia did not, and warned Genovese not to raise either subject again.[37]

The crowd that gathered in Havana on December 22 was reminiscent of Atlantic City in 1929. This time, Luciano and Lansky hosted, while the New York–New Jersey delegation included Genovese and Anastasia, Frank Costello, Joseph Bonanno, Gaetano Lucchese, Joe Adonis, Giuseppe Profaci, Giuseppe Magliocco, Michele Miranda, Anthony "Little Augie Pisano" Carfano, Joseph "Doc" Stacher, Longy Zwillman and Willie Moretti. Chicago sent Tony "Joe Batters" Accardo, brothers Charles and Rocco Fischetti, plus crooner Frank Sinatra to provide the meeting's entertainment. Stefano Magaddino came from Buffalo, while Carlos Marcello represented New Orleans with Costello partner Philip "Dandy Phil" Kastel. Moe Dalitz brought Cleveland's greetings to Lucky, and Santo Trafficante, Jr., carried the obligatory envelope of cash from Florida.[38]

After thanking the attendees for their money, Luciano "casually mentioned" that he had revised his 1931 opinion on the boss of bosses title, deciding that he should assume it after all. Anastasia supported the move, telling Lucky, "For me, you are the Big Boss, whether you like it or not. That's the way I look at it, and I would like to hear from anybody who don't feel the same way." Genovese remained silent, and Luciano later told biographers, "That was all I was after — first, to teach Vito a lesson in public without him losin' face and also to get the title without havin' to fight for it. So I won my first point, and frankly, I didn't give a shit what happened after that."[39]

The last comment was clearly disingenuous. Following the capture of a purely nominal title, Luciano moved on to discuss the global narcotics trade. Years later, he declared, "I told 'em I want 'em to get the hell outa that business, to stop it right then and there, and to forget it." Few students of the Cosa Nostra today believe that Luciano opposed drug trafficking. FBN agent Charles Siragusa claims that Luciano himself established the post-war heroin pipeline from Italy to the U.S., refining morphine base from the Middle East at a Palermo lab disguised as a candy factory. If Luciano *did* condemn the drug trade, his advice fell on deaf ears.[40]

Next up for discussion was the subject of Las Vegas, Nevada — or, more specifically, Ben Siegel's construction of the desert town's first lavish resort. Nevada, having legalized gambling in 1931, seemed the ultimate paradise for gangland investors bent on skimming untaxed profits from legitimate casinos. Siegel's Fabulous Flamingo had the syndicate's backing, but its endless cost overruns raised suspicion that Bugsy himself had been skimming. Moe Dalitz had investigated Siegel's operation and reported that the Bug's girlfriend, Virginia Hill, was bearing luggage filled with cash to Switzerland. Despite that finding, Lansky spoke on Siegel's behalf, convincing the delegates to see if he

Lucky Luciano nemesis Harry Anslinger (right) discusses drug-control policies with Assistant Secretary of the Treasury Stephen Gibbons (center) and Col. C.H.L. Sharman, chief of Canadian Narcotic Control (Library of Congress).

could turn a profit for them when the Flamingo opened on December 26. Nervous but hoping to recoup their losses with interest, the syndicate's directors agreed.[41]

Luciano later claimed that as the delegates prepared to leave, Genovese approached him for another private word. This time, Don Vito warned that Harry Anslinger had learned of Luciano's presence in Havana and would soon turn up the heat to have him ousted. Suspecting Genovese himself had tipped the FBN, Luciano claimed that he administered a beating that left Vito bedridden for three days, after which Luciano and Anastasia hustled him aboard a flight to New York, threatening to kill him if he ever spoke about the incident.[42] There may be nothing to the story, but the hatred between Genovese and Anastasia has been well established. It would ultimately lead to murder, and the fateful gathering at Apalachin.

Whoever tipped the FBN, Anslinger *was* aware of Lucky's hideout at the

Hotel Nacional. In February 1947, Anslinger wrote to Havana, asking the Cuban government to expel Luciano. When Batista dragged his feet, Anslinger went public, announcing that Cuba would receive no more U.S. medical supplies while Lucky remained in residence. Arrested on February 22, Luciano fought extradition but lost his case and was deported on March 20. Arriving in Italy on April 12, Lucky was arrested once more and sat in jail until May 14.[43] Rumors persist that he later returned to Mexico, and possibly reentered the United States, but nothing is confirmed.

Viva Las Vegas!

While Luciano suffered his travails in Cuba and in Italy, the clock ran down for Ben Siegel. Once an equal of Lucky and Meyer Lansky in the syndicate hierarchy, the Bug had fallen on hard times, and he could not redeem himself.

A short year earlier, Siegel had been triumphant in the struggle to seize control of Nationwide News Service, the Chicago-based firm that supplied American bookmakers with real-time race results. James Ragen, Sr., had managed Nationwide for owner Moses Annenberg, then took control when Annenberg was jailed for tax evasion in 1939. Chicago's Outfit craved control of Nationwide — and Siegel did his part, corraling California bookies — but Ragen stood firm until drive-by gunmen wounded him on August 15, 1946. From his hospital bed, Ragen named the shooters for FBI agents, but Director Hoover then withdrew protection, leaving Ragen to be poisoned under the eyes of his nurses. Ragen's affidavit disappeared, along with any hope of jailing his killers. Hoover did launch an investigation of the Outfit — inanely titled "CAPGA," for "Capone Gang," 15 years after Big Al's imprisonment — but it produced no prosecutions.[44]

Siegel's Flamingo flopped when it opened, still unfinished, on December 26, 1946. Closed two weeks later, it reopened with all facilities functional on March 1, 1947, and reported a $300,000 profit by May. Still, it was too little and too late. A sniper killed Siegel at Virginia Hill's mansion in Beverly Hills, California, on June 20, 1947. Within minutes of the shooting, syndicate gamblers Gus Greenbaum, Moe Sedway and Morris Rosen appeared to take command of the Flamingo, guiding it into an opulent future.[45]

Despite his personal failure, Siegel's vision for Las Vegas proved prophetic. A second resort, the Thunderbird, opened in September 1948, with Meyer Lansky pulling strings behind the scenes. Moe Dalitz and his partners opened the Desert Inn in April 1950. Other glitzy "carpet joints" included the Sahara (opened in October 1952, staked by the Outfit with New York partners), the

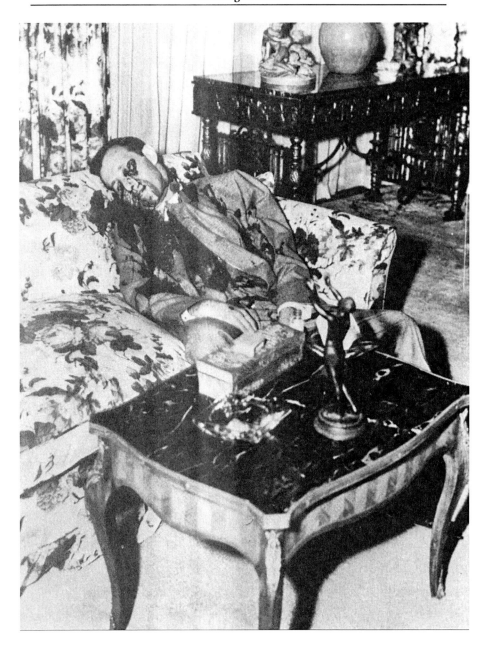

Benjamin "Bugsy" Siegel, executed for skimming funds from the Flamingo resort in Las Vegas (Library of Congress).

Sands (December 1952, owned by Lansky, Adonis, Costello, Stacher and others, with nine percent for Frank Sinatra), the Riviera (April 1955, run by Gus Greenbaum for Chicago), the Dunes (May 1955, bankrolled by New England mafioso Raymond Patriarca), the Hacienda (June 1956, reportedly "straight"), the Tropicana (April 1957, backed by Costello with Phil Kastel), and the Stardust (July 1958, another Dalitz venture).[46] Las Vegas would earn billions over time. No one can say how much was siphoned off the top for syndicate landlords.

· 5 ·

Bright Lights, Big Cities

Americans heard a great deal about organized crime as the 1940s closed. December 1948 brought a disclosure that mobsters nationwide were using war veterans as fronts for licensing of liquor stores and nightclubs. Nine months later, the Chicago Crime Commission and the American Municipal Association asked U.S. Attorney General J. Howard McGrath to launch a federal rackets investigation. FBI headquarters opposed the notion, and specifically declined to investigate links between mobsters and police in Providence, Rhode Island. The AMA repeated its plea in December 1949, amid reports that Mob bookies earned $15 billion annually ($136 billion today), but the Justice Department remained deaf and blind to what *The New York Times* called "respectable parasites."[1]

Agitation over mobsters was acute in New York, where state authorities denied boxing champion Joe Louis's bid for a beer franchise in February 1949, based on his ties to the Chicago Outfit. Further outrage briefly flared in August, with the revelation that Joe Adonis owned a conveyance firm that transported "all Ford automobiles" to Manhattan and environs. Political rivals blamed Mayor O'Dwyer for the spread of prostitution, drugs and gambling in New York City. Kings County's grand jury launched a probe of Brooklyn gambling syndicates in December 1949, and when Mayor O'Dwyer suggested legalized betting, Governor Dewey blasted the plan as "shocking, indecent and immoral."[2]

Finally, the response to local pleas for help would come, not from the Department of Justice, but from the U.S. Senate.

The Heat

Carey Estes Kefauver was born in Tennessee on July 26, 1903. He earned a law degree from Yale in 1927 and spent a dozen years in private practice before turning his hand to politics. Elected to Congress in 1939, he served nine years before winning a seat in the Senate. On January 5, 1950, when he introduced a resolution for the Senate Committee on the Judiciary to investigate organized crime's role in interstate commerce, Kefauver was still a relative stripling on Capitol Hill. [3]

Immediate opposition struck from several quarters. First, the Senate Committee on Interstate and Foreign Commerce claimed jurisdiction over the issue. While compromise could solve that problem, stronger opposition came from Senate Majority Leader Scott Lucas of Illinois and Nevada's Patrick McCarran, co-chairman of the Judiciary Committee, both of whom denied that any probe was warranted. Wisconsin's Joseph McCarthy, meanwhile, coveted the Mob investigation for himself but dropped it when his ties to Frank Costello were revealed, thereafter focusing on Communists. Outside the Senate, both Attorney General McGrath and J. Edgar Hoover proclaimed that chasing "hoodlums" was a strictly local matter. President Harry Truman, a product of Tom Pendergast's political machine, was inclined to agree.[4]

Murder resolved the stalemate in April 1950, when two mafiosi were slain at Kansas City's First Ward Democratic Party headquarters. Eager Republicans entered the fray, urging creation of a Special Committee to Investigate Crime in Interstate Commerce, with five members drawn from both

Members of the Kefauver Committee included (from left) Senators Herbert O'Conor, Lester Hunt, Estes Kefauver, Alexander Wiley and Charles Tobey (National Archives).

the Commerce and Judiciary Committees. Vice President Alben Barkley cast the tie-breaking vote that established the new committee on May 3, 1950, with Kefauver as its chairman.[5]

Over the next year, Kefauver's committee held hearings in 14 major cities nationwide, calling more than 600 witnesses to testify. Assistance came from Harry Anslinger's FBN, the Internal Revenue Service, and local authorities, while Hoover's FBI remained aloof. Associate committee counsel Joseph Nellis met Director Hoover, who told him, "We don't know anything about the Mafia or the families in New York. We haven't followed this." Columnist Jack Anderson later wrote that "Kefauver told me the FBI tried to block it.... Hoover knew that if the public got alarmed about organized crime, the job would go to the FBI. And he didn't want the job." Beyond feigning ignorance, Hoover established a squad of agents "to determine and document the nonexistence of organized crime." Assistant Director Alan Belmont obligingly reported that the "Maffia [*sic*] is an alleged organization.... The organization's existence in the U.S. is doubtful."[6]

Nonetheless, Kefauver forged ahead, collecting information on the Mafia and the larger syndicate. Some of the hearings were televised live, bringing surly mobsters into American living rooms nationwide. One curious aspect of the investigation was its focus on gambling, while avoiding most specifics of the ongoing narcotics trade. Authors Sally Denton and Roger Morris suggest that FBN agent George White, on loan to the committee from Anslinger's office, deliberately sidetracked the probe to avoid exposure of the federal government's collaboration with drug-dealing anti-communist factions in Europe and Asia.[7]

Kefauver's first interim report, published on July 20, 1950, summarized findings from Florida, where "groups of known gangsters, from diverse sections of the country, ... assemble primarily at Miami Beach." A second report, issued on January 29, 1951, declared that "organized crime does exist," and that "these operations could not continue without the protection of police and with the connivance of local authorities." A third interim report, released on April 17, 1951, found that "the Mafia ... has an important part in binding together into a loose association the two major criminal syndicates as well as many minor gangs and individual hoodlums throughout the country." At that juncture, Kefauver's panel only recognized two groups of organized criminals in America: New York's "Costello-Adonis-Lansky crime syndicate" and Chicago's "Accardo-Guzik-Fischetti" Mob, both operating through fronts nationwide.[8]

Kefauver's final report, published on August 31, 1951, recommended establishment of a National Crime Coordinating Council, staffed by members of "privately established local crime commissions," to serve as a clearinghouse for information on the syndicate, thereby facilitating prosecutions. To curb organized crime, the committee recommended federal legislation designed to "substantially eliminate the so-called wire services" via strict licensing, criminalize transmission of race results "obtained surreptitiously or through stealth," increase penalties for narcotics offenses, and impose "special" penalties for any sale of narcotics to minors. Other proposed statutes would have tightened restrictions on untaxed liquor and entry of illegal aliens into the United States.[9] None of the bills was adopted by Congress.

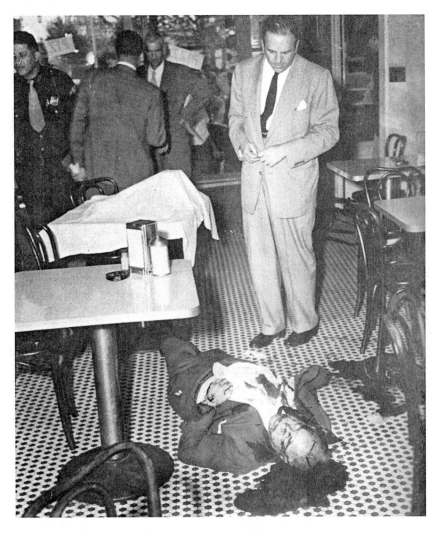

New Jersey mafioso Willie Moretti, murdered for speaking too freely before the Kefauver Committee (National Archives).

Finally, the committee cited 43 witnesses for contempt of Congress, based on their refusal to answer questions. The more notorious of those accused included Frank Costello and Joe Adonis from New York; Tony Accardo, Murray Humphries, Jake Guzik, Joseph Aiuppa and Rocco Fischetti from Chicago; Morris Kleinman, Lou Rothkopf and James Licavoli from Cleveland; Peter Licavoli from Detroit; Carlos Marcello and Phil Kastel from New Orleans; and Jack Dragna from Los Angeles. Of the 43, 22 defendants were finally convicted and sentenced to prison, but nearly all won reversal of their verdicts on appeal to the U.S. Supreme Court.[10]

Even so, some high-ranked mobsters fell as a result of the Kefauver heat. Willie Moretti, suffering from tertiary syphilis, spoke too freely before the committee in December 1950, and was slain as a result, at a New Jersey restaurant, on October 4, 1941. Mob-watchers blamed Albert Anastasia for that hit — and for the April 1951 execution of Philip Mangano in Brooklyn. Mangano's brother Vincent vanished the same day, clearing the way for Anastasia to assume command of the family. On the legal front, Meyer "Mickey" Cohen — Cleveland's front man in Los Angeles — was convicted of tax evasion in 1951, while Joe Adonis drew a two-year sentence for illegal gambling in New Jersey.[11]

Aftershocks

Pubicity surrounding the Kefauver hearings inspired creation of "little Kefauver committees" in various states nationwide. California Attorney General Edmund Brown was clearly premature when he declared his state "free of organized crime" in December 1952, but other jurisdictions claimed more substantive, if modest, victories. Oregon state police raided 100 illegal Clackamas County casinos in April 1951, seizing 115 gambling devices and 87 prisoners. Revenue agents in St. Louis used an obscure tax regulation to jail mega-bookie James Carroll. In Texas, where mafiosi Salvatore and Rosario Maceo ran wide-open vice in the "Free State of Galveston," state legislators found themselves obstructed by a mayor who asked, "If God couldn't stop prostitution, why should I?" Texas Rangers did it for him, but the job was not completed until 1957.[12]

New York had been the scene of Kefauver's most dramatic televised hearings, and state officials seemed determined to uproot the Mob. Governor Dewey had refused to testify before the Senate committee because it declined to visit him in Albany, but that fit of pique did not prevent him from dusting off his gangbuster's reputation. On March 28, 1951, Dewey created a five-member State Crime Commission with subpoena powers and a two-year mandate to investigate the underworld. At the same time, he empanelled a special grand jury to probe rampant gambling in Saratoga, a campaign that dealt Meyer Lansky his only conviction in September 1953.[13]

Despite legal challenges from Tammany Hall, the State Crime Commission survived and made life uncomfortable for various shady characters. Abraham Goldman, a deputy chief inspector with NYPD, resigned when his ties to Frank Costello were exposed. Reopening of the Abe Reles murder proved fruitless, but Mayor O'Dwyer suffered new embarrassment over his handling of Albert Anastasia. Some racketeers subpoenaed by the panel fled to California for the duration, while others struck a defiant pose. Anastasia stormed out of the hearing room after refusing to answer 97 questions, then squared off with the feds. Missing and murdered witnesses hampered his prosecution on tax-evasion charges, but ultimate conviction brought the mafioso a one-year sentence, rather than the maximum decade. Meanwhile, Anastasia beat a bid by Washington to strip him of his U.S. citizenship.[14]

Joe Adonis was less fortunate. Indicted with three codefendants on New Jersey gambling charges, he received a two-to-three-year prison term in May 1951. A second trial, for contempt of the Kefauver Committee, saw Adonis convicted again in February 1953, and while he ultimately beat that charge on appeal, a parallel perjury case threatened further jail time. Immigration agents had the last word, however, disproving the mobster's claim that he was born Stateside, rather than in Italy. Legal maneuvers stalled deportation until January 1956, when Adonis gave up the fight and returned to his homeland voluntarily, dying there in 1971.[15]

Gangland "prime minister" Frank Costello was also under fire. Slapped with a contempt charge for walking out on the Kefauver Committee, he rebounded with a Miami Beach interview, regaling friend Walter Winchell with his philosophy on gambling. "The Weather Bureau

Vito Genovese was stripped of his citizenship, but never deported (National Archives).

says tomorrow will be sunny," Costello proclaimed. "So you're a long-shot guy and you take a piece it will rain. Isn't everything in life a gamble?" Unamused, the IRS charged him with tax evasion and saw him convicted in May 1954. A five-year term in that case was upheld on appeal, but Costello defeated the government's bid to denaturalize him in December 1954.[16]

Vito Genovese also faced trouble from Immigration, whose agents sought to revoke his citizenship in November 1952. Adding insult to injury, the wife whose first husband Don Vito had murdered decades earlier now dragged him through divorce court, spilling details of his finances that humiliated the would-be boss of bosses and placed his New Jersey mansion on the auction block to satisfy late alimony payments. Unwilling to kill his ex despite the urging of other bosses, Genovese endured her testimony for years on end, including a 1955 Waterfront Commission hearing that detailed his labor racketeering in New Jersey, and another grand jury session in 1957. Despite her best efforts, however, the woman scorned could not send Genovese to prison.[17]

McClellan

Four years after Estes Kefauver closed his investigation of organized crime, two years after he failed to capture the Democratic presidential nomination, the Senate took another shot at racket-busting. This time, the vehicle was Joe McCarthy's Permanent Subcommittee on Investigations, but Wisconsin's disgraced Red-hunter was replaced as chairman by John Little McClellan of Arkansas, newly embarked on the third of his six Senate terms. While *The New York Times* declared that McClellan would tolerate "no more circuses," he was an outspoken opponent of organized labor, bent on using any probe of gangland to undermine unions.[18]

To that end, McClellan retained young Robert Kennedy, who had briefly served as counsel to McCarthy, resigned in July 1953, then rejoined the committee in February 1954. While Kennedy was far too liberal for McClellan's taste, especially on civil rights, he made a perfect front man for attacks on unions and Republicans. The McClellan Committee aimed its opening salvo at Murray Chotiner, a shady political operative who launched Richard Nixon's career with underworld support in 1946, raising enough questions about his ethics to make the GOP dispense with Chotiner's services in the 1956 presidential election.[19]

By January 1957, McClellan and Kennedy had a new committee to work with, and racketeers were — at least ostensibly — their primary target. Armed with extensive subpoena and investigative powers, the Select Committee on Improper Activities in Labor and Management focused its spotlight on the scandal-ridden International Brotherhood of Teamsters. Robert Kennedy's elder brother, Senator John F. Kennedy of Massachusetts, saw the crusade as a vehicle to boost his chances of securing the 1960 Democratic presidential nomination, while his father—friend and colleague of the nation's great ex-bootleggers—counseled restraint.[20]

The new committee first took aim at Teamster president Dave Beck and his top aides, based in Seattle, Washington. Union leaders did their best to stall the inquiry—Beck himself would plead his Fifth Amendment privilege 117 times—but obstructionism could not halt exposure of the fact that $322,000 had vanished from the Teamsters treasury under Beck's administration. Testimony from those who would speak linked the union to mobsters, organized gambling and vice. Beck declined to seek reelection in May 1957, ceding control of the Teamsters to Mob ally James Riddle Hoffa, but resignation would not spare him from prosecution. Convicted of embezzling union funds in February 1958, Beck received a 15-year sentence. A second conviction, for tax evasion in February 1959, added five years to that term. Mean-

Robert Kennedy (left), with an unidentified McClellan Committee staffer, confronts Jimmy Hoffa (right) during Senate hearings on the Teamsters Union (Library of Congress).

while, Teamster leaders defied calls for a cleanup of their brotherhood, result-ing in expulsion from the AFL-CIO in December 1957.[21]

Encouraged by their first victory, McClellan and Kennedy forged ahead. The next phase of their investigation, while turning up heat on the Teamsters and earning Robert Kennedy undying hatred from new IBT president Jimmy Hoffa, also expanded to scrutinize other Mob-infested unions, including the International Longshoremen's Association, the Hotel Employees and Restau-rant Employees Union, and the International Union of Operating Engineers. Racketeers were found in all of them, during 30 months of public hearings that involved some 1,500 witnesses, producing 20,432 pages of transcripts.[22]

In public statements, Senator McClellan railed against the mobsters who infested labor unions as "human parasites." On November 13, 1957, FBN agent Joseph Amato advised the committee that Vincent Squillante, an officer of New York Teamsters Local 813, was also a mafioso. Robert Kennedy, intrigued, asked, "Is there any organization such as the Mafia, or is that just the name given to the hierarchy in the Italian underworld?" Amato replied, "That is a big question to answer. But we believe that there does exist today in the United States a society, loosely organized, for the specific purpose of smuggling narcotics and committing other crimes.... It has its core in Italy and it is nationwide. In fact, international."[23]

Proof of Amato's claim would come one day later, from upstate New York.

· 6 ·

Rumors of War

Despite various state and federal investigations in the 1950s, life went on for mafiosi nationwide. In May 1952 FBN agents reported a small gathering of Italian-American mobsters on one of the Florida Keys. Two years later, the Cosa Nostra opened its membership rolls for the first time since 1932, when recruitment was halted to freeze various families at the strength they enjoyed following the Castellammarese War. Also in 1954, the FBN spied on Mafia meetings in Los Angeles, in a Chicago suburb, and in Morningside, New Jersey. Albert Anastasia entered federal prison in November 1954 and returned to his family in March 1956, two months before 35 known mafiosi rallied in New York City. FBN agents shadowed another sit-down at Binghamton, New York, on October 17–18, 1956. Among the topics raised in 1956 was Salvatore "Momo" Giancana's selection to replace "retiring" Chicago boss Tony Accardo. Only the latter of those meetings found the full Mafia commission represented, hewing to its rule of gathering at five-year intervals since 1931.[1]

Anastasia was the reigning mafioso in New York by 1956, but he still faced a deadly enemy in Vito Genovese. Since eliminating the Mangano brothers to become a boss in his own right, Anastasia had strengthened his alliances with Joe Adonis and Frank Costello, but that triad was shaken by Adonis's deportation and Costello's imprisonment during 1956. On a personal note, Anastasia had revealed a penchant for impulsive violence that led some mafiosi to privately dub him "The Mad Hatter."[2]

A prime example was the slaying of Brooklyn salesman Arnold Schuster on March 8, 1952. Days earlier, Schuster had made headlines in New York for his part in the capture of fugitive bank-robber Willie "The Actor" Sutton, a member of the FBI's Ten Most Wanted list. After spotting Sutton on the street, Schuster led police to their man, then enjoyed a whirl of celebrity that included televised interviews. Anastasia, watching Schuster on TV, ordered soldier Frederick Tenuto to execute Schuster. His reason: "I hate squealers." Tenuto carried out the contract, shooting Schuster once in each eye and twice in the groin. By the time Tenuto himself made the Bureau's Top Ten list in

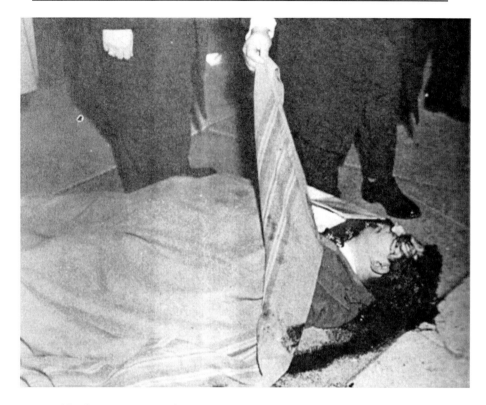

Arnold Schuster was murdered in New York on orders from Albert Anastasia for aiding in the capture of fugitive Willie Sutton (National Archives).

May 1950, he was already dead, killed on Anastasia's orders to cut the link between himself and Schuster's slaying. Headquarters dropped Tenuto from the list in 1964, after informer Joe Valachi confirmed his murder.[3]

While such episodes convinced some ranking mafiosi that Anastasia was mentally unhinged, Vito Genovese had more practical concerns. He still craved the boss of bosses title Lucky Luciano had denied him in 1946, with Anastasia's backing, and would stop at nothing to command the New York Mafia.

But first, he had to deal with Anastasia's strongest ally, Frank Costello.

Deposing the Prime Minister

The world of the Cosa Nostra was in flux when Frank Costello left federal prison on March 11, 1957. He had foiled Washington's plan to deport him, but two consecutive prison terms had weakened his grip on the reins of underworld power. Four months prior to his release from custody, Genovese had chaired a banquet in Manhattan, attended by 42 mobsters including Moe Dalitz among the non–Mafia diners. Unaware that one of their waiters doubled as a detective for the New York Police Department's Intelligence Division, the delegates debated Costello's forced retirement. A majority backed the move, and Costello, from prison, agreed in principle.[4]

Agreement was one thing; retirement was another, altogether.

Three weeks after Costello left custody, the Tropicana hotel-casino opened in Las Vegas. Costello partner Phil Kastel had spent $11 million to build "the Tiffany of the Strip," while his wife decorated the casino and hotel lobby. Nervous state authorities denied Kastel a gaming license, but that did not mean that either he or the Prime Minister were out, in terms of profiting from "skim." The untaxed cash flowed eastward, with no one the wiser, until Vito Genovese made his next move.[5]

On May 2, 1957, as Costello entered the lobby of his apartment building on Central Park West, a gunman stepped from hiding, called out, "This is for you, Frank!" and fired one shot that creased Costello's scalp. While the doorman identified Mafia soldier Vincent "The Chin" Gigante as Costello's assailant, Costello himself denied seeing the triggerman's face. Detectives searched Costello at the crime scene and retrieved a piece of paper from his pocket, reading "Gross casino win as of 4/26/57 ... $651,284"—a figure that precisely reflected the Tropicana's take over three weeks in Vegas. A grand jury convened in New York to investigate Costello's near-death experience and his Nevada ties, but stone silence earned the Prime Minister of gangland a 30-day workhouse sentence for contempt. Bailed out on May 22,

Frank Costello (left) is escorted by a police detective after he was wounded in a 1957 ambush (Library of Congress).

Francesco "Don Cheech" Scalice (left) **visiting Lucky Luciano in Italy, a year before Scalice's murder in New York (National Archives).**

Costello was free before authorities linked him to the Tropicana's counting room.[6]

Four days after that revelation, on June 17, unknown gunmen executed Anastasia Family underboss Francesco "Don Cheech" Scalice (or Scalise) in the Bronx. His passing elevated Carlo Gambino to underboss and, unknown to Anastasia, placed an ambitious schemer within striking range of the family throne. Police captured Vincent Gigante —variously described in headlines as a "hoodlum" and "ex-boxer"— two months later, on August 19. Friends of The Chin posted $100,000 bond on September 16, and conviction was hopeless in view of Costello's refusal to testify. Two days after he made bail, Gigante paid a $500 fine as a "scofflaw"— 50 dollars for each of 10 summonses he had ignored over time — and the attempted murder charge went up in smoke.[7]

Costello clearly recognized his need to deal with Genovese. Demoted to the rank of common soldier as a calculated insult, Costello retired to his mansion at Sands Point, Long Island. As a result of that surrender, Genovese allowed Costello to survive and keep the gambling interests that he shared with Phil Kastel around New Orleans.[8]

Genovese had good reason to be pleased, but he was not the victor yet. In Brooklyn, Albert Anastasia seethed over the treatment of Costello and the murder of Scalice. No one knew better than Don Vito that the Mafia's Mad Hatter was extremely dangerous when riled.

Parley in Palermo

In August 1957, 33 after since he first set foot in New York, Joe Bonanno returned to his native Sicily. Another 27 years would pass before Bonanno, in his self-serving memoir *A Man of Honor*, described the journey as a simple exercise in nostalgia.[9] The fact that he was less than candid comes as no surprise.

Mid-October found Bonanno at the Grand Hotel et des Palmes in Palermo, huddled with fellow mafiosi in a suite named for German composer Richard Wagner. Lucky Luciano presided at daily meetings between October 12 and 16, with New York delegates including Bonanno, his uncle/underboss Giovanni Bonventre, *consigliere* Frank Garofalo and family drug-runner Carmine Galante. Local families were represented by Giuseppe Genco Russo, boss of the Mafia in Mussomeli, Caltanissetta Province; Santo Sorge, a widely-traveled relative of Russo's from Mussomeli; Angelo La Barbera, recognized as the *capo mandamento* (regional captain) of three Mafia families in Borgo Vecchio, Palermo Centro and Porto Novo; Gaetano Badalamenti, the boss of Cinisi; Cesare Manzella, also from Cinisi; Tommaso Buscetta from Palermo; Calcedonio "Doruccio"

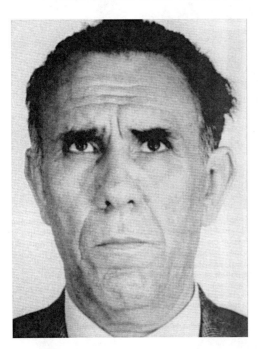

Sicilian mafioso Gaetano Badalamenti met with U.S. mobsters in Palermo, in October 1957 (National Archives).

Di Pisa, from Palermo's Noce neighborhood; and two cousins from Ciaculli, both named Salvatore Greco, known respectively as "Little Bird" and "The Engineer."[10]

The Palermo meeting's primary topic was heroin. The delegates established new supply routes and discussed means of circumventing America's new Narcotic Control Act, signed into law by President Dwight Eisenhower on July 18, 1956. Drafted in response to Harry Anslinger's depiction of a nation awash in deadly drugs, the law increased prison terms for drug offenses to a maximum of 40 years, while adding a life term — or death, if a jury decreed it — for sale of heroin to minors. Bonanno and his aides feared that such draconian penalties might tempt Mafia dealers to break the brotherhood's rule of silence (*omertà*)

Tommaso Buscetta attended the same meeting at Palermo's Grand Hotel et des Palmes (National Archives).

if convicted, in a bid to spare themselves. Despite that concern, the New Yorkers agreed to receive and sell regular shipments of heroin processed in Sicily and in Marseilles— the fabled "French Connection," operated with help from Corsican mobsters.[11]

A second achievement of the Palermo meeting was the establishment of Sicily's first Mafia commission, dubbed the Cupola or "Senate." Larger than its model in America, the Sicilian commission included 13 members representing various factions from the Province of Palermo. Original members included three delegates from the Grand Hotel conference: Salvatore "Little Bird" Greco, Calcedonio Di Pisa, and Cesare Manzella. Other Palermo members included Salvatore La Barbera, brother of Angelo; Antonio Matranga from Resuttana; Mariano Troia from San Lorenzo; Michele "The Cobra" Cavataio from Acquasanta; Lorenzo Motisi from Pagliarelli; Salvatore Manno from Boccadifalco; Mario Di Girolamo from Corso Calatafimi; Francesco

Sorci from the Santa Maria di Gesù; Giuseppe Panno from Casteldaccia; and Antonio "The Shrewd One" Salamone from San Giuseppe Jato.[12]

Delegates at the Grand Hotel et des Palmes celebrated their success with a 12-hour banquet, held in a seafood restaurant on Palermo's waterfront. Bonanno's attitude incensed a waiter, who remarked on his arrogance to a coworker, apparently not knowing that the boorish diner spoke Sicilian. Bonanno responded by hurling a pitcher of ice water at the startled server's head. On recognizing his mistake — and Bonanno's status in the Mafia — the waiter offered a tremulous apology.[13]

Exit the Mad Hatter

While Joe Bonanno charted global heroin routes in Palermo, Albert Anastasia faced critical problems in New York. Rumors claimed that Anastasia had paid his triggerman-nephew James "Jimmy Jerome" Squillante to kill family underboss Frank Scalice in June, after Anastasia caught Scalice selling Mafia memberships for $50,000 apiece. Another version of the story calls Squillante a Genovese soldier, acting on orders from Don Vito. Three months later, on September 19, Squillante also liquidated Joseph Scalice, to silence threats of avenging his brother's murder. Joseph left a lucrative garbage-haul-ing business, which Anastasia was pleased to absorb despite impending Senate hearings on that topic.[14] Such eliminations may have troubled new underboss Carlo Gambino — or signaled to Vito Genovese that Anastasia was losing control of his family.

Yet another problem was Anastasia's ambition to trespass on Meyer Lan-sky's Cuban gambling preserve. Lansky's partners in Havana included Moe Dalitz, now established in Las Vegas, and mafioso Santo Trafficante, Jr., ele-vated to command of the Tampa family with his father's death in August 1954. Author Hank Messick, without citing sources, claims that Trafficante swore a blood oath of allegiance to Lansky in autumn 1957, at the Hotel Nacional office of Cleveland mobster Sam Tucker, with mafioso Charles "The Blade" Tourine on hand as a witness. According to Messick, Trafficante pledged to help Lansky "and the organization he represents" eliminate Anastasia.[15]

An alternate scenario, prefered by authors who cast the Cosa Nostra as the dominant force in U.S. organized crime, involves a plot between Vito Genovese and Carlo Gambino. Both stood to gain from Anastasia's removal: Genovese by eliminating a dangerous longtime rival who wanted him dead; Gambino by elevation to boss in his late master's place. Together, various historians assert, they schemed to execute the Mob's "Lord High Executioner" at the earliest opportunity.[16]

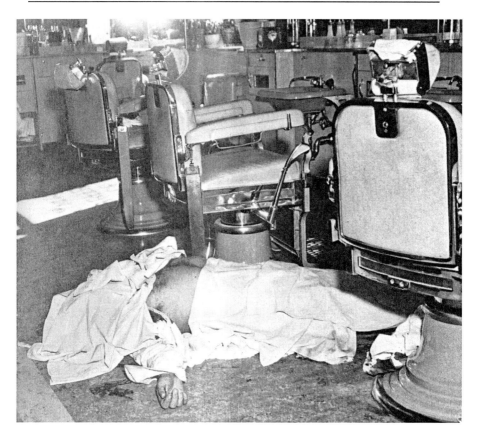

Albert Anastasia was murdered at a New York City barber shop (National Archives).

Whichever version is the truth, if either, all sources agree that Trafficante visited Anastasia on October 24, 1957. He registered as "B. Hill" at Broadway's Park Sheraton Hotel (now the Omni Park Central), where Arnold Rothstein had been shot after a card game in November 1928. Trafficante abruptly checked out of his suite on October 25, two hours before Anastasia stopped for a shave at the Park Sheraton's barber shop. (Messick says that a phone call from Florida precipitated Trafficante's sudden exit.) Despite Anastasia's obsession with personal security, bodyguard-chaufffeur Anthony Coppola went for a stroll, leaving his boss unguarded in the barber's chair. Anastasia's face was swathed in steaming towels when two gunmen masked by scarves entered the shop and killed him with five point-blank shots.[17]

Despite assignment of 100 detectives to Anastasia's slaying, and a reckless claim that the case was "near solution" in early November, the Mad Hatter's

murder remains officially unsolved. The only suspects publicly advanced —
by true-crime authors, rather than police — were the three Gallo brothers:
Albert ("Kid Blast"), Joseph ("Crazy Joey"), and Larry. A police informant
later claimed that Joey Gallo called his murder team "the barbershop quintet,"
an odd remark since he had only two brothers, and ballistics evidence
restricted the Park Sheraton firing squad to two men. Faulty arithmetic aside,
another drawback to the theory is that all three Gallos were soldiers in Joe
Profaci's family until they led defectors in rebellion against their boss, four
years after Anastasia's murder. No persuasive theory has yet been suggested
for Profaci's meddling in the three-way Anastasia-Genovese-Lansky feud.[18]

Whoever fired the shots that snuffed out Anastasia's life, his passing left
New York's five families unbalanced. Hank Messick says that Anastasia had
called a meeting of 100 ranking mafiosi, scheduled to convene on October 28,
in hope of obtaining support for his intended war on Jewish mobsters nationwide. His pitch against the "Kosher Nostra" would have shattered the national
crime syndicate forged between 1929 and 1934, striving to assert Mafia dom-
ination of organized crime throughout the United States.[19] Sudden death
scotched that plan and averted the catastrophic war, but there would still be
a Mafia summit.

Vito Genovese sent out the invitations, summoning his brethren to a
gathering on November 14, at Apalachin, New York.

· 7 ·

The Sit-Down

Lucky Luciano had established a tradition of the Mafia's commission rallying at five-year intervals, most recently in 1956. Now, the events of 1957 forced the panel's first sit-down for an emergency since Luciano was convicted of white slavery in 1936. Preparations for the unexpected meeting were hashed out at a preliminary caucus held in Livingston, New Jersey, on November 10.[1]

Vito Genovese favored a meeting in Chicago, where security was guaranteed by the Outfit's connections to local police and politicians, but an ongoing IRS investigation of Windy City boss Tony "Big Tuna" Accardo prompted second thoughts. Stefano "The Undertaker" Magaddino, boss of Buffalo, proposed instead that delegates should return to the site of their 1956 meeting, which had passed without a hitch. The site: Joe Barbara's estate at Apalachin, New York.[2]

Joe the Barber

Founded in 1836, the hamlet of Apalachin covers 1.5 square miles of ground in Tioga County, situated six miles west of Endicott. Its name, in the extinct Unami language formerly spoken by Lenape tribesmen in the Hudson Valley, translates as "from where the messenger returned." In the early 1900s, residents of Endicott, across the Susquehanna River in Broome County, labeled it "The Nob," regarding its inhabitants—especially the Italians employed at the Endicott Johnson Shoe Company — as suspicious characters engaged in criminal activities including gambling, prostitution, and Black Hand extortion.[3]

That image had changed by the end of World War II. Apalachin claimed fewer than 900 year-round residents in 1950, out of 29,880 for Tioga County at large, and crime was rare. Most locals left their doors unlocked at night, with no fear of intruders. There were still Italian criminals in the vicinity, but they were affluent, ostensibly respected citizens.[4]

Their leader, and boss of the regional Mafia family, was Giuseppe Maria Barbara, known to his neighbors as Joseph Barbara, Sr., and to his cronies in gangland as "Joe the Barber." Born in Castellammare del Golfo, Sicily, on August 9, 1905, he immigrated to the States at age 15 or 16 and was naturalized in 1927. During Prohibition, Barbara lived in Endicott, serving as an agent for Santo Volpe's family, based in Pittston, Pennsylvania. Police detained Barbara at Wyoming, Pennsylvania, on January 5, 1931, on suspicion of murder, but later dropped the charge. Seven months later, on August 8, NYPD officers arrested Barbara for possession of a submachine gun used in a Mob execution. Again, Joe beat the rap. Pennsylvania State Police nabbed him on suspicion of a third slaying, on February 10, 1932, but again the case went nowhere. A year later, on February 21, 1933, Barbara was questioned in the strangling of Scranton bootlegger Samuel Wichner. Investigators also traced multiple phone calls to his home from a Syracuse pastry shop owned by the city's preeminent heroin dealer.[5]

Santo Volpe retired from Mafia affairs in 1933, ceding his family—with interests in coal mining and control over several United Mine Workers locals—to successor Giovanni Sciandra. Sciandra ruled the roost until persons unknown gunned him down in 1940, and while homicide detectives regarded Joe Barbara as a leading suspect in that murder, no prosecution resulted. Suddenly in charge, Barbara had attained a measure of respectability. Married in May 1936, he sired two sons and a daughter. In 1944 he bought a 58-acre tract of land at Apalachin and erected a $250,000 fieldstone mansion on McFall Road ($3.1 million today). His one and only criminal conviction came in 1946, when feds caught him buying 300,000 pounds of sugar for manufacture of untaxed liquor. Barbara paid a fine on that charge, then rebounded with the purchase of a Canada Dry soft-drink bottling plant and a distribution franchise for Gibbons Beer, manufactured in Wilkes-Barre, Pennsylvania.[6]

Giuseppe "Joe the Barber" Barbara, Sr., host of the Apalachin meeting (National Archives).

Mob-watchers suspected that Barbara ran bootleg liquor under cover of

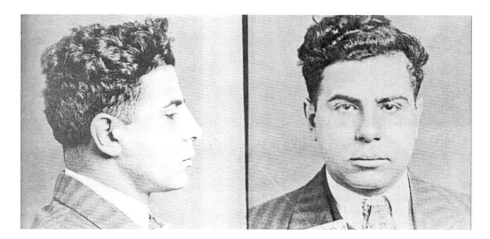

Carmine Galante was jailed for speeding after a Mafia meeting at Apalachin, New York, in 1956 (National Archives).

his soda operation, but they never proved it. Meanwhile, Joe the Barber gave money to charity, expanded his business to dominate the beer and soft-drink market around Binghamton, New York, and generally impressed the Powers That Be with both his business acumen and generosity. When Barbara applied for a pistol permit under New York's strict Sullivan Law, Endicott's police chief provided a reference.[7]

Barbara hosted the Mafia commission's quinquennial meeting at his Apalachin estate in October 1956 without mishap, although he could not be responsible for guests once they left his home. Shortly after the gathering, a state trooper stopped Bonanno Family underboss Carmine Galante for speeding through Windsor, New York. Galante's typically pugnacious attitude sent him to jail, where investigators learned of his recent stop at Apalachin. Soon afterward, a flying squad of officers from West New York, New Jersey, turned up in Windsor, offering bribes for Galante's release. Troopers refused the payoff, and Galante wound up spending 30 days in custody. More critically for Joe the Barber, the arrest and bribe attempt placed him under ongoing scrutiny by the New York State Police.[8]

That incident would have dire consequences for the Mafia at large.

Talking Points

By all accounts, the Apalachin meeting had at least four topics slated for discussion. First and foremost was the spate of bloodshed in New York, beginning with the May attempt to murder Frank Costello, followed by the June execution of Frank Scalice and Anastasia's ambush in October. Despite his reputation as the underworld's Mad Hatter, Anastasia still had loyal friends in the Mafia. Two of his *caporegimes,* Aniello Dellacroce and Armand Rava, were primed for war against Vito Genovese, and might pose an intrafamilial threat to Carlo Gambino if they suspected Anastasia's successor of complicity in the barbershop assassination. Worse yet, the battle might spread to include the Lucchese Family, seen as Genovese allies—and beyond New York to Florida, where Santo Trafficante, Jr., was another suspect in the death of Anastasia. In order to secure his new enhanced authority, even to save his life, Don Vito had to plead his case for killing Anastasia and convince his fellow bosses that preemptive action had been necessary.[9]

A closely related matter involved Mafia's investments in Cuba. Tampa's Trafficante and Calogero Minacore of New Orleans—alias Carlos "The Little Man" Marcello—had interests in Havana that would later tie them to a convoluted web of CIA conspiracies. Both had resented Anastasia's moves toward Cuba, as had Meyer Lansky (not invited to the Apalachin meeting), and boss Frank DeSimone of Los Angeles, successor to Jack Dragna at Dragna's death in February 1956.[10] Would Genovese, in turn, now claim a piece of Cuba's action for himself? Would that touch off a power struggle between the Cosa Nostra and the larger, multiethnic syndicate including Lansky, Longy Zwillman, the Chicago Outfit, and the Dalitz group from Cleveland, now established as legitimate casino owners in Nevada?

Third on the list of topics to discuss was international narcotics trafficking. Groundwork for increased collaboration between Sicily and New York's reigning Cosa Nostra families had been established at the Grand Hotel et Des Palmes in Palermo, nine short days before Anastasia's murder at the Park Sheraton Hotel. Despite repeated claims that the American Mafia "outlawed" drug-dealing, various families were deeply immersed in the traffic from their beginnings. In addition to the drug labs supervised by Lucky Luciano, heroin had flowed from Turkey to the States through Marseilles, France, since the mid–1930s, refined and packaged by Corsican mobsters. That "French Connection" would endure until the early 1970s, supplying 90 percent of America's black-market heroin — 5,000 pounds per year, by the FBN's best estimate. To maximize their profits and prevent a replay of the Prohibition-era liquor wars, the mafiosi growing rich from "smack" required some means of formal regulation.[11]

Finally, the delegates were slated to discuss division of authority within Manhattan's Garment District. Racketeers had long plagued the district and its thriving industries. Partners Lepke Buchalter and Gurrah Shapiro had dominated labor racketeering in the neighborhood from 1927, when they executed Jacob "Little Augie" Orgen and assumed command of his gang, until Thomas Dewey convicted them both of extortion a decade later. Shapiro's imprisonment and Lepke's subsequent execution cleared the field for other operators, including the Lucchese Family. By 1957, Lucchese's son Robert was active in the Garment District, collaborating with Lucchese brother-in-law Joseph "Joe Palisades" Rosato and Thomas Gambino, son of Don Carlo. Further sharing of the spoils demanded formalized agreement under seal of the commission.[12]

The Lineup

Who would attend the Apalachin conference? All families across the country were invited — and, apparently, some guests from Italy. Immediately after the event, *The New York Times* reported 65 persons arrested, but the list appended to that article included only 57 names. Two months later, the *Times* claimed that 60 were jailed, while authorities believed that "at least sixty-four" had been present. Despite passage of more than half a century, no two reports of the convention manage to agree on how many attendees were detained by the police, much less the number or identity of those who got away.[13]

A combination of arrest records, circumstantial evidence, and educated speculation indicates that the following Mafia families were represented at Joseph Barbara's estate on November 14, 1957:

• *The Barbara Family.* As host of the event, Joe the Barber was responsible for care and feeding of his guests, as well as matters of security. FBN spokesmen later claimed that son Joseph Jr., only 21 years old in 1957, handled all arrangements for the gathering, including motel reservations for the delegates. Family underboss Rosario "Russell" Bufalino, born in Montedoro, Sicily, in September 1903, had immigrated as a teenager and found his way to Buffalo, where his rap sheet listed arrests for petty larceny, receiving stolen goods, conspiracy to obstruct justice, drug trafficking, and fencing stolen jewelry. Other family members confirmed as attendees included: Dominick Alaimo, born at Montedoro in January 1910, with arrests since 1932 including robbery, plus federal counts of violating labor and liquor statutes; Ignatius Cannone, born in New York City in November 1925, with charges filed since age 21 for disorderly conduct and resisting arrest; *caporegime* Anthony "The Gov" Guarnieri, born at Utica, New York, in May 1910, arrested since 1945 on charges including illegal gambling, possession of firearms, and felonious assault; Bartolo Guccia, born at Castellammare del Golfo in December 1891, arrested in the U.S. since 1916 for possession of a pistol, breaking and entering, bootlegging, and murder; Pasquale "Patsy" Monachino, born at Realmonte, Sicily, in January 1908, with a clean record prior to Apalachin; older brother Salvatore "Sam" Monachino, also born at Realmonte (February 1893), with no preceding rap sheet; James David Osticco, born in Pittston, Pennsylvania, in April 1913, charged with violating the Volstead Act in 1931; Angelo Sciandra, born at Pittston in November 1923, never arrested prior to 1957; Pasquale "Patsy" Sciortino, born in Cattolica Eraclea, Sicily, in March 1915, arrested in 1951 for violating the Immigration Act of 1924, still under INS investigation when he came to Apalachin; Pasquale "Patsy" Turrigiano, another Castel-lammarese, born in August 1906, jailed since 1928 on counts of larceny, assault, and Volstead violations; and Emmanuel "Manny" Zicari, born at Siculiana, Sicily, in February 1900, arrested in 1934 for counterfeiting.[14]

Two other Barbara Family members were suspected of attending the Apalachin meeting, but remain officially unconfirmed as delegates. Cuban-born Salvatore "Vicious" Trivalino, birth date unknown, found his way to Florida in 1909 and reached New York a decade later, reportedly joining the Barbara Family in 1949 with a record of 21 arrests. William Medico of Pittston, born around 1906, was arrested in 1931 on a Volstead charge. By 1957, with brother Philip, he ran Medico Industries, employing James Osticco as the company's traffic manager.[15]

• *The Genovese Family.* Don Vito was the gathering's prime mover. Underboss Gerardo "Jerry" Catena, born in South Orange, New Jersey, in January 1902, boasted arrests since 1923 for robbery, hijacking, bribing a fed-eral juror, and suspicion of murder, with extensive interests in vending machines, real estate, trucking, labor unions, and oil leases. *Caporegime* Michele "Big Mike" Miranda, born in a suburb of Naples in July 1896, had logged arrests since 1915 on charges including disorderly conduct, vagrancy, and suspicion of murder. Another *caporegime,* Salvatore "Charles" Chiri, was born at Villa Scalia, Sicily, in August 1888 and was registered as a resident alien in New Jersey since December 1940. He had managed to avoid police since arriving in the States. Hotel records from Scranton, 50 miles distant from Apalachin, indicate that Joseph "Socks" Lanza — a participant in Oper-ation Underworld, still boss of the Fulton Fish Market in 1957 — also planned to attend the Apalachin gathering, but no evidence of his arrival had been found.[16]

• *The Gambino Family.* Led by a newly-minted boss allied with Vito Genovese, the former Mangano-Anastasia Family was a potential time-bomb nestled in the heart of the Cosa Nostra's capital city. Still years away from preeminent status as New York's de facto boss of bosses, Carlo Gambino could go the way of his five murdered predecessors if Genovese failed to make his

case before the commission. *Consigliere*-turned-underboss Joseph Biondo, AKA "Joe Bandy" or "Little Rabbit," was born at Barcellona Pozzo di Gotto, Sicily, in April 1897, immigrating to New York in time for Prohibition. He had joined in Lucky Luciano's plot against Salvatore Maranzano, and secured his new post by abetting Carlo Gambino's treachery against Anastasia. New *consigliere* Joseph "Staten Island Joe" Riccobono, born in Palermo during April 1894, boasted arrests since 1930 on charges including conspiracy, extortion, and carrying concealed weapons. *Caporegime* Armand Rava, New York born in January 1911, with arrests since 1929 for bootlegging, extortion, drug trafficking, numbers racketeering and vagrancy, remained stubbornly loyal to Albert Anastasia's memory. More pragmatic *capos* included second-generation mafioso Constantino Paul Castellano, born in Brooklyn during June 1915, jailed since 1934 on counts of civil contempt and robbery with violence; and Carmine "The Doctor" Lombardozzi, another Brooklyn native, born in December 1913, with arrests since 1929 for rape, homicide, and unlawful entry.[17]

Police escort Carlo Gambino, successor to Albert Anastasia (National Archives).

• *The Lucchese Family.* Led by Gaetano Reina until his murder early in the Castellammarese War, then by Gaetano Gagliano until his death from natural causes in 1951, this clan now bore the name of boss Gaetano "Three-Finger Brown" Lucchese. Born in Palermo, in December 1899, Lucchese immigrated to New York in 1910, and logged his first conviction—for auto theft—in 1921. He was present when Lucky Luciano's borrowed Jewish gunmen killed Salvatore Maranzano in 1931, and emerged from the shakeup as Gagliano's underboss, holding that post for 20 years before ascending to the throne. Considered a Gambino ally, Lucchese named Stefano LaSala—alias "LaSalle"—as his underboss, with Vincent "Nunzio" Rao as *consigliere.* Born in Palermo during June 1898, Rao emigrated to New York before World War I and started piling up arrests in 1919, on charges including grand larceny, homicide, and illegal posses-sion of firearms. Lucchese *caporegimes* included Gio-vanni "Big John" Ormento, born in New York City during August 1912, with federal nar-cotics convictions in 1937 and 1941; and Palermo native Joseph Rosato, born in Janu-ary 1904, with arrests since 1928 on charges of homicide and disorderly conduct. Other prominent family members suspected of attending the Apalachin conference were Carmine "Mr. Gribbs" Tra-munti, a New Yorker born in October 1910, and comparative youngster Aniello Migliore, born in Queens, New York, during October 1933. Despite his youth, Migliore reportedly earned some $50,000 per day ($397,000 today) from illegal gam-bling in New York City, after pay-ing tribute to his boss.[18]

Gaetano "Three-Finger Brown" Lucchese (National Archives).

• *The Bonanno Family.* Ruled by the closest thing to a surviving "Mustache Pete," the Bonanno clan was a potential wild card at Apalachin. Boss Joseph Bonanno, with a record of arrests from 1930 including grand larceny, posses-sion of an unlicensed firearm, and transporting machine guns, was no particular friend of any other

Natale "Joe Diamonds" Evola (National Archives).

Cosa Nostra boss in New York City, barely hiding his contempt for any outfit that accepted non–Sicilians as "made" members. Former underboss Giovanni Bonventre, with arrests from 1943 for burglary, kidnapping, and endangering the health of a child, loved Sicily so much that he returned to live there during 1950, serving as a conduit of information between Bonanno and Lucky Luciano. Bonventre would appear in 1957 for the Apalachin meeting, but would not supplant new underboss Carmine Galante, born in East Harlem during February 1910, with the most recent of his numerous arrests occurring after the commission's last gathering, in 1956. Before that, he had served nine years in prison for wounding a policeman and a six-year-old bystander during a 1930 hijacking. *Caporegimes* attending Joe the Barber's sit-down included Natale "Joe Diamonds" Evola, Brooklyn born in January 1907, with arrests since 1930 for coercion, federal narcotics violations, and firearms possession; and Anthony Riela, born in Terranova, Sicily, in August 1896, suspected but never charged in two 1944 murders, and arrested in 1955 for operating a brothel.[19]

• *The Profaci Family.* Last but not least among New York City's five Mafia families, the gang led by Giuseppe "Don Peppino" Profaci preserved a measure of neutrality in the conflict between Genovese and Anastasia. A native of Villabate, Sicily, born in October 1897, Profaci faced charges of rape and theft in 1916, emigrating to America upon release from prison in 1921. He tried Chicago first, then moved on to New York in 1925 and logged his first arrest three years later, at the abortive Mafia conference in Cleveland. The IRS sued Profaci in 1953, seeking more than $2 million in unpaid taxes, while the Justice Department lunched an ultimately unsuccessful bid to revoke Don Peppino's naturalized citizenship the following year. Underboss Giuseppe "Fat Joe" Magliocco was Profaci's brother-in-law, born at Portella di Mare, Sicily, in June 1898, and arrested in Cleveland with Profaci and a concealed pistol in December 1928. Joining the family's top men at Apalachin was *caporegime* Salvatore "Sam" Tornabe, born in 1897, known to non-mafiosi as a salesman for Magliocco's Sunland Beverage Company in Manhattan.[20]

The other New York family represented at Apalachin, based in Buffalo and with a branch in Rochester, locally known as "The Arm," was run by Stefano Magaddino. Born in Castellammare del Golfo during October 1891, the chief advocate of meeting at Joe Barbara's estate reached New York in 1909 and logged his first arrest in 1921, on suspicion of killing a New Jersey mafioso. Underboss John Charles Montana, born in Montedoro, Sicily, in June 1893 and established on U.S. soil since age 14, may be the American Mafia's most unusual member: from running errands for the Mob on Buffalo's West Side, he organized a fleet of taxi cabs in 1922, won election to Buffalo's Common

Council in 1927, and was reelected to a second term in 1929, becoming chairman of the Housing and Slum Clearance Committee, as well as the Labor Relations and Compensation Committee. Montana ran for Congress in 1936, but New York Republicans were out of favor during that Depression year. In 1938 he tried again, abandoning the GOP, but lost a second time, accepting as his consolation prize appointment to a commission that revised New York's constitution with 10 amendments. In 1943 Montana served as chairman of Buffalo's Zoning Board of Appeals. In 1956 the Erie Club chose Montana as Buffalo's "Man of the Year."[21]

Family *caporegime* Antonio Magaddino was drab by comparison to Montana, and limited in influence despite his blood tie to elder brother Stefano. Born at Castellammare del Golfo in July 1897, this Magaddino logged multiple arrests in his homeland between 1916 and 1929, on charges including murder, rape and robbery. Benito Mussolini's purge of mafiosi drove him to America, serving Stefano and the family from Niagara Falls. Two other *caporegimes* attending the Apalachin sit-down were Rosario "Roy" Carlisi and James LaDucca. Carlisi was born in Chicago in April 1909, logging arrests since 1937 for federal liquor violations, gambling, contempt and malicious mischief.

John Charles Montana, the personification of the Mafia's merger of politics and legitimate business (National Archives).

LaDucca, a Buffalo native born in October 1912, dabbled in various rackets without compiling a rap sheet before Apalachin. Other family members attending the meeting included Dominick D'Agostino, born in Reggio Calabria, Italy, in December 1889, arrested since 1930 on charges of income tax evasion and contempt, convicted on a federal narcotics rap; the Falcone brothers, Salvatore and Joseph, born at Sciacca, Sicily, in August 1891 and January 1902 respectively, with Salvatore relocated to Florida by 1946; Samuel Lagattuta, born in Palermo during April 1896, with arrests since 1933 including counts of arson,

New Jersey mafioso Frank Majuri (National Archives).

possession of a concealed weapon, and suspicion of murder; Rosario "Roy" Mancuso, Buffalo born in January 1907, arrested since age 13 on a list of charges including juvenile delinquency, burglary, robbery, assault with intent to kill; the Valenti brothers, Frank and Constenze, both natives of Rochester born respectively in September 1911 and February 1926, with Frank's arrests dating from 1933 on charges of counterfeiting, extortion, liquor-law violations, murder, and assault and battery. One source also places Patsy Mancuso, brother of Rosario, at the Apalachin meeting, but no known evidence documents his attendance.[22]

New Jersey harbored two Mafia families during the 1930s, both considered satrapies of stronger clans in New York City. One, based in Newark, was led by Gaspare D'Amico until 1937, when he botched an attempt on Joe Profaci's life and fled the country, leaving his turf up for grabs by New York's five families and the gang led by Stefano Badami in Elizabeth, New Jersey. Unidentified assassins killed Badami in 1955, whereupon Filippo Amari succeeded him. On the eve of Apalachin, Amari retired to his native Sicily, ceding control of the New Jersey family to Nicholas Delmore. While he would not attend the gathering at Joe Barbara's estate, Delmore sent newly appointed underboss Frank Majuri, born in New York City during April 1909, with arrests since 1935 for bootlegging, bookmaking, and probation violations. Joining Majuri in Apalachin were *caporegime* Louis "Fat Lou" LaRasso, born in Elizabeth, New Jersey, in November 1926, and family member Alfred Angelicola, born in January 1914.[23]

Giuseppe "Joe" Ida (or Idi, in some accounts) assumed command of Philadelphia's Mafia family after boss Joseph "Joe Bruno" Dovi died from natural causes in October 1946, expanding the clan's influence to Atlantic

City and South Jersey. A native of Fiumare di Muro, Calabria, born in June 1890, Ida had avoided jail thus far, while posing as a salesman for the DeAngelis Buick Agency in New Brunswick. Joining him at Apalachin were underboss Dominick Olivetto, born in Camden during December 1906 or January 1907 (reports vary), boasting arrests since 1932 for bootlegging, gambling and larceny, and enigmatic Antonio "Mr. Miggs" Polina (or Pollina).[24]

Pennsylvania's other Cosa Nostra family, based in Pittsburgh, was led in 1957 by John Sebastian LaRocca, alias "John LaRock." Born at Villarosa, Sicily, in December 1901 or 1902 (accounts differ), LaRocca immigrated with his family in 1910, working as a coal miner until he sought the path of least resistance with organized crime. Sentenced to three years in prison for assaulting a woman in 1922, he emerged to rise through the Mafia's ranks and succeeded boss Frank Amato when failing health forced Amato's retirement in 1956. Joining LaRocca on his trip to Apalachin were *caporegimes* Michael James Genovese — born in Pittsburgh's East Liberty district in April 1919, arrested since 1936 on charges including assault, robbery, and carrying a concealed weapon — and Gabriel "Kelly" Mannarino, born in October 1916 at New Kensington, Pennsylvania, where he operated the Ken Iron and Steel Company. Mannarino's rap sheet listed arrests since 1933 for bootlegging, gambling, and violation of Pennsylvania's Uniform Firearms Act. One source lists another Pittsburgh delegate to Apalachin as Louis Pagnotti, operator of a coal company, whose son and grandson inherited both the firm and Pagnotti's penchant for felony indictments.[25]

New England Mafia boss Raymond Loreto Salvatore Patriarca and his underboss, Henry Tameleo, avoided the Apalachin meeting, sending *consigliere* Frank "The Cheeseman" Cucchiara in their stead. Born at Salemi, Sicily, in March 1895, lately operating from Watertown, Massachusetts, Cucchiara had compiled a record of arrests since 1925 including possession of morphine, illegal possession of dynamite, and suspicion of murder. FBN spokesmen also claimed that ex–New England boss Filippo "Philip" Buccola, retired to Sicily in 1954, came back for Joe the Barber's gathering, reporting that he was observed in Boston roughly two weeks earlier. A wire-tapped conversation also caught Buccola referring in advance to the convention, but hard evidence of his attendance remains elusive.[26]

Cleveland boss Giovanni "John Scalish" Scalici had come a long way since the 1930s, when he worked at Moe Dalitz's Pettibone Club for $100 a week. Native born in September 1913, with arrests for burglary and robbery dating to 1930, Scalish had succeeded Alfred Polizzi when Polizzi retired in 1944, to explore new frontiers of gambling and construction work in Florida. *Consigliere* John DeMarco would accompany Scalici to Apalachin. Also registered at a nearby motel, but otherwise erased from conference history, was reputed family *caporegime* Charles "Curly" Montana, spelled "Montano" on one list of suspected delegates. [27]

Detroit should have been represented at the meeting, and indeed, boss Giuseppe "Joe Z" Zerilli did present his driver's license to a clerk in Binghamton who rented him a car on November 14, after the Barbara event broke up. Born in Terrasini, Sicily, in December 1897, Zerilli emigrated at age 17, arriving four years before Michigan lawmakers offered the nation a preview of Prohibition. While one account describes him as a founder of the early Purple Gang, Zerilli was not eligible for that strictly–Jewish syndicate. In charge of Motor City's Mafia since 1936, when predecessor Guglielmo "Black

Cleveland *consigliere* John DeMarco (National Archives).

Bill" Tocco faced a charge of tax evasion, Zerilli ironically found himself named in newspaper reports as the boss of a new "Purple Gang," when the old name proved too irresistible to drop. Another speculative Motown delegate was Anthony "Tony Jack" Giacalone, born in January 1919, later widely known for his association with the Teamsters Union and its president, James Riddle Hoffa.[28]

Chicago's multiethnic Outfit was arguably the strongest crime family outside of New York City, and while it should have been represented at Apalachin, no evidence has surfaced placing any of its members on or near Joe Barbara's estate. Boss Salvatore "Sam" Giancana — alias "Momo" or "Mooney" — was born in the Windy City during June 1908 and had worked his way up from the juvenile Forty-Two Gang to serve Al Capone as a chauffeur and triggerman, finally ascending to replace "retired" boss Tony Accardo in 1956. After offering his city as a venue for the 1957 meeting, Giancana may have felt insulted by rejection — certainly he gloated, afterwards— but it seems doubtful that he would have shunned the crucial sit-down altogether. Several authors state with confidence that he attended, listing Giancana among those who managed to escape unseen. Two sources also list Chicago underboss

Left: Salvatore Giancana offered Chicago as a safe location for the Mafia gathering in November 1957 (National Archives). *Right:* "Retired" Chicago godfather Tony Accardo regretted selecting Giancana as his successor (National Archives).

Frank "Strongy" Ferraro as an Apalachin visitor, but evidence of his attendance is ephemeral.[29]

Despite Chicago's strength, admittedly exaggerated in many reports, Illinois also boasted two more small, quasi-autonomous Mafia families. One, operating from the state capital at Springfield, was led by Frank Zito. Born in Palermo during February 1893, Zito later compiled a record of arrests in Illinois dating from 1931, on charges that included bootlegging and suspicion of murder. FBN agents claimed that Zito collaborated with St. Louis mafiosi to flood Illinois with narcotics. He would be among those caught at Apalachin in November 1957. Meanwhile, upstate in Rockford, Antonio Musso established his Mafia clan during Prohibition, ruling the roost until poor health retired him in 1957. Successor Joseph Zammuto was born at Aragona, Sicily, in April 1899, emigrated in 1913, and was naturalized in 1936, five years after he paid a $208 fine for carrying a concealed weapon. Preferring the concealment of legitimate fronts, Zammuto bought Rockford's Dr. Pepper bottling plant in 1954. Police would note his registration at a motel close to Apalachin, but he slithered through their net.[30]

While situated virtually next door to Chicago, and amenable to dealings with the Windy City's Outfit, Milwaukee, Wisconsin, harbored its own substantial Mafia family. Five bosses ruled the clan from 1918 to 1952, when John Alioto assumed command, grooming son-in-law Frank "Frankie Bal" Balistrieri as his underboss. Born in May 1918, Balistrieri — also called "Mr. Big," "Mr. Slick," and "Mad Bomber" — was college-educated and had spent six months in law school before turning criminal full-time. Alioto apparently missed the Apalachin conference, but police would find Balistrieri's registration card at a local motel, in the wake of their raid.[31]

The St. Louis family is another that should have been represented at Apalachin, though no evidence proves any member attended. Anthony "Tony Lap" Lopiparo had arrived from Kansas City in the 1940s to find five rival gangs battling for turf in St. Louis. By the end of World War II he ruled the Gateway City's Cosa Nostra with assistance from underboss Ralph "Shorty" Caleca. No source names either as an Apalachin delegate, but two claim that St. Louis was represented by future boss John "Johnny V" Vitale as a substitute. Born on the city's North Side in 1909, Vitale distinguished himself as a high school athlete and earned a paltry living as an usher during the Depression, before he turned to crime as a protégé of mafioso Anthony "Tony G" Giordano. Reporters later claimed that Vitale could "kill with kindness," rarely a method preferred by the Mob.[32]

Farther west, in Kansas City, control of the Mafia rested with Giuseppe Nicoli "Nick" Civella. A son of Italian immigrants, born in March 1912, Civella had a record of arrests dating from age 10 on charges that included auto theft, bootlegging, larceny, theft, robbery with firearms, gambling, and vagrancy. In the early 1940s, as a Democratic Party precinct worker, Civella forged close ties with local boss Charles Binaggio. Following Binaggio's murder in April 1950, Civella served as underboss to successor Anthony Gizzo, claiming the throne when a heart attack killed Gizzo in April 1953. By the time he went to Apalachin in November 1957, Civella had led his family into the lucrative world of legal gambling in Las Vegas, Nevada. With him at the autumn gathering was *caporegime* Joseph Filardo, born at Castelvetrano, Sicily, in August 1898, arrested since 1922 on charges including blackmail, bootlegging, suspicion of murder, and multiple violations of federal food and drug laws.[33]

The Mafia's outpost in Des Moines, Iowa, described by some authors as a branch office of the Chicago Outfit, was run by Luigi Tomaso Giuseppi Fratto, also known as Louis Fratto, "Lew Farrell" and "Cock-eyed Farrell." Born in Chicago, in July 1908, Fratto distinguished himself as a labor racketeer under Al Capone, before moving on to Des Moines. Established as that city's top mafioso by 1940, he was also a cousin of ferocious Mob hit man Felix "Milwaukee Phil" Alderisio. Brother Frank "Frankie One-Ear" Fratto was also a contract killer, suggesting that Luigi had no shortage of lethal talent available. Two sources name Fratto as a "likely attendee" at Apalachin, but cite no evidence confirming it.[34]

One certain delegate was Santo Trafficante, Jr., traveling from Tampa to New York as "Louis Santos." Born in Tampa during November 1914, Traffi-cante had logged arrests since 1946 on charges including bribery, running bolita games (the Cuban version of "numbers"), and conspiracy to violate gambling statutes. Following his father's death from natural causes in August 1954, Trafficante took over the family business and was suspected of involve-ment in Albert Anastasia's murder three years later. He might have missed the Apalachin meeting, after a Florida judge sentenced him to five years on a 1954 bribery conviction, but that verdict was overturned on appeal. Deeply involved with Meyer Lansky in Cuban gambling, Trafficante was particularly interested in the upcoming discussion of Havana.[35]

In New Orleans, home of America's premiere Mafia family, control of the Cosa Nostra had descended from the infamous Matrangas and Sylvestro "Silver Dollar Sam" Carolla to Calogero Minacore, better known as Carlos "The Little Man" Marcello. Born to Sicilian parents in Tunisia, in February 1910, Marcello reached Louisiana with his family before his first birthday. After dropping out of school, Marcello organized a gang of teenage bandits and logged his first arrest, for bank robbery, in 1929. He dodged conviction in that case, but drew a nine-to-12-year sentence for another heist in 1930. Subsequently pardoned, Marcello formally joined the Mafia in 1935, then was jailed again in 1938 for smuggling marijuana. Another year in prison hardly fazed him, and he reigned supreme in the Crescent City following Sam Car-olla's 1947 deportation, planting outposts from Texas to Tennessee. Despite the family's wealth and influence, no reports place Marcello at Apalachin. One account claims that his brother Joseph attended the meeting, but no proof has thus far emerged.[36]

Dallas, dismissed by some authors as an outpost of the New Orleans Mafia, actually harbored its own Cosa Nostra family from Prohibition onward. Sicilian immigrant Carlo Piranio arrived from Louisiana in 1910 and estab-lished the local clan, with brother Joseph serving as his underboss. Soldier Joseph Francis Civello, born in Baton Rouge in February 1902, logged his first Dallas arrest in July 1928, for blasting Joe DeCarlo with a shotgun at the St. Paul Drug Store. DeCarlo, on his deathbed, called the shooting accidental, thus sparing Civello from indictment. He received a 15-year federal sentence for narcotics trafficking in 1937, but emerged from Leavenworth to rise through the Piranio Family ranks, succeeding Joe Piranio at his death in 1956. Motel records prove that underboss Joseph Campisi joined Civello for the Apalachin gathering, though he eluded the police. Born in 1918, Campisi opened Campisi's Egyptian Restaurant in 1946 and received one of the city's first liquor licenses, later expanding the enterprise into a thriving chain still operated by his family. Two sources add another Dallas delegate to Apalachin, soldier John Francis Colletti, but if he was in the neighborhood, he left no trace.[37]

Denver's Mafia had survived raids by the 1920s Ku Klux Klan and trimmed dead wood during an early–1930s feud between the rival Carlino and Smaldone families. Brothers Clarence, Clyde, and Eugene Smaldone emerged victorious in 1933, ruling the Mile-High City's Italian underworld until prosecutions sidelined them in the 1940s. That cleared the way for James "Black Jim" Colletti, born at Lucca Sicula, Sicily, in October 1897. Colletti's

Los Angeles mafioso-lawyer Frank "One Eye" DeSimone (left) consults with Mafia client John Rosselli (Library of Congress).

Denver rap sheet listed arrests since 1925 on charges of vagrancy, drunkenness, disorderly conduct, and suspicion of murder. Sometimes erroneously listed as a scout for the Bonanno Family, Colletti *was* partnered with Joe Bonanno in the Colorado Cheese Company. His underboss-brother, Vincenzo Colletti, registered at a motel near Apalachin in November 1957, but unlike James, he managed to elude authorities.[38]

California claimed three Cosa Nostra families in autumn 1957. The largest, in Los Angeles, lost notorious boss Jack Dragna to a heart attack in February 1956. Successor Frank "One Eye" DeSimone was born in Pueblo, Colorado, in July 1909, then moved to California with his parents, as a child. His father, Rosario "The Chief" DeSimone, had supervised L.A.'s Sicilian rackets briefly, in the 1920s, and his son continued in the family business after graduating from from the University of Southern California Law School in 1933, later serving as defense counsel for a rogue's gallery of mafiosi. Underboss and distant DeSimone relative Simone Scozzari, born in Palermo during January 1900, had entered the U.S. illegally at 23. His rap sheet listed multiple arrests for bookmaking, and he saw action in Jack Dragna's wars with Mickey Cohen, but he favored real estate investments as a cover. He owned the stylish Venetian Club in Los Angeles, until heat from the Apalachin raid forced it to close in 1958.[39]

In San Francisco, 340 miles north of Los Angeles, Francesco Lanza had emerged triumphant from a Mafia turf war in 1932, reigning until his death from natural causes in July 1937. Anthony Lima succeeded Lanza, running the family until jurors convicted him of grand theft in April 1953. Next in line was Michael Abati, who named James "Jimmy the Hat" Lanza — son of Rosario — to fill Abati's former post as underboss. Lanza would attend Apalachin in Abati's place, his presence verified by a motel registration.[40]

Forty miles northwest of San Francisco, San Jose claimed its own small Cosa Nostra clan, led by Onofrio Sciortino, born in Sicily in April 1891. With underboss Giuseppe Xavier Cerrito, Sciortino founded the San Jose family in 1942, staking a claim to gambling, loan-sharking and prostitution. Cerrito, better known as "Joseph," was born in Palermo during January 1911 and managed to avoid contact with the police, covering his tracks with income from a Lincoln-Mercury dealership in Los Gatos. While Sciortino did not attend the Apalachin meeting, authorities found Cerrito's registration at the same motel where Jimmy Lanza had a room reserved.[41]

FBN agents also suspected three foreign mafiosi of attending Joe Barbara's cookout, including two from Canada and one from Sicily. The Canadians, if they were present, represented the Cotroni Family of Montreal, Québec. Boss Vincenzo "Vic the Egg" Cotroni ran the clan, with aid from *caporegime*-brother Giuseppe "Pep" Cotroni, while Luigi Greco handled duties as the family's underboss. No source claims that Vic Cotroni made the trip to Apalachin, but Harry Anslinger's agents insisted that Greco and Pep were on hand to discuss the global distribution of heroin. While logical enough — Montreal is only 270 miles northeast of Apalachin — no evidence survives to document their presence.[42]

Likewise, no substantive proof supports the presence of the FBN's alleged Sicilian delegate to Apalachin, boss Giuseppe Settacase from Agrigento. Born in 1898, he had attended the Grand Hotel et Des Palmes meeting in October 1957 and was surely interested in heroin smuggling. Wiretaps maintained by the FBI and Canada's Royal Canadian Mounted Police caught Settacase discussing the Apalachin sit-down's aftermath, deriding American mafiosi for their public humiliation, but if the transcripts document his personal attendance, no such statements have surfaced in print.[43]

Thus stands the lineup, documented and suspected, for the gathering at Joseph Barbara's estate. The delegates had come from near and far to chart the future course of their "honored society," but even the commission's best-laid plans could go awry.

· 8 ·

Busted!

On Wednesday, November 13, 1957, residents of Apalachin left their beds reluctantly, feeling an autumn chill. The day began at 28 degrees, and even at high noon the temperature would not climb past 48. Throughout the day, pedestrians would be surprised by spitting rain showers and flakes of early snow that melted upon contact with the ground.[1] It was a good day to stay warm and dry indoors, but Sergeant Edgar Dewitt Croswell did not have that option as he drove the six short miles from Vestal's New York State Police barracks to the nearby Parkway Motel with his partner, Vincent Vasisko.

A Woodstock native, born in July 1913, Croswell had graduated from his hometown high school in the Great Depression, quickly finding out that "jobs were scarce; you took about the first thing that came along." In Croswell's case, that was a short stint with the Kingston Police Department, followed by a tour of duty as a detective for the Sears, Roebuck & Company's mail-order division, tracking deadbeats and stolen merchandise. Croswell subsequently returned to Kingston, joining the town's fire department "because the pay was better," then joined the state police in August 1941. After 11 months on uniformed patrol, he graduated to the Bureau of Criminal Investigation, where he would spend the rest of his career. Divorced by 1957, at age 44, Croswell lived at the Vestal barracks, consumed by his job. As he told *The New York Times,* "My hobby is police work."[2]

Vincent Vasisko was 13 years younger than Croswell, born at Endicott, New York, in July 1926. Various reports describe him as a trooper or investigator for the state police at age 31, with trooper listed as the lowest rank, investigator one step higher.[3] In either case, Croswell was in charge as they made the trip to Apalachin on November 13.

As Croswell later told the tale, he was contacted by the Parkway's owner, with a complaint that one of the motel's guests had paid for his room with a bad check. Croswell and Vasisko were in the motel office, discussing the problem with the owner's wife, when Joe Barbara, Jr., entered the lobby. He asked the registration clerk for three "double" rooms, to be occupied on Wednesday

The main street of Apalachin, New York, in 1957 (National Archives).

and Thursday nights by delegates to a "convention of soft-drink people." Barbara paid for the rooms, but could not name the individuals. He simply knew that six men would be coming, possibly arriving late that night.[4]

Croswell recognized young Barbara by sight, and also knew his father as a local soft-drink bottler. Beyond that, all published accounts report that Croswell was intensely interested — "obsessed," some authors say — by the illicit life of Barbara's father. Their first encounter, according to one report, was a "more than acrimonious" meeting in 1944. No details of that incident survive today, and other reports contradict that version. Some claim that Croswell had merely heard rumors of Joe the Barber's Mafia affiliation, others that he had maintained covert surveillance on Barbara's Apalachin estate for 12 to 18 months prior to autumn 1957. Still other accounts ignore the Parkway Motel encounter completely, claiming that Croswell's attention was only drawn to Barbara on November 14, when flashy cars with out-of-state license plates began streaming through Apalachin.[5]

Croswell, in his later statements, said that eavesdropping on Joe the Barber's son inspired him to take a closer look at the upcoming "soft-drink convention." From Vestal, Croswell and Vasisko drove past Barbara's Endicott bottling plant, found nothing out of place, then rolled on another seven miles to scout the Barbara estate on McFall Road, in Apalachin. There, the officers saw either two or four intriguing vehicles (reports differ). One belonged to

Patsy Turrigiano—no surprise, considering his known association with Joe Barbara and their parallel criminal records. Two others, some reporters say, were a blue Cadillac with Ohio tags, and a coral-and-pink Lincoln licensed in New York. The Lincoln, Croswell told reporters afterward, belonged to James LaDucca from the Magaddino Family. The Caddy later turned up at the Parkway Motel, where Cleveland mafiosi Giovanni Scalici and John DeMarco had registered.[6]

That night, before going to sleep at the Vestal barracks, Croswell telephoned his boss, Inspector Robert Denman, in Sidney, New York, 27 miles northeast of Binghamton, to report his suspicion of a gangland summit in the making. Afterward, he called two agents of the Internal Revenue Service's Alcohol and Tobacco Tax Division based in Binghamton, Kenneth Brown and Arthur Rustin. Both agreed to join him in surveillance on Joe Barbara's estate the following day.[7]

Every Man for Himself

Thursday in Apalachin saw a replay of the prior day's weather, with an overcast that threatened rain. It was cool enough for visitors who gathered at Joe Barbara's estate to wear their topcoats if they left the house — and that

A view of Joseph Barbara's home in November 1957 (National Archives).

was where the preparation of their feast was underway, 220 pounds of steak, veal chops and ham grilling to order on the barbecue. The meat alone had cost Barbara $432, but it was a small price to pay for the honor of hosting the august assemblage.[8]

By noon, outside of the estate's perimeter, Sergeant Croswell watched the gathering with Vincent Vasisko and their IRS companions, Agents Brown and Ruskin. They wrote down license numbers for the vehicles parked in Barbara's driveway, while watching a dozen or so "soft-drink men" dressed in silk suits and camel's hair great coats, shoes polished to a mirror shine. Croswell later said the group "looked like a meeting of George Rafts," referring to the film star who had made his reputation playing gangsters on the silver screen and socializing with the likes of Bugsy Siegel in real life.[9]

And then, something went wrong.

Exactly what transpired remains a matter of dispute. Some stories claim that Barbara's guests saw Croswell and company from the patio and alerted their host to the presence of spies. A second version claims that Bartolo Guccia was returning with some fish for grilling when he saw the officers lurking near Barbara's home. A third tale credits Barbara's wife, Josephine, with spotting the watchers and warning her husband. Joe, in turn, allegedly recognized Croswell from prior encounters, alerting the assembled mafiosi that the sergeant "hates Italians and calls them guineas." That account, penned long after the fact by an author who was nowhere near the scene, goes on to quote Barbara as saying of Croswell, "He'll think nothing of framing anyone of you men by planting a gun or some dope in your car just because you're Italian and a friend of mine. Men, you better leave now and watch those troopers closely so they can't plant anything in your car, should they stop you and search it."[10]

That warning, author Gary Hafer claims, sent some of Joe the Barber's guests rushing to their vehicles, while others asked if there was any way to flee the grounds on foot. Barbara supposedly answered, "In the back of the house is a footpath that leads through the woods to the main road and past the spot those bastards have blocked off. Once you get on the main road, have the driver of your car pick you up there." Thus began a double exodus, some of the delegates departing by car, while others sprinted for the woods— in plain view of Croswell and his fellow officers. Later, Vincent Vasisko remarked, "If they stood still, nobody would have touched them. We would have just gone home."[11]

It is a rule of thumb, however, that whenever someone runs away from the police, the runner instantly invites detention and interrogation. So it was that afternoon, as Croswell and the others watched at least a dozen men break for the trees on foot, while flashy cars began to jockey for position in Barbara's driveway. The four lawmen set up a hasty roadblock and immediately called for backup from the New York State Police. Another 15 officers arrived within the next half-hour.[12]

Each car approaching the roadblock was stopped, its occupants identified and questioned, then released since the police had no cause to arrest them. First in line was a car occupied by Dominick Alaimo and Emmanuel Zicari. Next came Russell Bufalino, riding in a Chrysler Imperial with Vito Genovese, Gerardo Catena, Joseph Ida and Dominick Olivetto. Joe Profaci rode in another car, while a fourth carried Carlo Gambino. Some refused to state their business; others claimed that they had come to "visit a sick friend" — a reference to Joe Barbara's 1956 heart attack. All were soon released, and the assembled troopers — lacking valid search warrants — made no move to approach Barbara's house, leaving researchers to speculate on how many guests remained inside, out of sight.[13]

The mafiosi who had bolted for the woods, however, were less fortunate. Their strange behavior cleared Croswell to hold them for questioning at the Vestal barracks, if only he could catch them. And that, as it turned out, would be no problem. "Those city boys didn't have a chance," Croswell said. "With their fancy shoes and their hats and coats snagging on branches, we could grab them easy. One by one we rounded them up, bedraggled, soaking wet, and tired. There are no sidewalks in the wood." Vincent Vasisko added, "All the [police] cars had to do is patrol the roads. They had to come out sooner or later. You see a guy in a silk suit and a white fedora, you say, 'He doesn't belong in the woods!'"[14]

Even so, it was one o'clock the next morning before state police completed their roundup. Some of the fleeing mafiosi had discarded guns and cash — Apalachin residents reported finding hundred-dollar bills scattered around the countryside for months after the raid — but others went to Vestal with their pockets full. In all, police found their suspects carrying nearly $300,000 in cash. The poorest delegate had $450, while one who described himself as unemployed carried $10,000.[15]

Who's Who?

Confusion still surrounds the guest list for Joe Barbara's big barbecue. *The New York Times,* working from lists provided by the state police, initially claimed that 65 persons were seized in the raid. A day later, that figure was scaled back to 58 known mobsters in attendance, plus two unnamed Barbara employees. In January 1958 the *Times* added four new names to a list of 60 compiled by state troopers.[16] Those initially identified as Apalachin delegates on November 16 included the following mafiosi, with names shown as spelled and alphabetized (sometimes incorrectly) in the *Times*:

- *Joseph Barbara, Sr.*
- *Joseph Barbara, Jr.*, not found at his father's estate, but charged with third-degree assault on November 15 for kicking *New York Journal American* photographer Charles Carson, when Carson tried to take his picture.[17]
- *Joseph Bonanno*, caught in a corn field. Bonanno later denied attending the sit-down, claiming that he met Stefano Magaddino for a private talk in nearby Endicott, while two of his men went hunting near Apalachin and were caught in the state police dragnet. One of them, Bonanno said, was carrying his driver's license, leaving Bonanno "dumbstruck by the perverted whimsy of life." Since none of those detained were fingerprinted, Bonanno's alibi can neither be refuted nor confirmed.[18]
- *"John" Bonventre*
- *"Russell" Bufalino*
- *"Roy" Carlisi*
- *Ignatius Cannone*
- *Paul Castellano*
- *Gerardo "Cateno"*
- *"Charles Chieri"* [Salvatore Chiri]
- *Joseph "Ciuello"* [Civello]
- *James Colletti*
- *Frank Cucchiara*
- *Dominick D'Agostino*
- *John DeMarco*
- *Frank DeSimone*
- *Natale Evola*
- *Joseph Falcone*
- *Salvatore Falcone*
- *Carlo Gambino*
- *Michael Genovese*
- *Vito Genovese*
- *Anthony Guarnieri*
- *"Bartalo" Guccia*
- *Joseph Ida*
- *Louis "La Rasso"*
- *James LaDucca*
- *"Sam Lagatutte"* [Lagattuta]
- *Carmine "Lomardizzi"* [Lombardozzi]
- *Antonio Magaddino*

- *Joseph "Magliocci" [Magliocco]*
- *Frank Majuri*
- *Rosario Mancuso*
- *Gabriel Mannarino*
- *Michele Miranda*
- *Sam Monachino*
- *Patsy Monachino*
- *John Montana*
- *Dominick "Oliveto" [Olivetto]*
- *"John" Ormento*
- *James Osticco*
- *"Joseph" Profaci*
- *Vincent Rao*
- *Armand Rava*
- *Anthony Riela*
- *Joseph Riccobono*
- *Joseph Rosato*
- *"Louis Santos, of Havana,"* caught in the woods and unrecognized as Santo Trafficante, Jr.[19]
- *"John Scalish"*
- *Angelo Sciandra*
- *"Patsy" Sciortino*
- *Simone Scozzari*
- *Salvatore Tornabe*
- *"Patsy" Turrigiano*
- *Frank Valenti*
- *"Costenze" Valenti*
- *Emmanuel Zicari*
- *Frank Zito*

Those added to the roster by the *Times* in January 1958 included Dominick Alaimo, "Nick" Civella, Joseph Filardo, and "Neil" Migliore. Alaimo had been stopped at Croswell's roadblock but excluded from the former list. An Apalachin merchant subsequently identified Civella and Filardo as the men who used his telephone to call a taxi following the raid, while Migliore was involved in a minor traffic accident near Apalachin on November 15, presumed to be in town on Mafia convention business.[19]

Concerning mafiosi who escaped the raid at Barbara's estate, estimates range from 12 or 13, offered by Croswell at the time, to 50 or more. Hotel registrations confirm the presence of missing mobsters Alfred Angelicola, Frank Balistrieri, Joseph Campisi, Joseph Cerrito, Vincenzo Colletti, Gaspar

Police mug shots of Kansas City mafioso Nicholas Civella (National Archives).

DiGregorio, Frank Garofalo, James Lanza, Charles Montana, John LaRocca, and Joseph Zammuto in the general vicinity, though none of them was apprehended by police. Officers found unspecified items of clothing owned by Stefano Magaddino in Barbara's barn, and retrieved Carmine Tramunti's business card from the woods nearby, though someone else could have dropped it. Soon after the raid, Joseph Zerilli used his Michigan driver's license to rent a car in Binghamton, bound for home in Detroit. Finally, Joe Barbara's housekeeper later identified Carmine Galante as one of several guests who remained indoors on November 14, and thus eluded police.[20]

Various sources name 20 more mafiosi as "likely" or "probable" delegates to Apalachin, but none offers any supporting evidence. Those listed by some authors and omitted by others include Joseph Biondo, Philip Buccola, John Colletti, Giuseppe

Giuseppe Zerilli was traced to the Apalachin meeting through his driver's license (National Archives).

Cotroni, Frank Ferraro, Louis Fratto, Anthony Giacalone, Salvatore Giancana, Luigi Greco, Joseph Lanza, Stefano LaSalle, Gaetano Lucchese, Joe Marcello, William Medico, Patsy Mancuso, Louis Pagnotti, Anthony Polina, Giuseppe Settacase, Salvatore Trivalino, and John Vitale.[21]

The final tabulation: 58 mobsters certainly attended Barbara's cookout, with at least 17 more (and probably 19) in the immediate vicinity, while addition of 20 speculative delegates brings the "possible" count to 97.

First Inquisition

For those detained by Sergeant Croswell, the ordeal extended beyond mere embarrassment. Apparently confessing to use of "third-degree" tactics, Croswell frankly told *The New York Times*, "We gave them a rough time at the station house, but we couldn't even make them commit disorderly conduct there. These guys are never indignant."[22] He left details to the reader's imagination, but the raid occurred nine years before the U.S. Supreme Court's ruling in *Miranda v. Arizona* ordered police to warn arrestees of their rights to silence and legal representation, desisting from all questioning once a prisoner asks for a lawyer. We can only guess how Croswell and his fellow troopers handled the interrogation of their suspects. Afterward, no one appeared to care.

After taking off their shoes and emptying their pockets, the collected mafiosi answered questions stiffly but politely. Most claimed that they had come to see Joe Barbara and check on his recuperation from the latest heart attack. Their simultaneous appearance was a mere coincidence. James LaDucca claimed he was chasing a deer through the woods when state troopers nabbed him. Carmine Lombardozzi also said that he was hunting, but had failed to bring a gun or hiking gear because he planned to purchase everything required in Apalachin. James Osticco told police that he had come to Barbara's estate "to fix a pump." John Montana said he was driving to Pennsylvania when his brakes failed near Ithaca, New York, and he made his way to Barbara's house in hopes of finding a mechanic. On arrival, he had been surprised to see "some kind of party" underway but did not ask its purpose. He was drinking tea with Barbara's wife when the commotion started, and Montana ran into the woods. "It was just human nature," he said, "that I would ask myself, 'What am I doing here?'"[23]

Even that small admission cost Montana dearly, later on, but for the moment he and all the others were released, no charges filed. Croswell and company were later villified in print for turning their prisoners loose, but they had no choice at the time. Although the assembled delegates boasted nearly 300 arrests among them, including 100 convictions on various charges, none of them were fugitives from justice at the time, nor were they seen committing any crime. Most laid claim to one or more legitimate businesses in their home cities.[24]

Embittered as he may have been by failure to build cases on the spot, Croswell was forced to send the mobsters on their way. But he had lit a fuse that would burn rapidly from Apalachin into New York City, Albany, and finally to Washington, D.C. The Mafia had been embarrassed for a second time, and on a grander scale than the debacle delegates had faced in Cleveland, 29 years earlier.

Conspiracy?

Perhaps because reports of the Barbara meeting's chance exposure seemed improbable, or details have been rearranged so frequently, the Apalachin raid has spawned several gangland conspiracy theories. The most persistent swirl around Meyer Lansky and the so-called "Kosher Nostra" element of America's national crime syndicate, including such high-powered Jewish mobsters as Longy Zwillman, Joseph "Doc" Stacher, Phil Kastel, and Moe Dalitz and his Cleveland partners, lately relocated to Las Vegas. Mob historian T.J. English writes that "a few Jews" were present at Apalachin, while author John Davis says Lansky and Stacher declined invitations to attend, but no evidence supports either claim.[25]

Davis, indeed, goes further, claiming that Lansky and Stacher avoided the meeting — along with alleged invitees Frank Costello and Carlos Marcello — "because they knew the conclave would be raided and they didn't want their names taken down by the police." How could they know a raid was planned? "Because," Davis wrote, "they, in concert with Carlo Gambino, planned the raid themselves."[26]

According to Davis, all concerned in the plot had reason to despise Vito Genovese and seek his humiliation. Costello, of course, had nearly been murderd on Don Vito's orders, just six months before Apalachin. Marcello had been partnered with Costello in New Orleans gambling since the 1930s. Lansky was a close ally of both mafiosi, as well as exiled Lucky Luciano — who recalled Genovese's attempts to unseat him as boss of bosses and may have suspected Don Vito of framing him for white slavery in 1936. Gambino's motive is the most obscure, considering his very recent collaboration with Genovese in killing Albert Anastasia, but Davis answers that objection, as well. "It was worth the risk," Davis writes, "to ensure the undermining of Genovese. Almost *anything* was worth the risk if it would diminish Genovese's power and curb his ambitions." And, in fact, when Genovese was jailed on drug charges in 1959, Gambino would emerge as the dominant leader among New York City's five families.[27]

Other journalists suggest or take for granted Lansky's role in the Barbara bust. Hank Messick notes Lansky's "amusement" at the Mafia's embarrassment, while Mike La Sorte and John William Tuohy confidently name Lansky as Sergeant Croswell's tipster. Tuohy claims that Lansky feared execution "for raising the price of dope" to Mafia vendors, but his tale is marred by a spurious claim that Carlo Gambino "was conspicuously absent" from Apalachin.[28]

Whether the meeting was deliberately sabotaged or not, by someone in attendance or across the continent, exposure of the sitdown would have unexpected consequences for the rich and powerful on both sides of the law.

· 9 ·

Playing Catch-Up

The Apalachin raid was an overnight sensation, trumpeted in headlines nationwide. Sam Giancana, whether present or a no-show for the actual event, was quick to make his feelings known. A wiretap caught him chastising Stefano Magaddino via telephone. "I hope you're satisfied," Chicago's boss told Buffalo's godfather. "Sixty-three of our top guys made by the cops." Sounding almost sheepish, Magaddino answered, "I gotta admit you were right, Sam. It never would have happened in your place."[1]

Joe Bonanno later wrote that Magaddino was "seduced by vanity," moving hastily to advance himself in the wake of Albert Anastasia's death. Someone else took that condemnation a lethal step further, lobbing a hand grenade through the kitchen window of Magaddino's home on Dana Drive, in Lewiston, soon after Apalachin. The "pineapple" failed to explode, but Don Stefano got the message.[2]

In Manhattan, supposed retiree Frank Costello took a more sanguine view of the affair, telling a friend, "Why the hell they just didn't sublet the 17th Precinct in Manhattan for the day, is beyond me. That way they could have saved the travel."[3]

Some lower-ranking mafiosi were amused by the public humiliation of

Stefano Magaddino survived an assassination attempt following the Apalachin conference (National Archives).

their overlords. Speaking to author Peter Maas, informer Joe Valachi later said, "I'll tell you the reaction of all us soldiers when we heard about the raid. If soldiers got arrested in a meet like that, you can imagine what the bosses would have done. There they are, running through the woods like rabbits, throwing away money so they won't be caught with a lot of cash, and some of them throwing away guns. So who are they kidding when they say we got to respect them?"[4]

One Apalachin delegate who missed most of the furor was 60-year-old Salvatore Tornabe, ostensibly a salesman for Joe Magliocco's Sunland Brewing Company. Authorities were still puzzling over the contents of a note retrieved from his pocket on November 14, written partly in English and partly in Italian, when Tornabe died from natural causes in Manhattan, on December 30. The note several times mentioned "Acqua-Velva," variously interpreted as a reference to Aqua Velva shaving lotion or, more probably, to Antoinette Acquavella, common-law wife of mobster Carmine Galante.[5] In either case, Tornabe was beyond interrogation.

Newspapers had a field day with the Apalachin bust, none more so that the stately *New York Times*. Unfortunately, its reporters never figured out how many thugs were finally identified and questioned by police during the raid, much less what they intended by their gathering. Amidst high-minded calls for crackdowns on the Mob and recitation of the rap sheets held by various attendees, *Times* stories published in November 1958 and April 1959 proclaimed the meeting's purpose "still a mystery."[6]

Top Hoodlums

No one, presumably, was more surprised by Apalachin than FBI Director J. Edgar Hoover. After denying the Mafia's existence for two decades, he woke on November 15, 1957, to find himself proved wrong. It may not be literally true, as Curt Gentry writes, that Hoover learned of the raid from his morning paper "with his cairn terriers nipping at his heels," but the effect was nonetheless startling.[7]

Over the two months prior to Croswell's raid, Hoover had delivered two speeches proclaiming that America's primary internal threat was the shrunken and aging Communist Party. On September 19, in Atlantic City, the director lamented that "technical" rather than "logical" interpretations of the law prevented his G-men from hounding Reds into prison. One month later — and five days before the Anastasia killing in New York — Hoover told an audience in Washington, D.C., that the Communist Party had found a "renewed lease on life" through "a major campaign to influence American teenagers."[8] Now, he faced irrefutable proof of collaboration among mobsters across the country, frequently declared impossible by bureau headquarters.

Hoover's first, predictable reaction was blind fury. Incapable of owning up to a mistake, much less an implication of collusion with the underworld, Hoover surveyed headquarters for someone to blame. His first target, Assistant Director Alan Belmont, had served since February 1950 as chief of the FBI's Domestic Intelligence Division. Clearly, if a Mafia existed without Hoover's knowledge, Belmont should have warned his boss. Loyal to a fault, Belmont accepted formal censure for his "failure," while absolving his subordinates.[9]

Unsatisfied with one victim, Hoover sought another. The next logical candidate was Louis Burrous Nichols, chief of the Crime Records Division from May 1941 until he was promoted, in October 1951, to serve as third in command of the Bureau. Who better to have warned the chief if gangsters had established a nationwide network behind Hoover's back? Unfortunately, Nichols had retired 12 days before the Apalachin bust — and went to work for Schenley Industries, a distilling empire owned lock, stock, and whiskey barrel by Mob associate Lewis Solon Rosenstiel. Rosenstiel's ex-wife recalled occasions when Meyer Lansky fawned over her husband, calling him "Supreme Commander." She was also the primary (if somewhat suspect) source of claims that Lansky blackmailed Hoover with photos of the director in drag. Despite his relocation, Nichols phoned Hoover several times with offers of help during the Apalachin "crisis," but Hoover refused to take his calls.[10]

Hoover was desperate for information on the previously nonexistent Mafia, but there was none to speak of in the bureau's files. Field offices in Albany and Buffalo disclaimed responsibility for Apalachin, each insisting that the hamlet lay within the other's jurisdiction. Inquiries to other offices across the nation turned up next to nothing. Out of Dallas, for example, came the word that Joe Civello was regarded merely as "a counselor for the Italian community at large." Robert Kennedy, as counsel for the McClellan Committee, asked FBI headquarters for any available information on the Apalachin delegates, later recalling that 40 were unknown to the FBI, while the slender files on others consisted chiefly of newspaper clippings. Adding insult to injury, Kennedy then tried Harry Anslinger's FBN, which "had something on every one of them."[11]

Enter William Cornelius Sullivan, an agent since 1941, assigned to the Domestic Intelligence Division since June 1954. As chief of that division's Central Research Section, he offered to produce a detailed survey of the Mafia from its beginnings to the present day, which ought to prove the bureau's "inside" knowledge. Hoover gratefully accepted, but the final monograph would not be finished until summer 1958, since it required digestion of several hundred published books and countless other documents.[12] While Sullivan and company were laboring on his behalf, Hoover needed a quicker fix.

His answer was the Top Hoodlum Program, inaugurated on November 27, 1957. A letter of that date, dispatched to every FBI field office, ordered each special agent in charge to compile of list of ten "top hoodlums"— no more, and no less— within the jurisdiction of his office. For some areas, such as New York City and Chicago, Hoover's dictum required selection of ten among hundreds of mobsters. Other field offices, such as those in Anchorage, Alaska, and Salt Lake City, Utah, would be forced to pad their lists with two-bit miscreants. In no case could an order from the boss be sidestepped without courting punishment, transfer to a less desirable post, or outright dismissal. (Throughout his 48-year tenure, Hoover fought successfully to exempt all FBI employees from the Civil Service, leaving all at the mercy of his arbitrary whims without legal recourse.[13])

Until quite recently, all published sources agreed that the Top Hoodlum Program was launched soon after the Apalachin raid. Whether the particular author was FBI-friendly or highly critical, none disagreed that Hoover's new interest in the Mob dated from sometime in the second half of November 1957.[14] Even the FBI's Web site agreed, on two separate pages devoted to the bureau's illustrious history. One read:

> November 14, 1957: New York State Trooper Edgar Croswell uncovered a conference of crime bosses who had gathered from across the country on the estate of Joseph Barbara in Apalachin, New York. In response to the exposure of a nationwide criminal syndicate, Director Hoover instituted the Top Hoodlum program to develop information about prominent criminal leaders and their activities.[15]

Another page confirms it, reporting that:

> Croswell's important detective work exploded nationally. Concerns had been expressed that a secret network of connected criminal enterprises existed. But many, including FBI Director J. Edgar Hoover, had disagreed. They said crime was a serious problem, but there was no evidence that a conspiratorial web linked racketeers across the country. Now there was evidence. Hoover got to work, ordering his field executives to develop maximum information on crime bosses in their areas of jurisdiction. This "Top Hoodlum Program" produced a wealth of information about organized crime activities.[16]

Retired FBI Assistant to the Director Cartha Deloach was the first to amend history, nearly a quarter-century after Hoover's death. Writing in 1995, he claimed that the Top Hoodlum Program began "some months before the police stumbled onto the Apalachin meeting," but still in 1957. After Croswell's raid, Deloach proclaims, "suddenly our Top Hoodlums Program became more urgent. And it began to pay off in the most concrete way possible — in arrests and convictions." Curiously, even with a wealth of bureau files to draw from, he cites no prosecution occurring prior to 1962.[17]

More recent still is a new addendum to the FBI's Web site, asserting that Hoover launched the Top Hoodlum Program on August 25, 1953, after the New York City field office voiced concern over "rising mobster activity." That was the same year, we recall, when Hoover formed a team of agents to "document the nonexistence of organized crime." Again, no evidence is offered, and the new Web page claims no successful prosecutions before the early 1960s.[18]

Opposing those still-undocumented claims, we have a mountain of testimonial and documentary evidence. Memoirs published by retired agents William Turner and William Roemer, Jr. (self-described head of the Top Hoodlum unit in Chicago), confirm that the program was initiated in November 1957. A letter from the Society of Former Special Agents of the Federal Bureau of Investigation, sent to Ohio Congressman Michael Oxley in February 1993 to aid in his posthumous defense of Hoover against a scathing new biography, asserted that the program was inaugurated in 1958. Stranger still, the two contradictory pages dating the Top Hoodlum Program from November 1957, quoted above, remained in place on the bureau's Web site as this book went to press. Finally, and conclusively, memos surviving in the FBI's files on "Top Hoodlums" Carmine Galante and Abner "Longy" Zwillman reveal beyond any doubt that bureau field offices received their first notice of the program's existence on November 27, 1957.[19]

Assuming for the sake of argument that Deloach and the FBI's contradictory Web page were correct, how could the peerless FBI, which needed only three years to kill or capture "every major gangster" of the 1930s, pursue hundreds of mafiosi from 1957 — or 1953! — into the next decade without filing a single felony charge? The answer, according to Deloach and other apologists, lies with slackers in Congress. According to Deloach, "Jurisdiction was our major problem. We simply were not allowed to pursue the mob unless it clearly violated federal law." The amended FBI Web site agrees, stating: "It's important to understand: at the time, most racketeering activities— including gambling and loan sharking — were beyond our jurisdictional reach."[20]

In fact, as Deloach must have known, local crimes are still beyond the Bureau's reach today, in most cases. Interstate crimes, however, have fallen under FBI jurisdiction from the agency's beginning, many including activities common to organized crime. A partial list of federal statutes that Hoover ignored with regard to the Mob includes:

• The Sherman Antitrust Act of 1890, criminalizing "every contract, combination in the form of trust or otherwise, or conspiracy, in restraint of trade or commerce among the several States, or with foreign nations." Aimed specifically at outlaw monopolies, the law was twisted for decades into a weapon for disrupting labor unions.[21]

• The Mann Act of 1910, banning transportation of women across state lines for "immoral purposes." Written specifically to crush "white slave" rings, the law was used almost exclusively by G-men to prosecute individuals—particularly black celebrities—who traveled with their lovers.[22]

• The Clayton Antitrust Act of 1914, closing loopholes in the Sherman Act with respect to price-fixing and other acts typical of criminal monopolies, ignored by the FBI while leaving its enforcement to the Antitrust Division of the Justice Department.[23]

• The Dyer Act of 1919, punishing interstate transportation of stolen cars. While gangsters ran hot-car rings nationwide, Hoover used the law to pursue petty thieves and claim credit for autos recovered by local police.[24]

• The Volstead Act of 1920, banning alcoholic beverages. Hoover opposed the Prohibition Bureau's transfer from the Treasury Department to Justice in 1930 and its subsequent merger with the FBI — then called the Division of Investigation — in 1933, remaining aloof from the "dry" agents under his command and failing absolutely to curb their corruption.[25]

• The Lindbergh Law of 1932, penalizing interstate kidnapping. While used extensively by Hoover in high-profile ransom cases, it applied equally (but was never used) in cases of interstate "one-way rides" favored by gangland hit men. Hoover preferred to treat those kidnap-murders as a "local problem."[26]

• The National Firearms Act of 1934, regulating ownership of machine guns, silencers, and other "gangster weapons." While primarily assigned to Treasury for transfer-tax collection, the law could be enforced by any federal agent. Hoover ignored it completely, except where Depression-era bandits were concerned.[27]

• The National Stolen Property Act of 1934, granting the FBI jurisdiction over interstate transportation of any and all stolen goods. Hoover applied it selectively, ignoring the black-market smuggling trade that has long been a staple of organized crime.[28]

• The Fugitive Felon Act of 1934, covering interstate flight to avoid prosecution, incarceration, or giving testimony. It clearly covers gangsters "on the lam" from justice. Hoover used the statute against mobsters rarely, when it suited him, generally in cases such as the stage-managed Lepke Buchalter "arrest" guaranteed to give him front-page coverage.[29]

• The Hobbs Act of 1951, passed specifically to punish racketeering with a ban on any actual or attempted robbery or extortion affecting interstate commerce. Hoover belatedly "discovered" the law after Apalachin, but still produced no prosecutions until the early 1960s.[30]

Finally, the Bureau's record makes it clear that Hoover found ways to justify investigation, harassment, arrest and prosecution of virtually *anyone* when he was motivated to do so, usually in political cases or when driven by personal spite. FBI claims that it lacked all jurisdiction over mob activities prior to 1961 simply will not hold water.

Kicking and Screaming

While Hoover awaited the results of William Sullivan's Mafia research, calls for swift action echoed from coast to coast. On January 15, 1958, New York Assemblyman William Horan proposed creation of the state's own "Little FBI" to battle gangsters. Governor Averell Harriman accepted that suggestion six months later, creating a 50-man unit "similar to the Federal Bureau of Investigation," designed to conduct "a forthright attack against criminal elements operating anywhere in the state."[31] While such efforts conformed to Hoover's long-standing description of racketeering as a state or local issue, he could not dodge the tacit implication of FBI failure.

Worse news arrived on April 10, 1958, when U.S. Attorney General William Rogers announced the creation of a new Special Group on Organized Crime within the Justice Department's Criminal Division, dismissed by some FBI apologists as "a two-year experiment."[32] The unit, led by former federal prosecutor Milton Wessel, was indeed scrapped after barely two years of operation, but that outcome resulted from Hoover's personal opposition.

From the start, Attorney General Rogers said, Hoover resisted participation in the anti-Mafia campaign with "kicking and screaming." FBI memos record his description of Wessel as a "Pied Piper" and "a real rat," while members of the Special Group were branded as people who "look at 'Mr. District Attorney' on TV too frequently." The new unit's chief in Chicago, future Illinois governor Richard Ogilvie, says Hoover "ordered that the FBI files, containing the very information that we needed on organized crime, were to be closed to us. Furthermore, he forbade any agents even to talk to the Special Group." Small wonder, then, that Wessel would report "our unit was dissolved because we had aroused the jealousy of older agencies that resented our authority over crimes in their jurisdiction."[33]

The very jurisdiction that FBI spokesmen claimed not to possess.

"Baloney!"

Assistant FBI Director Alan Belmont received William Sullivan's completed Mafia monograph on July 9, 1958. The 375-page document, including extensive reference citations, was split between descriptions of the Mafia in

Sicily and the United States. It also included Sullivan's formal request that copies of the monograph be disseminated "to all field offices, Legal Attaches [FBI outposts in foreign countries], the Attorney General, and Harry J. Anslinger, Commissioner of the Bureau of Narcotics, U.S. Treasury Department, in view of his interest in and cooperation in furnishing valuable information concerning the Mafia."[34]

Given Hoover's well-known hatred of Anslinger, that addendum should have warned Belmont, but he passed the monograph to Leland Boardman, third in command at the time as assistant to the director. Boardman, in turn, sent the report to Hoover with a note stating that he, Boardman, would study it when he had time. Hoover immediately wrote across the monograph's cover: "The point has been missed. It is not now necessary to read the two volume monograph to know that the Mafia does exist in the United States."[35]

Buoyed by that hasty vote of confidence, Sullivan ordered immediate distribution of 25 copies to various Justice Department officials, with one sent to Harry Anslinger. Delivery was made as Hoover went to lunch with constant companion Clyde Tolson — and finally began to read the monograph. Enraged by what he saw on paper, and the news that copies were in circulation, Hoover ordered Sullivan to "retrieve it at once." Agents scrambled to reclaim all copies of the monograph — including one snatched literally from the hands of an assistant attorney general.[36]

Having endorsed the monograph and its conclusions sight-unseen, Hoover now branded its contents "baloney" and banned any mention of Sullivan's findings at Bureau headquarters.[37] Among the statements that infuriated Hoover, once he got around to reading them, were:

• "The Mafia exists in Sicily as a vicious, domineering, unique form of organized criminality" that "developed powerfully after 1860" and remained pervasive to the date of writing.[38]
• "While it does not appear that Sicily is 'world headquarters' for the Mafia, as some claim, some degree of coordination appears to exist between the Mafiosi in Sicily and those in the United States."[39]
• "The present-day Mafia controls crime to the extent that it dominates certain criminal operations wherever it can, pushing crime to the limit beyond which further trespass would mean either the destruction of the productive society upon which it feeds or a popular rising against it in a wave of reprisal that would encompass the destruction of its elements."[40]
• "The most outstanding feature of the ... Mafia organization ... was its evasion of precise, clear-cut pinpointing by the authorities. This revealed a quality of adaptability no doubt due in large part to a lack of formal imped-

imenta such as ... the constitution, bylaws, and formal administrative techniques of the more conventional type of organization."[41]

• In America, the transplanted Mafia constituted "a special criminal clique or caste composed primarily of individuals of Sicilian origin or descent who comprise a distinct but related segment of the whole of organized crime; a segment which takes on the characteristics of a lawless brotherhood."[42]

• "It would be absurd to think that the American counterpart of the traditional Mafia of Italy is a distinctly outlined, conventional type of organization. It would be equally absurd to think that because it is not, it has no existence at all."[43]

• "In order to plan, direct, and coordinate their criminal operations, top Mafia leaders from all parts of the country have met from time to time over a period of years," beginning with the Cleveland gathering in 1928, continuing periodically until the Apalachin meeting. Other sit-downs had occurred since 1946 in Atlantic City; the Florida Keys; Los Angeles; River Forest, Illinois; Chicago; Mountainside, New Jersey; New York City; Binghamton, New York; and Livingston, New Jersey.[44]

• And finally, the Mafia "represents one of the most ruthless, pernicious, and enduring forms of criminality ever to exist in the United States."[45]

Beyond doubt, Sullivan had done his best to let Director Hoover off the hook, stressing repeatedly the Mafia's obsession with concealment, its distinction from the Old World gangland hierarchy, and the fact that despite "insistent allegations of the existence of the Mafia in the United States, there have been also denials."[46] It was all in vain, however, since the data Sullivan collected proved not only the existence of a Mafia, but the disturbing fact that Hoover and his agents had completely missed at least nine major gatherings of top hoodlums within the past decade alone, together with their daily operations spanning the United States.

For the director's sake, that had to be "baloney." Nothing else would do. Nor would the new Top Hoodlum Program salvage Hoover's reputation as a gangbuster. Despite a rash of newly-authorized — and blatantly illegal — wiretaps, burglaries and bugging targeting selected mobsters from Manhattan and Chicago to Las Vegas and beyond, the Mafia was still not Hoover's top priority. Clinging to his obsession with left-wing political dissent and its suppression by whatever means his agents could devise, legal or otherwise, Hoover had little time to spare for chasing mobsters. In 1959, two years after the Apalachin raid, his New York City field office had 400 agents assigned to the Communist Party — and only four to the Top Hoodlum Program.[47]

Close to Home

Tioga County naturally had an interest in the Cosa Nostra's choice of Apalachin as a meeting place. Three weeks after the raid, on December 4, District Attorney George Boldman announced plans to convene a grand jury investigation of the Barbara gathering. The panel, he declared, would be "exclusively involved in the meeting and the purposes thereof." On December 19 a pool of 36 locals was chosen, from which 23 would be empanelled as grand jurors on January 3, 1958. With an eye toward the future, Boldman also chose another panel of 36 to serve as trial jurors, should any Apalachin delegates be criminally charged. Boldman added that "it would not surprise us" if some witnesses were jailed for contempt.[48]

The grand jury convened in Owego, with Sergeant Croswell called as its first witness on January 14. While he regaled the panel with descriptions of November's raid, attorneys for subpoenaed mafiosi briefed reporters on their strategy. Their clients would refuse to answer any questions, to avert the threat of double jeopardy if they were charged in multiple jurisdictions. Frank Costello had used that ploy in 1957, when he refused to testify under a grant of immunity before New York County's grand jury concerning his near-fatal shooting, and while he was jailed for contempt, his appeal was pending.[49]

The panel's first reluctant witness was Josephine Barbara, née Vivana, wife of Joe the Barber. When approached by two state troopers bearing her subpoena on January 15, she had dropped the summons in the snow, snapping, "I can't take that!" Still, service was completed, and she appeared on January 24. Before the panel, she refused to answer any questions, citing both marital confidentiality and her Fifth Amendment privilege against self-incrimination. In return, she received a new subpoena, requiring a second appearance on February 6.[50]

Joseph Profaci was the first Apalachin delegate called

Giuseppe "Don Peppino" Profaci (National Archives).

to testify in Owego, on January 28. He refused to answer any questions and was ordered to return on February 18. February 4 was a busy day for the grand jury, as D.A. Boldman questioned Joe Barbara, Jr., Michele Miranda, Dominick D'Agostino, Joseph Civello, Antonio Magaddino, James Colletti and John Montana — who repeated his tale of sipping tea with Josephine Barbara. John Ormento, Emmanuel Zicari and Patsy Turrigiano stonewalled the jury with Fifth Amendment pleas on February 6. Frank Zito did not make it to the jury room, hospitalized on February 24 after a "heart ailment" struck at him at an Owego motel.[51]

Anthony Riela (National Archives).

Boldman filed his first contempt charge against Anthony Riela, described in print as a Newark motel operator, after Riela declined to answer 17 questions. Arraigned on February 25 and held in lieu of $1,000 bond, Riela faced a maximum sentence of 17 years if convicted on all counts. Roy Carlisi was indicted on the same charge two days later, pleading not guilty when he faced County Judge Francis Clohessy on March 7. Carlisi posted bond, with his case and Riela's adjourned until April 3.[52]

In fact, Riela would not face trial until October 1958. He waived trial by jury, and Judge Clohessy convicted him of all 17 counts on October 15. Ten days later, Riela received a 60-day sentence and was fined $4,250, then released on bond pending appeal. Carlisi stalled his trial for seven months and took his chances with a jury, which convicted him of 15 counts on May 5, 1959. On May 18 he received a 60-day sentence to match Riela's, and a slightly smaller fine of $3,750. Riela lost his first appeal on December 31, 1959, before the Appellate Division of the State Supreme Court, but fought on to win reversal of the judgment from New York's Court of Appeals on April 21, 1960. That panel ruled that refusal to answer questions about one event may constitute a crime, but it cannot support 17 separate charges.[53]

There ended justice at the county level for the Apalachin delegates, with questions forever unanswered. Other venues would be left to try their best and hope for more enlightening results.

Partisan Gangbusters

Given the longstanding symbiotic relationship between mobsters and corrupt public officials, Apalachin was bound to be politicized. Republican assemblymen fired the first salvo at outgoing Democratic Governor Harriman on December 2, emerging from a caucus at Manhattan's Roosevelt Hotel to demand that he appoint a special rackets prosecutor and convene an extraordinary grand jury to investigate the Barbara barbecue. *The New York Times* endorsed that proposal, despite a concession that it was "conceived in a lather of anti-Harriman politics." So did State Attorney General Louis Lefkowitz. Republican legislators sought a $500,000 appropriation for the proposed inquiry, but insisted that the money should not go to New York's State Commission of Investigation, created by Thomas Dewey and currently led by Harriman appointee Arthur Reuter — whom, they said, "did not have enough power to conduct a thorough investigation." Reuter countered that it was "amazing" for the GOP to offer any criticism of his panel, "in view of the fact that they have cut the appropriations for this office to the bone."[54]

Governor Harriman countered on December 11, inviting all of New York's 62 district attorneys to join in a statewide purge of organized crime, beginning with a conference at Albany in one week's time. The day before that meeting was convened, December 15, Republican leaders called for the creation of a "clearing house" on racketeering, dubbed the Division of Law Enforcement, led by a new assistant attorney general. That move, they said, should "transcend political considerations and political differences," and "should not be impeded through unseemly bickering." Democratic D.A.s Frank Hogan of New York County and Edward Silver from Brooklyn were cool to that proposal, advising Governor Harriman that it "would not be useful or helpful in the present situation." Attorney General Lefkowitz, a staunch Republican, then chided Harriman for his failure to tackle the Mob "head-on." He told the *Times*, "I am somewhat disappointed, frankly, with his way of coping with organized crime ... the way he acted is not an effective means of coping with the problem. You cannot fight it by appointing a committee." Instead, Lefkowitz hoped to lead "one massed drive against organized mobster operations" statewide.[55]

In his annual address to the state legislature, on January 8, 1958, Governor Harriman countered Lefkowitz's plan with a proposal for a three-member state crime commission to replace the panel chaired by Arthur Reuter. The war on crime and other problems was impeded, Harriman declared, by the "tight money policy" of the Eisenhower administration. State Republican chairman Judson Morhouse fired back, condemning Harriman's speech as a "do-it-yourself eulogy in which he claims credit for everything except creation and blames President Eisenhower for failing to correct any flaws in that."[56]

The New York Times found "more politics than concern for law enforcement in the current hullabaloo about crime and gangsters" in New York and New Jersey. Labor racketeering had increased, the paper granted, but traditional gangs like that of Al Capone were "hardly in existence in this area any more." On the same day that the *Times* published that fanciful opinion, January 12, Carmine Galante resurfaced in his role as poster child for civic corruption. Assemblyman William Passannante, a Democrat from New York's First District on Long Island, told reporters that he had been asked to intercede on Galante's behalf in the 1956 speeding case. So had two Republican legislators, Joseph Carlino of Long Island and Daniel Dickinson, Jr., from Broome County. None had helped the mafioso, they averred, though ex-mayor Donald Krame wound up representing Galante in court. "After I got into it," said Kramer, "I became aware of his record and advised him to plead guilty."[57]

Partisanship marked every effort to uproot the Cosa Nostra in New York. In January 1958 the legislature's Republican majority passed a bill granting Attorney General Lefkowitz broader investigative powers, then defeated two Democratic measures to relax restrictions on electronic "bugging." In April, GOP Congressman Kenneth Keating accused Governor Harriman of a "whitewash" and "a disgraceful cover-up of corruption and vice" in New York. Harriman, said Keating, had "blatantly ignored his duty" by failing to order an investigation of the Apalachin meeting. Harriman replied that Keating seemed to be "running hard for governor."[58]

In fact, Keating had his eye on the U.S. Senate, defeating D.A. Frank Hogan to claim the seat of incumbent Irving Ives, who declined to seek reelection in 1958. An actual GOP gubernatorial contender, Paul Williams, took his case to New York's Rotary Club on July 10, 1958, with a lecture on the Mafia's activities and a proposal for new legislation requiring published statements of net worth from all convicted racketeers. Carmine DeSapio, youngest and last boss of Tammany Hall, charged that Williams had "indicted two million Italo-Americans in New York State ... with willful and filthy libels." Judson Morhouse fired back with a demand that Governor Harriman repudiate DeSapio's "morally indefensible smear." Money ultimately triumphed in November, as Standard Oil heir Nelson Rockefeller defeated incumbent Harriman by a margin exceeding 600,000 votes.[59]

License Revoked

State authorities professed amazement at the number of Apalachin delegates who held liquor licenses and gun permits. On December 3, 1957, Thomas Rohan, chairman of the State Liquor Authority, met with Governor

Harriman, afterward telling reporters that the board would move to revoke any licenses held by alleged mafiosi "wherever evidence warrants such action. In all other cases, information will be held for consideration in connection with application for renewal of licenses."[60]

Armed with broad discretionary power to rescind licenses or deny renewals, the Liquor Authority announced license reviews of six Apalachin delegates on December 4. Those named included Joseph Magliocco, president of Brooklyn's Sunland Beverage Corporation; Ignazio Cannone, owner of a licensed restaurant in Endicott; brothers Sam and Patsy Monacchino, operators of the Super Beverage Company in Auburn; John Montana, president-director of Buffalo's Frontier Liquor Corporation; and Roy Carlisi, also from Buffalo. A seventh Apalachin attendee, Salvatore Tornade, held a liquor solicitor's permit, while the wife of an eighth, left unnamed, was also licensed.[61]

At a public hearing convened on December 16, the Liquor Authority announced tough new rules for licensees. A license henceforth could be lifted if its holder engaged in "improper conduct" off of licensed premises, refused to testify in any legal proceeding, or lied under oath. First to fall under the new rule was Joe Magliocco, whose license for wholesaling beer was revoked on April 2, 1958. Specific charges included omitting a prior arrest from his application and attending the Barbara meeting. The board also called for forfeiture of Magliocco's $2,500 "good faith" bond with the state. Magliocco appealed that ruling and won a court order mandating some unspecified lesser punishment. New York's Court of Appeals refused to hear the Liquor Authority's appeal in November 1958, leaving board spokesmen to complain that no less-severe penalty existed. By then, it was a moot point, since Magliocco had left the beer business. In March 1959 the Liquor Authority announced that it had revoked ten licenses within the past year, eight of them held by Apalachin delegates.[62]

Possession of concealable firearms — strictly regulated since 1911 by New York's Sullivan Act — was the other bone of contention. Under that law, possession of unlicensed pistols was a misdemeanor, while carrying a hidden gun without a permit was a felony. On December 3, 1957, Brooklyn Assistant District Attorney Edward Panzarella and Kings County D.A. Edward Silver announced a review of their files dating from 1920, to determine whether any Apalachin delegates had sought or received gun permits. Broome County D.A. Louis Greenblott planned a similar review, but Joe Barbara, Sr., beat him to it, surrendering his license, .32-caliber pistol and five rounds of ammunition on November 23.[63]

To aid in local inquires, NYPD created a special 15-member squad on December 5, 1957, assigned to review all 22,909 of the city's Sullivan permits. The microscope would focus first on seven "hoodlums," one of them deceased, who had applied for and in some cases received gun licenses. Because the law required each applicant to list character references, the seven cases would require investigation of 88 persons. Four Apalachin suspects on the list included: Joseph Magliocco, granted a permit in April 1945, which was renewed annually until its revocation on November 28, 1957; Vincent Rao, whose applications were denied in 1929 and 1933; Frank Valente, rejected in 1949 and again in 1951; and Joe Profaci, granted a permit in 1930, which he renewed yearly until its revocation in 1946. Profaci had appealed that decision, winning another permit in December 1947, but renewal was denied in April 1948.[64]

On December 7, 1957, Police Commissioner Stephen Kennedy issued an order forbidding NYPD officers from selling firearms to civilians under any circumstances. Previously, members of the force could sell their surplus pistols to permit holders as long as they recorded the buyer's name and the weapon's serial number. Joe Magliocco had obtained two pistols by that very means. Patrolman Joseph Pointer sold Fat Joe a .32-caliber revolver in April 1945, while Patrolman Edward Hurley furnished a .38-caliber weapon around the same time. Both were confiscated, with a third gun, when authorities revoked Magliocco's permit. Also seized were guns owned by five other New Yorkers, three of whom had vouched for Joe Profaci's character, and two who served as references for Magliocco. Two of Magliocco's brothers also lost their guns and permits as the cops cleaned house.[65]

Meanwhile, police wired prosecutors in Cayuga, Niagara and Oneida counties that Sullivan permits were held by Apalachin delegates Patsy Sciortino of Auburn, Dominick D'Agostino of Niagara Falls, and Joseph Falcone in Utica. Vince Fiore, Utica's deputy police chief, told investigators he had known Falcone before joining the force in 1929, and had regarded him as a respectable citizen "until recently." Falcone had been licensed to carry a gun on some undisclosed date, but his permit was revoked in 1939, then restored in 1945. When questioned, Deputy Chief Fiore could not say where Falcone's gun had been during the six years he was banned from owning it.[66]

In a sideshow to the main event, Arthur Grasso—owner of the Park Sheraton barber shop where Albert Anastasia got his last shave—also lost his gun permit and .32-caliber pistol thanks to "evasiveness in answering questions concerning his alleged association with notorious characters who frequented his shop." On another front, Joe Falcone and Buffalo's James LaDucca were also stripped of their licenses to serve as notaries public.[67]

Weeding the Garden State

New Jersey authorities tried to match New York's zeal in pursuing Apalachin delegates. In Trenton, on November 29, 1957, State Attorney General Grover Richmond, Jr., issued subpoenas for eight attendees, demanding their appearance before Mercer County's grand jury. The list included Vito Genovese, Gerardo Catena, Anthony Riela, Frank Majuri, Charles Chiri, Louis LaRasso, Dominick Olivetto, and Joseph Ida. Genovese, Catena, Olivetto and Ida kept their dates with the grand jury on December 3, answering questions "up to a point," then ducked behind the Fifth Amendment. Anna Genovese, separated from Don Vito since 1950, resisted facing the panel, but the threat of a contempt charge brought her to Trenton on December 17, where she denied any knowledge of Apalachin.[68]

Frank Majuri had more immediate problems in Elizabeth, New Jersey, where he was on probation for a July 1957 bookmaking conviction when he made the trip to Apalachin. On December 4, Union County Judge Milton Feller revoked Majuri's probation, invoking the previous one-to-two-year prison term and ordering Majuri to pay the $2,095 remainder of his original $3,000 fine. The appellate division of Newark's Superior Court affirmed that ruling and ordered Majuri's incarceration on December 16, 1957.[69]

Two days later, New Jersey's State Law Enforcement Council announced that it had "uncovered a link" between unnamed public officials in northern New Jersey and "some character" involved with the Apalachin meeting. Chairman Joseph Harrison told reporters, "The council is very, very anxious that the link be fully investigated. It will take time. Right now, we have a puzzle and we are trying to put the pieces together." Critics charged that the Republican-dominated council, established in 1952 and scheduled to disband in January 1958, sought to extend its life by fabricating crises. Even so, the mere suggestion of a scandal prompted Bergen County prosecutor Guy Calissi to declare that his jurisdiction was clean. On January 2, 12 days before its scheduled dissolution, the council announced impending public hearings to explore New Jersey "aspects" of the Apalachin sit-down. Chairman Harrison planned to call at least 10 witnesses, but withheld their names because publication "might make it more difficult for us to reach some of them."[70]

Those hearings focused on the incident wherein New Jersey police allegedly tried to bribe state troopers following Carmine Galante's October 1956 arrest in Windsor, New York. The troopers in question — Sergeant Croswell and partner Vince Vasisko — testified on January 6, naming Captain Chris Gleitsmann and Detective Sergeant Peter Policastro from West New York as the pair that approached them, seeking to purchase Galante's release. Policastro dodged 100 questions by resorting to the Fifth Amendment, while Chief of Police Frederick Roos was a no-show, sidelined with ulcers. The supposed prime mover in the bribe attempt, West New York Director of Public Safety Ernest Modarelli, had dropped out of sight on December 30, along with witness B.B. Azarow, whose Mob-owned vending machine company boasted a direct telephone line to West New York police headquarters. On January 7, John Courtney, secretary of the West New York Board of Education, testified that he had seen Modarelli the previous night, alive and well in North Bergen.[71]

On the same day, Captain Gleitsmann and Sergeant Policastro stormed out of the hearing room, defying orders to testify. Outside, Gleitsmann told his story to reporters, claiming that Sergeant Croswell had solicited a bribe for Galante's release. In response, Gleitsmann said, "I put my hand up or finger." Asked what that meant, he replied, "I laughed at him again. See, I didn't say anything about money. I don't know what went through Croswell's mind, because we were kidding." As for the contention that he dropped Safety Director Modarelli's name, Gleitsmann conceded, "I may have said it for effect."[72]

The Law Enforcement Council's hearings closed on January 7, followed closely by Governor Robert Meyner's announcement that the panel would disband as scheduled, one week later. Further investigation of the bribe attempt passed to Hudson County's grand jury, which returned five indictments on February 3, 1958. Those charged with attempted bribery included Ernest Modarelli, Chief Roos, Captain Gleitsmann, Sergeant Policastro, and a fifth defendant identified only as "John Doe." Their case subsequently dropped out of the headlines, but Policastro resurfaced years later as a bagman for local mafioso Joseph Zicarelli. Arrested on new bribery charges in 1970, Policastro testified for the state, resulting in Zicarelli's conviction. A brain tumor killed Policastro on September 8, 1971.[73]

Undesirable

Several of the Apalachin delegates were aliens, while 18 more were naturalized American citizens. Nine days after Croswell's raid, Commissioner of Immigration and Naturalization Joseph Swing began examining the files of all concerned, in hopes of deporting any undesirables. William King, district director of the Immigration Bureau in Buffalo, told reporters, "If we find that any of these men gained citizenship in an illegal manner, or through fraud, we'll take action."[74]

In fact, that action had begun even before the Apalachin gathering, with revocation of Vito Genovese's citizenship in 1955. The government accused him of bad character and a fraudulent application for citizenship, the latter charge admitted on appeal by Genovese, with the peculiar explanation that lying did not matter, since the events he concealed would not have prompted rejection. The United States Court of Appeals for the Third Circuit rejected that argument on September 18, 1956, but more appeals followed and a new hearing was pending when Sergeant Croswell raided Joe Barbara's cookout.[75] As we shall see, Don Vito soon had other legal problems that eclipsed his immigration difficulties.

On December 16, 1957, immigration agents arrested Russell Bufalino at his home in Kingston, Pennsylvania, and drove him to Manhattan for a deportation hearing. Bufalino had never pursued naturalization, and authorities now sought to deport him on grounds that he had failed to provide annual notification of his address, as required by law for aliens. Prosecutors also charged that Bufalino had left the country several times, re-entering on each occasion with false claims that he was born in America. Two days before Christmas, the Board of Immigration Appeals freed Bufalino on $10,000 bond, with a hearing on his deportation set for January 2. On that date, Bufalino received an 18-day delay in execution of his deportation order. Back in court on March 10, Bufalino refused to identify two of the men who rode with him to Apalachin. Confronted with motel receipts showing that he rented rooms for Joe Civello and Simone Scozzari, Bufalino told the court, "I'd be lying if I said that I could remember their names."[76]

By then, Scozzari faced his own immigration problems, arrested and held for deportation in Los Angeles on January 22, 1958. Prosecutors claimed that he had entered the U.S. illegally in 1923, as a shipboard stowaway. Scozzari fought that charge, postponing the inevitable for more than four years, but was finally deported to Italy on June 13, 1962. Bufalino, for his part, waged a long and costly battle with Immigration that ultimately proved successful, despite his loss of various appeals. He would remain in the United States, a recognized illegal alien engaged in daily crimes, for the remainder of his life (some of it as a federal prisoner convicted of extortion and conspiracy).[77]

Equally successful was Carlo

Rosario "Russell" Bufalino (National Archives).

Gambino, summoned for a deportation hearing as an illegal alien on November 3, 1958. Gambino had time to answer 10 preliminary questions before "an apparent heart attack" abruptly ended the proceedings and sent him to the hospital, scheduled to appear again on November 19. Gambino admitted stowing away to reach America in 1921, but claimed that crime was superseded by Immigration procedures carried out when he returned from a visit to Canada in 1935. The United States Court of Appeals for the Second Circuit denied Gambino's latest appeal of his deportation order on January 7, 1970, but like Bufalino, he fought on. Despite a loss before the Supreme Court in June 1970, Don Carlo still prevailed. The Immigration and Naturalization Service granted Gambino an indefinite stay on November 5, 1971, citing his poor health. Thus relieved of worry, he survived another five years as New York's de facto boss of bosses.[78]

Next in line was Joe Profaci, naturalized in 1927, now facing loss of U.S. citizenship for failure to disclose arrests in Sicily, before he immigrated in 1921. Profaci's lawyers claimed their client simply misunderstood the question relating to prior arrests, assuming his interrogators only cared about events occurring in the States. On appeal of his deportation order, the Court of Appeals for the Second Circuit agreed, finding that "since good moral character during the prescribed five year period in this country was the sole test of good moral character, ... and naturalization could not be denied on account of arrests prior to the five years of residence in the United States, it could honestly have been thought that the examiner was not interested in earlier, foreign, arrests." Profaci's deportation order was reversed, with orders for dismissal.[79]

On June 5, 1959, U.S. Attorney John Henderson filed papers in Buffalo to revoke the citizenship of Apalachin delegate Dominick D'Agostino. The charge was fraud, specifically allegations that D'Agostino lied about his marital status and prior arrests when questioned by naturalization examiners in 1926. *The New York Times* reported that filing but carried no follow-up stories. The *Utica Observer-Dispatch* claimed that a verdict on D'Agostino's case was still pending in December 1962. Inquiries to sources in Buffalo, as well as the U.S. Bureau of Citizenship and Immigration Services, produced no further information on D'Agostino's case by press time for this book. Neither does his name appear in the U.S. Social Security Death Index, although that list is incomplete.[80]

Finally, the feds went after Anthony Riela, filing their motion to revoke his naturalization in Newark on August 23, 1960. According to U.S. Attorney Chester Weidenburner, Riela lied repeatedly on his May 1933 application for citizenship, filed in Brooklyn. False answers included his name, date and place of birth, marital status, address of residence, and names of supporting witnesses. It seemed to be a slam-dunk for the government, and while Riela's lawyers appealed his deportation order, the Court of Appeals for the Third Circuit affirmed the order on November 4, 1964.[81] As in the D'Agostino case, however, no further data was available from government files or media sources concerning final disposition of Riela's case at press time for this work.

On balance, we may safely say that federal attempts to rid the nation of selected Apalachin delegates bore mixed results at best.

Watchdogs

Despite their political wrangling, New York state legislators managed to proceed with an investigation of the Mob. Edward Donovan, former chairman of the New York State Correction Commission, had been named in July 1957 to lead the Joint Legislative Committee on Government Operations, commonly known as the "watchdog committee." Eleven days after the Apalachin raid, Donovan announced that his committee would investigate the meeting, with private interrogations scheduled to begin December 12. The panel issued subpoenas for 36 New Yorkers identified as Apalachin delegates, with two— Joseph Falcone and Rosario Mancuso— seeking dismissal of their summonses on grounds that the hearings constituted a discriminatory "fishing expedition." Justice Frank Delvecchio in Syracuse rejected those appeals, and the inquisition forged ahead.[82]

First on the witness stand, as in Tioga County, was Sergeant Edgar Croswell, this time claiming that he was alerted to the meeting by advance orders for special cuts of meat, requested by Joe Barbara from the local Armour factory on November 5, 1957. John Ormento came next, admitting his address, then claiming his Fifth Amendment privilege in response to nine more questions before he was dismissed subject to recall. Joe Barbara, Jr., led the parade on December 13, acknowledging his role in making hotel reservations for his father's guests, but he disclaimed any further knowledge of the gathering or its agenda. He was followed to the stand by John Ormento, pleading the Fifth 83 times on his second appearance; Anthony Guarnieri, with 55 refusals to answer; Joe Profaci, ducking 31 questions; and Joseph Falcone, balking at 42. Seven more Apalachin attendees repeated that performance on December 14: Michele Miranda, dodging 32 questions; Natale Evola, pleading the Fifth 21 times; Paul Castellano, 44; Roy Carlisi, 40; James LaDucca, 28; Antonio Magaddino, 24; and Dominick D'Agostino, 17.[83]

Three witnesses broke the pattern on December 20, attempting to explain away their presence at Barbara's estate. John Montana repeated his story of failed brakes and teatime with Barbara's wife, following a luncheon with Governor Harriman, Italian Prime Minister Mario Scelba, and 43 other guests. Ignatius Cannone claimed that he had dropped in to ask Joe the Barber's advice on purchasing a draught beer system, but left without speaking to Barbara, since his host was busy with "strangers." Emanuel Zicari, described as "an Endicott shoe worker," said he was too sick for work, so called on old friend Barbara instead, only to find himself pressed into service making coffee for "an awful lot of people." Two other witnesses, Vincent Rao and Joseph Riccobono, declined to offer any information other than their names, on grounds of self-incrimination. Detecting a 60-minute discrepancy in Montana's testimony, concerning his time of arrival at Barbara's house, the watchdog committee referred his case to Buffalo District Attorney George Meyl "for such action as he deems necessary and proper under the circumstances."[84]

Montana was not charged with perjury, but his Apalachin arrest and attempts to placate authorities—including subsequent testimony before the McClellan Committee—still cost him dearly. Public association with the Apalachin delegates doomed his political career, while Montana's failure to "take the Fifth" resulted in virtual underworld ostracism, starting with demotion from his post as *consigliere* of the Magaddino Family. Still, he remained a wealthy, reasonably well-respected businessman, with interests extending beyond Buffalo to Ontario's Fort Erie Race Track, where he served as director of its jockey club.[85]

John Cusak, district supervisor of Harry Anslinger's FBN, appeared before the watchdog committee on January 9, relating his bureau's conviction that narcotics distribution was a major theme of the Apalachin meeting. In support of that contention, Cusak cited the attendance of convicted drug traffickers John Ormento, Dominick D'Agostino, and "Joseph Civillo" from Dallas. Cusak specifically named Ormento as "one of the most active and important narcotics violators in the United States." Russell Bufalino followed Cusack to the witness stand, acknowledging his name before retreating under cover of the Fifth Amendment to avoid all further questions. Simultaneously, in a nearby hearing chamber, Senate Majority Leader Walter Mahoney described his prior legal representation of Buffalo's Frontier Liquor Corporation, founded in 1947 by John Montana. Senator Mahoney recalled meeting Montana at various social functions, but denied ever doing business with him personally.[86]

January 13 brought a shift of focus, as the watchdog committee grilled assemblymen Joseph Carlino, Daniel Dickinson and William Passannante concerning their involvement in Carmine Galante's 1956 traffic arrest. All three repeated their stories of dropping Galante's case as soon as they recognized his Mafia ties, claims happily accepted by committee chairman William Horan. Any further scrutiny of sitting lawmakers, Horan advised the press, would result in his inquiry being "dragged off the trail," and was thus unacceptable.[87]

Horan's panel did issue a summons for non–Apalachin attendee Meyer Lansky, but never succeeded in questioning him. Initially served on February 12, as he left court from a preliminary hearing on a nuisance vagrancy charge, Lansky was ordered to appear on February 20. That hearing was postponed when Lansky's lawer was required on other business in federal court. Rescheduled to testify on March 7, Lansky won yet another delay and was subsequently forgotten. Meanwhile, he beat the vagrancy rap on February 27 when Magistrate Reuben Levy dismissed the charge. Still, Meyer did not escape the media melee entirely unscathed: on February 20, Cuba's Minister of the Interior barred Lansky from returning to the island that had made him rich since Prohibition.[88]

Finally, the watchdog committee's sole achievement was a report published on March 30, 1958. That document recognized the Apalachin sitdown as "strong evidence" for the existence of "an active association or organization of criminals whose operations are nation-wide and international," possibly emanating from the "ancient stronghold" of Sicily. It also complained that there was "no effective means for the quick obtaining and collation of pertinent information" on organized crime. Particularly targeted for criticism were police who gathered data on at least five "Apalachin-type meetings" between 1952 and 1956, without pursuing any meaningful investigations. That said, the committee dissolved on April 29, leaving the task of rooting out the Mafia to other hands, already waiting in the wings.[89]

In Contempt

Governor Harriman's replacement for the watchdog committee was a new State Commission of Investigation. On April 25 Harriman identified his choices for the four-man panel: Jacob Grumet and Myles Lane from New York City, John Ryan, Jr., of Buffalo, and Goodman Sarachan from Rochester. Lane and Goodman were Democrats, while Grummet and Sarachan were Republicans. Lane, as Manhattan's U.S. attorney, had filed tax evasion charges against Frank Costello. Grumet had aided Thomas Dewey in his prosecutions of Waxey Gordon and Lepke Buchalter, before serving as Chief of the Homicide Bureau in the New York County District Attorney's Office. Ryan served as Buffalo's chief city judge. Sarachan was a Supreme Court justice in the Seventh Judicial District. Sworn in on April 30, each would receive a $15,000 annual salary while pursuing a broad investigation of narcotics, illegal gambling, and labor racketeering.[90]

The panel spent three months reviewing files collected by the now-defunct watchdog committee, then issued a flurry of subpoenas in early August 1958. None of the subjects were identified before hearings convened on August 12, but Chairman Lane told reporters that several had not been subpoenaed before. The first two summoned, Apalachin delegates Frank Valenti and Rosario Mancuso, were granted blanket immunity but still refused to testify, whereupon both were charged with "willful and contumacious refusal to answer material and relevant questions." Both were jailed without bond by Supreme Court Justice Morris Spencer "until such time as you are willing to appear before the commission and answer such questions as may be propounded to you."[91]

Thus the pattern was established: any mobster who refused to talk would be locked up indefinitely, not for any crime committed on the streets, but for observing the code of *omertà*. Next in line, on August 13, were Joseph Riccobono and Paul Castellano. Attorney Joseph Brill, representing Riccobono, called the panel's offer of immunity "hollow and a mockery," but Governor Harriman had no time for legal niceties. Vacationing at Elmira, he told reporters, "We've got to end this business of people's refusing to answer questions on matters in the public interest. These people have got to be forced to talk." The Appellate Division of New York's Supreme Court upheld the jailings on August 14, and Apalachin guest Michele Miranda joined his cohorts in custody the following day.[92]

Public hearings resumed on August 20, with Carmine Lombardozzi and Costenze Valenti called to testify. Both knew what to expect, and both remained stubbornly silent. They were ordered to jail, but received a brief stay while New York's Court of Appeals considered fresh pleas from the five mafiosi already confined. Judge Charles Desmond heard their arguments and rejected them on August 22, whereupon Lombardozzi and Valenti brought the total of caged hoods to seven. Five of those held — Castellano, Mancuso, Miranda, Riccobono and Valenti — asked U.S. Supreme Court Justice John Marshall Harlan II to free them pending appeal of their charges, but he refused on September 3.[93]

While those in jail continued their fruitless appeals, subpoenaed witness Joseph Falcone considered his options and dropped out of sight, missing his scheduled date with the commission on September 11, 1958. Instead, the panel received a letter from Dr. James Douglas of Utica, saying that Falcone was immobilized by pain resulting from surgery several months earlier. Chairman Lane announced plans to proceed "very vigorously" against Falcone, perhaps compounding a contempt citation with charges of conspiracy to obstruct justice, then issued a summons for Falcone's physician. Dr. Douglas answered all the questions posed to him, thus becoming the first commission witness to avoid incarceration. While awaiting Dr. Douglas, the commissioners grilled Joseph Rosato but received no answers to their inquiries.[94]

On November 6, 1958, with the first anniversary of the Apalachin raid fast approaching, Sergeant Joseph Benanati of the New York State Police Criminal Intelligence Unit briefed the commission on his futile efforts to serve Joe Barbara, Sr., with a subpoena. Visiting the Barbara estate on September 30, he was informed by Josephine that husband Joe was "sick in bed," while she was likewise too ill to accept the document on his behalf. Benanati then marched around the house with a loudspeaker, audible from one-fifth of a mile, calling in vain for Barbara. Joe Junior also testified that day, reporting that his father had been ill since January 3, when Junior had assumed command "as assistant to the president" at Barbara's bottling plant. Jacob Grumet, replacing Myles Lane as commission chairman, warned Joe Jr. and his lawyer, "You know that we are going to apply for a warrant for his arrest, and it's my suggestion that he answer our subpoena. I think he could avoid a lot of trouble by answering our subpoena, because we are intent on examining him."[95]

Illness sounded good to scheduled witnesses Joseph Rosato and Joseph Profaci, when they sought and received postponements of their testimony on December 2. Antonio Magaddino won postponement on the same day, since his lawyer was tied up in court on another matter. Anthony Guarnieri was the first Apalachin delegate to answer questions, on January 13, 1959, claiming that he delivered three shirts to Joe Barbara on the day of the meeting, and "took for granted" that the other guests had come to wish Barbara a speedy recovery from his latest heart attack. Afterward, Chairman Grumet told reporters, "You can quote me as saying I don't believe his story."[96]

Samuel Lagatutta hewed to the expected line on January 14, pleading the Fifth to 90 questions. Stefano Magaddino ducked 37 questions of his own, but for undisclosed reasons was not granted immunity. On January 15, Lagatutta found himself in court with Joe Rosato, ordered to show cause whey they should not be jailed for contempt. Neither offered any viable defense, but while Lagatutta was caged, Rosato eluded police. Joe Profaci recovered from his latest bout of illness long enough to testify on January 27, claiming that he was en route to Pennsylvania in November 1957 when his chauffeur took "a wrong turn in a road" and brought him to Endicott, New York, by accident. Once there, Profaci decided on a whim to visit Barbara, then left after an hour and was stopped by state police. "If his story was true," Chairman Grumet opined, "then he certainly asserted his constitutional privilege frivolously."[97]

Subpoena-dodgers vexed the commission in early 1959. Joe Barbara, Sr., remained elusive, deploying attorneys to oppose a contempt citation based on his refusal to accept a summons. Commission chief counsel Eliot Lumbard filed a brief against Barbara with the State Supreme Court's Appellate Division on February 6, condemning Barbara's "distorted, ritualized game of 'you catch me' in total abandonment of common sense." The commission's first annual report, issued on March 15, claimed that many other "long-entrenched underworld leaders" had fled the state to avoid interrogation and contempt citations, thereby disrupting the Mafia's "smooth operations." Pleased with itself, the panel described its procedure as "the first time that participants in the Apalachin meeting have not been allowed to come through a revolving door into a hearing and back home again. This time they went from the hearing to jail, where they will remain until they comply with the order of the court."[98]

How much compliance was required to win their freedom, though? Brothers Costenze and Frank Valenti tested the waters on March 17, announcing through their lawyers that they "desire[d] to answer the questions as soon as possible." Both addressed the commision on March 18, with questions including who invited them to Apalachin, the number of delegates present, who addressed the gathering, and whether any public officials attended. Frank told the panel that his brother planned to visit Joseph Barbara and "I had time to kill, so I went along." No meeting was held, he insisted. Rather, he passed his time eating, drinking, and "admiring the scenery." As for the raid, Frank professed total ignorance: "State troopers? I didn't see no state troopers. I couldn't have cared less if J. Edgar Hoover was there. I hadn't done anything." Costenze echoed his brother's account, describing their trip to Apalachin as "a social call on a friend." Incredulous, Chairman Grumet dismissed the testimony as "very well rehearsed," "unequivocally unworthy of belief," and "a sham designed to impede the commission's investigation."[99]

Back in jail, the brothers filed new motions seeking liberty, on grounds of their alleged cooperation. Supreme Court Judge Edgar Nathan, Jr., deferred ruling on the plea until March 25, but set bond at $50,000. Strapped for cash, the Valentis remained in custody — and were disappointed again when Nathan dismissed their writ of habeas corpus, finding that the brothers "had not complied with the order of the court, which directed them to give truthful testimony."[100]

On April 14 the commission served subpoenas on Vito Genovese, Russell Bufalino, John Ormento and Natale Evola, commanding all four to appear for questioning on May 12. Joe Barbara, Sr., had also been served in the meantime, and was scheduled to appear on May 25. Frank Valenti caught a break on May 7, when the State Supreme Court's Appellate Division found his March testimony sufficient to absolve him of contempt. Brother Costenze, on the other hand, would stay in jail, since his "purported answers are palpably false and evasive, designed to obstruct." Frank posted $15,000 bond on May 13 and breathed free air for the first time in six months.[101]

Vincent Rao faced the commission on May 11, 1959, after ducking subpoenas for more than a year. He claimed his Fifth Amendment privilege in declining to answer 20 questions, then was dismissed with an order to return on June 9. New chairman John Ryan told reporters that immunity had not been granted, since the panel had to learn if Rao was facing any active prosecutions. On his second appearance, with immunity granted, Rao called himself "a victim of circumstance." He rode to Apalachin with Joseph Rosato and Salvatore Tornabe, since deceased, believing the occasion was "a buffet luncheon." He did not meet his host, Rao said, and spoke to no one else. "I wasn't properly introduced," he insisted. "I didn't know them. I'm not that forward." He had dodged subpoenas in Miami, registered at a hotel as "Victor Rizzo," Rao explained, because "I didn't want to be embarrassed." The performance, though transparent, was enough to spare him from citation for contempt.[102]

Vito Genovese met the commission one week later, testifying under a grant of immunity. Don Vito claimed he was invited to Joe Barbara's estate by "Mike Miranda and Jerry Catena, whom I knew," relying on their description of Barbara as "a businessman" who might buy steel from Genovese. Playing the victim, Genovese claimed that the trip had ruined his life, resulting in his subsequently being "framed" on a narcotics rap. "I should have broken both my legs," he said, "before accepting that invitation."[103]

While Genovese was excused, his cohorts grew increasingly restless in jail. Carmine Lombardozzi, facing trial in federal court with 26 codefendants on charges related to the Apalachin meeting, sought release from New York's Civil Prison on bail matching his $15,000 federal bond. His also sent a telegram to Governor Rockefeller, offering cooperation with the State Commission of Investigation. Paul Castellano pitched a similar offer July 17, after losing his joint appeal with Michele Miranda to the U.S. Supreme Court on June 29. Joe Riccobono soon joined the penitent team, with Lombardozzi the first to testify, on July 20. He had accepted friend Carlo Gambino's invitation to the Barbara estate, he said, although he did not know the host. Lombardozzi dined, drank, and played pinochle with friends in Barbara's garage, but they discussed no business. Castellano and Riccobono described the same card game in their testimony on July 21, which was dismissed by the commission as "false," "inherently incredible," and "clearly evasive." Still, it was enough to liberate Castellano and Riccobono, though Supreme Court Justice Frederick Backer ordered Lombardozzi to remain in jail, deeming his statement "palpably false."[104]

New York's Court of Appeals dealt Costenze Valenti another defeat on July 8, 1959, ruling that he must remain in custody until he answered the commission's questions honestly. Three weeks later, Valenti asked the Supreme Court for a transfer from civil prison to Rochester's jail on compassionate grounds, to facilitate visits from relatives. Justice Birdie Amsterdam deferred judgment, while Deputy Commissioner Nathan Skolnik told the court, "Valenti may attain his immediate freedom by truthfully and candidly answering the commission's questions, but he totally avoids this remedy." Justice Birdie approved Valenti's transfer on August 21, but a state appeal delayed the move. Ultimately, Valenti served more time on his contempt charge than any other Apalachin delegate, released after 16 months on December 11, upon submitting $15,000 bond. In January 1960 he was slapped with perjury charges, but the Supreme Court's Appellate Division dismissed that case on March 15, 1960.[105]

Michele Miranda sought to win his freedom on August 12, 1959, with a return appearance before the commission. This time, Miranda — the first Apalachin witness so far to admit knowing Joseph Barbara — claimed he was invited to a barbecue where 60-odd guests spent their time discussing the scenery, weather, and their host's poor health. Barbara, he said, "looked very bad," prompting another guest to call a doctor. Miranda left before the physician arrived, after speaking briefly to Vito Genovese. Chairman Ryan called Miranda's testimony "incredibly false, evasive," and geared to obstruct the commission, but the Supreme Court's Appellate Division freed Miranda on November 20.[106]

Rosario Carlisi, already convicted of contempt before Tioga County's grand jury, faced the state commission on August 13, 1959, and refused to answer any questions despite an offer of immunity. Back for a return engagement the following day, Carlisi still refused and was remanded into custody by Supreme Court Judge Louis Capozzoli. Tired of jail after a week, Carlisi agreed to talk and was freed on $5,000 bond, with an order to "testify fully and truthfully" at his next hearing, on October 5. On that date, he told the panel that he traveled to Apalachin with Joseph Falcone and James LaDucca at the "casual invitation" of Russell Bufalino, understanding the event to be a barbecue. Chairman Ryan judged that testimony "false and incredible," asking Justice John Flynn to revoke Carlisi's bond and return him to jail.[107] Absence of any further coverage suggests that Carlisi remained at liberty.

Joe Barbara, Jr., took a different approach on October 5, when he pled guilty to giving the commission "contumacious" answers during November 1958 testimony. Facing a maximum sentence of three years in prison, Barbara instead received one year's probation on December 18, from General Sessions Judge Mitchell Schweitzer. Between those events, in November, Rosario Mancuso grudgingly agreed to testify about the Apalachin gathering. Like his cohorts before him, Mancuso claimed his visit was intended to lift Joe the Barber's spirits following his heart attack. Supreme Court Justice Jacob Markowitz released Mancuso on November 27, after 15 months in custody.[108]

Despite his panel's failure to elicit anything resembling credible testimony, Chairman Sarachan tried to look on the bright side, telling reporters that the commission still planned to "crack" the Apalachin mystery someday. Even while lying, Sarachan declared, the witnesses had "added pieces to the puzzle." In any case, he claimed, "this particular crowd is pretty much out of business. I don't mean that organized crime is at an end, but a younger group will have to take over. The older leaders are on the run."[109]

Which must have come as startling news to Russell Bufalino, Carlo Gambino, Paul Castellano, Gerardo Catena, Joe Magliocco and the rest — not to mention Santo Trafficante, Jr., Sam Giancana, Joe Zerilli, John Scalish, and others beyond the commission's short reach.

On December 21, 1959 — one day after Sarachan's self-congratulatory press conference — the commission announced that its next round of hearings, scheduled to grill seven out-of-state witnesses, would be postponed until mid-January 1960. In fact, the various Apalachin delegates from Pennsylvania, New Jersey, Ohio and Texas universally defied New York's subpoenas and were not compelled to testify.[110]

· 10 ·

Trial and Error

For ardent Mob-watchers it was not good enough simply to question Apalachin delegates, or even jail them briefly for refusal to cooperate with their inquisitors. If they were truly members of a criminal conspiracy spanning the nation — or the globe — whose crimes included countless murders, they should be locked up forever, even executed if the law permitted it.

But how? Based on what evidence?

Around New York, authorities sought any charge available to build a case.

Exit the Barber

Apalachin, in a very real sense, ruined life for Joe Barbara, Sr. Ailing before the raid, he now found himself under siege. Agents of the State Liquor Authority raided his Endicott bottling plant on November 26, seizing ledgers and other records "to study for possible law violations." Barbara had already surrendered his beer-distributing license, but sued for return of papers related to his soft drink business. In that, at least, he was successful, obtaining an order from the state Supreme Court that required liquor agents to show cause for seizing the records.[1]

It was a small win, and the last for Joe the Barber. Federal prosecutors indicted him for tax evasion in March 1959, while state investigators hounded him, denouncing claims of poor health as a fraud, and finally obtained a court order requiring Barbara's appearance before the State Investigative Commission, though no date was set and he never actually testified. On September 24, 1958, Barbara listed his Apalachin estate for sale at a rumored price of $125,000 — 50 percent below its value based on press reports. Local builder LaRue Quick and Realtor Russell Terry of Vestal, New York, bought the property on May 21, 1959, and Barbara moved to nearby Endicott, but he had no time to enjoy his retirement. Stricken by a final heart attack on May 27, he lapsed into a coma two days later and died at Johnson City's Wilson Memorial Hospital on June 17. Only four Apalachin delegates—Anthony Guarnieri, Bartolo Guccia, Pasquale Turrigiano and Emmanuel Zicari—attended Barbara's funeral service on June 22. Ten months later, on the night of April 16, 1960, unknown prowlers burned a six-foot cross at Barbara's grave site and left a note reading: "We will get your pals one by one. The Gypees." Broome County authorities branded the incident a case of "stupid vandalism," to which they attached "no particular significance."[2]

Six days after that bizarre incident, LaRue Quick and Russell Terry broadcast plans to open Barbara's estate as a tourist attraction, charging visitors one dollar per head to tour the site "where crime met its Waterloo." The entrepreneurs planned to employ 35 locals, while promising guests a lake and swimming pool, a driving range and restaurant, but none of those amenities existed when the first tourists arrived on April 24, 1960. Instead, they made do with a short-order stand peddling 35 cent hamburgers and 15 cent sodas, and a 50 cent "Apalachin Joe barbecue." Adding insult to injury, *Mad Magazine* treated readers to a faux advertisement for "Lawless Manor in the Heart of the Underworld at ... Appalachin [*sic*], N.Y.," where guests could "live high while laying low" for a mere $198 per night (paid in unmarked bills).[3]

Full-time Apalachin residents protested the estate's exploitation, and local officials backed their constituents, denying Quick's application for a commercial zoning variance. Quick appealed that ruling to Tioga County's Supreme Court, which quashed the town's objections. Fighting on, opponents of the Mafia theme park took their case to the State Supreme Court's Appellate Division, which upheld the ban on July 27, 1960. More appeals ensued, but Quick lost again, on December 1, 1960, and sold the property in 1961.[4]

Dragnets

From Manhattan to Hollywood, everyone in post-Apalachin America wanted a piece of the Mafia. On July 31, 1959, *The New York Times* announced three programs in production for television's fall lineup. CBS planned two shows—a drama titled "The Meeting at Apalachin" from *Westinghouse Desilu Playhouse* (producers of the controversial "Untouchables" series) and an untitled feature from *Playhouse 90*—while NBC touted a program called "Mafia," based on unspecified "actual files." Desilu's production aired belatedly on January 22, 1960, with pseudonyms used for all the players except Edgar Croswell, but it was scooped by the September 1959 theatrical release of director Edward Cahn's *Inside the Mafia,* wherein bloody mayhem ensues during a gangland gathering at "Apple Lake, New York."[5]

Back in real life, authorities pursued the Apalachin delegates with sudden, unaccustomed vigor. One week after Croswell's raid, the NYPD arrested Joe Profaci, Natale Evola and Paul Castellano, grilling the trio for several hours about Albert Anastasia's murder, then releasing them without charges. The following day, November 23, officers detained Michele Miranda, Joseph Riccobono and Carmine Lombardozzi for questioning. On November 24 authorities slapped Frank Majuri with a charge of violating probation and ordered Louis La Rasso to testify at his hearing the next day. That morning — November 25 — police hauled in Armand Rava and Salvatore Tornabe, releasing them both after nightfall. In the predawn hours of November 27 raiders struck the homes of 15 New York racketeers, including Michael Genovese. That afternoon found Vincent Rao in an interrogation room, while Mineola officers added John Ormento to their list of 17 reputed mafiosi held for questioning.[6]

The initial frenzy faded during the winter, but trouble continued for various Apalachin visitors — and some who never came within 1,000 miles of Barbara's estate. Sal Tornabe racked up 10 traffic citations after the gangland gathering, but he dodged payment when garage attendant Charles Francoviglia claimed responsibility for the violations on December 5, 1957. Magistrate James LoPiccolo challenged Francoviglia's story in Brooklyn's Traffic Court, then slapped him with a 10-day jail term in addition to a $50 fine. Tornabe's worries ended forever when he died three weeks later, on December 30.[7]

Lucky Luciano with unidentified friends at his home in Naples, Italy (National Archives).

Lucky Luciano, questioned in Naples, denied any part in the Apalachin gathering. "They're still trying to frame me," he told reporters afterward. "Until I read all that trash in the papers, I never heard of Apalachin. I still don't know where it is, and I don't care. I'm clean. I even pay my income tax. They got nothing on me and never will have." And he was right. Despite continual surveillance and rumors of an impending narcotics indictment, he died a free man on January 26, 1962, killed by a heart attack at Naples's Capodichino Airport.[8]

Three Apalachin visitors fought back in court for the bad publicity stemming from the November raid. On February 12, 1958, Patsy Sciortino joined the Monachino brothers in announcing plans to sue Sergeant Croswell for "false imprisonment, false arrest, defamation of character and defamation of standing in the community." With lawyer Joseph Monachino representing father Sam and his co-plaintiffs, the litigants charged that Croswell's raid would adversely affect the Monachino beer distributorship and Sciortino's one-man bleach business. Each plaintiff sought $100,000 for his detention on November 14, plus another $400,000 for Croswell's publication of their names—a total of $1.5 million in alleged damages. Only Sciortino followed through on the threat, filing his case in August 1958, then he withdrew it 10 months later, with attorney Monachino citing "the difficulty of proving a monetary loss."[9]

Other Barbara well-wishers were too busy ducking indictments to think of filing their own claims. Federal prosecutors charged Dominick Alaimo with Taft-Hartley violations in March 1959, and jurors convicted him two years later. In Utica, investigation of Apalachin delegates Joseph Falcone and Rosario Mancuso uncovered a web of corruption that imperiled Oneida County's entrenched Democratic political machine. With Sergeant Croswell serving as his lead investigator, Special Prosecutor Robert Fisher forced the resignations of Utica Police Chief Leo Miller and Deputy Chief Vincent Fiore, while indicting Streets Superintendent Joseph Bollettieri on fraud and larceny charges. By October 1959, five locals stood convicted of operating brothels, and 13 Mob-connected bookies were awaiting trial. Falcone and Mancuso wriggled through the dragnet, but they had worn out their welcome.[10]

On December 17, 1959, New York City's Health Department summoned Vincent Rao to Housing Court, where he was charged with permitting rats to infest a tenement he owned in East Harlem. According to the state, Rao had ignored "stern warnings" to eradicate the vermin that besieged his tenants. Rao missed his court date, prompting issuance of an arrest warrant, but he ultimately dodged conviction as a slumlord. In May 1960 the State Investigating Commission added charges that Rao had conspired with mafioso Anthony Carfano and various contractors to inflate the cost of erecting a

Anthony Carfano and Janice Drake, murdered in September 1959 (National Archives).

clubhouse at the Yonkers Raceway by some $4 million. Carfano—alias "Little Augie Pisano"—had nothing to fear from the charges, since unknown gunmen had executed him in Queens with girlfriend Janice Drake on September 25, 1959.[11] Once again, Rao slipped through the net and avoided conviction.

Carmine Lombardozzi was next in line for indictment, named as one of 47 defendants charged with a $2 million stock swindle on May 18, 1960. According to the Securities and Exchange Commission, Lombardozzi, his individual codefendants, and three indicted corporations had conspired to inflate stock prices for Canada's Atlas Gypsum Corporation, peddling shares worth 20 cents each for as much as $3 apiece. Lombardozzi was not among those convicted in that case, but similar charges—and worse, including assaults on police officers and FBI agents—would dog him through the next two decades.[12]

"A Close-knit, Clandestine, Criminal Syndicate"

McClellan Committee counsel Robert Kennedy had quizzed FBN agent Joseph Amato about the Mafia in Washington one day before the Apalachin raid. Six weeks later, on December 23, 1957, Kennedy announced a "brand-new investigation" into labor and industrial racketeering, telling reporters that the probe "has its roots in the Apalachin conclave." Another four months passed before committee member Irving Ives, senator from New York, announced a full-scale investigation of the Mafia itself, including "the entire list" of Apalachin delegates, among 100 subpoenaed gangsters. Those sub-poenas were issued in mid–May 1958, with hearings scheduled to begin on June 30.[13]

In June 1958 the committee's membership included Chairman McClellan and Vice Chairman Ives; future presidential candidates John F. Kennedy (D–Mass.) and Barry Goldwater (R–Ariz.); Frank Church III (D–Idaho), future investigator of CIA and FBI abuses; future Watergate inquisitor Sam Ervin (D–N.C.); and Karl Mundt (R–S.D.), former stalwart member of the House Un-American Activities Committee. Robert Kennedy remained in his role as chief counsel, aided by chief clerk Ruth Young Watt.[14]

Two members of the committee, worlds apart in their political philos-ophy, came to the hearings burdened with a history of Mob involvement. Kennedy's father, Joseph Kennedy, Sr., had been a high-society bootlegger during Prohibition, closely affiliated with Meyer Lansky, Moe Dalitz, Frank Costello and other leaders of the fledgling national crime syndicate — and, as we shall see, those ties endured for decades after repeal. Goldwater, in turn, was a crony of notorious figures in Arizona and Las Vegas, with Moe Dalitz

Willie Bioff, slain by an Arizona car-bombing in 1955 (National Archives).

prominent among them. When a car-bombing killed former pimp and extortionist Willie Bioff in 1955, Goldwater attended his funeral, thus exposing their friendship and financial entanglements. Three years later, in December 1958, Goldwater mourned the passing of another crony: mobster and casino manager Gus Greenbaum, knifed to death with his wife at their Arizona estate.[15]

None of those issues rated mention as the hearings convened in Washington. Chairman McClellan opened with a statement that "there exists in America today what appears to be a close-knit, clandestine, criminal syndicate. This group has made fortunes in the illegal liquor traffic during prohibition, and later in narcotics, vice, and gambling. These illicit profits present the syndicate with a financial problem, which they solve through investment in legitimate business. These legitimate businesses also provide convenient cover for their continued illegal activities."[16] All true, but the exclusive focus on mobsters of Italian heritage would produce a distorted view of American organized crime.

Although committee leaders had announced the issuance of subpoenas for 100 mafiosi, including all identified Apalachin attendees, only 24 witnesses were called to testify between June 30 and July 3, when the hearings adjourned. Five of those — Sergeant Croswell, Capt. James Hamilton of the Los Angeles Police Department, Thomas O'Brien from NYPD, Martin Pera from the FBN, and Daniel Sullivan of the Miami Crime Commission — spoke for law enforcement. Three others were committee staffers. Of the remaining 11, ten were known or suspected Apalachin attendees: Russell Bufalino, Vito Genovese, James LaDucca, Louis LaRasso, Thomas Lucchese, Rosario Mancuso, Michele Miranda, John Montana, Joe Profaci and John Scalish.[17]

The testimony from authorities was perfectly predictable. Sergeant Croswell — misspelled "Crosswell" in committee transcripts — described his first interaction with Joe Barbara during the Second World War, detailed Barbara's criminal record, and moved on through details of the Apalachin raid. Agent Pera warned that mafiosi involved with narcotics were making a "concerted effort" to penetrate labor unions and industry — which, in fact, had begun decades earlier. Captain Hamilton described a parallel effort by "the Sicilian group [and] others" to infiltrate unions and legitimate business. Dan Sullivan detailed the ongoing migration of midwestern mobsters to Florida, where they had purchased hotels and other above-board concerns. Thomas O'Brien had participated in post-Apalachin interviews, but added nothing of substance.[18]

The Apalachin delegates subpoenaed by McClellan likewise offered few surprises. Vito Genovese set the standard, claiming his Fifth Amendment privilege while refusing to answer 150 questions. Russell Bufalino and Joe

Profaci were close behind, with 92 and 91 refusals, respectively. James LaDucca declined to answer 77 questions; Rosario Mancuso, 71; Louis LaRasso, 52; and John Scalish, 34 (including his wife's maiden name). Thomas Lucchese ducked 82 questions, but answered many others pertaining to his birth and immigration, old arrests, and his sundry legal businesses. He explicitly denied Mafia membership, any knowledge of drug-trafficking, and involvement in any illegal business—though he took the Fifth when questioned about gambling.[19]

Michele Miranda's interrogation verged on comic opera at times, thanks to his fractured English. "I decline myself on the ground that it may incriminate myself," he told the panel at one point, and at another: "I decline to answer myself on the ground I incriminate myself." Attorney Abraham Brodsky felt obliged to tell the senators, "This is not an act. That is the way he speaks." Growing frustrated at last, Chairman McClellan told Miranda, "Let's try to expedite this. You growl out something, and if it means anything, besides this answer that 'I decline to answer on the ground that it may tend to incriminate me,' say so. Proceed now. Growl it out. Mr. Reporter, get the best you can out of the growl and put it down."[20]

Only John Montana struck a pose of full cooperation with the panel, answering all questions posed to him without pleading the Fifth Amendment. He admitted knowing many mobsters through the liquor industry, after repeal, but claimed that he had not researched their backgrounds, "because if [they] received a license I felt that the State of New York had done it." The seeming bid for full disclosure showed frayed edges, however, when Montana told his version of the Apalachin meeting. Leaving Buffalo with Antonio Magaddino for an appointment at Russell Bufalino's Medico Industries in Pittston, Pennsylvania, Montana drove into a rainstorm and found the windshield wipers of his new Cadillac inoperable. Next, his brakes failed, and in the absence of a handy garage, Montana drove to the nearby home of business associate Joe Barbara, who had "ten or fifteen mechanics to take care of his trucks." On arrival, Montana parked in front of Barbara's garage and entered his house, leaving Magaddino in the Caddy. While Montana drank a cup of tea with Barbara and his wife, "somebody" entered and "said there was a roadblock."[21]

"Then, of course, I didn't have any alternative," Montana said. "I could not drive my car, Mr. Kennedy, so the next thing I could do was to walk." Why not drive away? "Because there is a steep hill. The state trooper will tell you it is a very steep hill and with no brakes—going up it was all right but coming down I wouldn't have been safe." Why leave at all? "Maybe I should have stayed there, Senator, but that was my best judgment. When I saw the commotion, I was no part of it, and I thought I would walk away from it."

Strangely, although he had already identified several Apalachin attendees as business associates, Montana insisted that he recognized no one at Barbara's home on November 14.[22]

Senator Ives had trouble swallowing Montana's story. "You are a well-balanced individual," he told the witness. "After all is said and done, just because somebody yells 'roadblock,' every time that happens you don't go dashing through the woods, do you? After all, you are a rational person, rather than any other type."

"Well, there is always the first time, Senator," Montana replied. "That is what happened."

"Do you mean to tell me," Ives bored in, "you are losing your equilibrium as you are getting older?"

"I hope not," Montana answered.

"Well, all right," said Ives, ending the ordeal. "That is the only way to explain such an irrational thing as you did."[23]

While the McClellan hearings finally revealed no new information concerning the Apalachin conference, the attendant publicity ruined Montana. His reputation as Buffalo's "Man of the Year," a member of the city's mercantile elite, was soiled beyond redemption by the Barbara raid and its aftermath. At the same time, Montana's public efforts to redeem that reputation by violating *omertà* cost him the trust of fellow mafiosi. Stripped of his rank as *consigliere* of the Magaddino Family and forced to retire, he would stand with the others at trial in days to come, but any vestige of respect was lost.[24]

Arrivederce, Don Vitone

Apalachin's biggest loser was the man who called the meeting: Vito Genovese. Despite ongoing claims that mafiosi shunned drug trafficking by order of the brotherhood, Don Vito and his cohorts were neck-deep in heroin. The FBN had eyes on Genovese, their interest redoubled after Apalachin, but the agency could find no solid evidence against him — until 1958.

Two versions of Don Vito's fall Puerto Rican four-time loser Nelson "The Melon" Cantellops in a pivotal role. Prior to attaining courtroom stardom, Cantellops had been convicted of obtaining money under false pretenses (1949), attempted forgery (1952), and possession of marijuana (1956). In 1957 he received a five-year term for peddling heroin, and was cooling his heels in Sing Sing when FBN Agent Anthony Consoli learned of The Melon's supposed connection to Genovese from a street informant. According to the bureau's version of events, Consoli charmed Cantellops by securing his transfer to a more comfortable lockup, where the grateful pusher told all to Assistant U.S. Attorney William Tendesky, agreeing to testify against Genovese and company in court.[25]

The *other* version has a rather different twist. According to authors John Tuohy, Hank Messick, and others, Frank Costello met with Meyer Lansky and Genovese Family member Vincent "Jimmy Blue Eyes" Alo to plot Genovese's removal. In this account, Nelson Cantellops not only worked for Genovese, through John Ormento, but also doubled as a part-time courier for Lansky. Cognizant of his imprisonment, the trio sent a representative to Sing Sing, persuading The Melon to contact an FBN agent, whose name the visitor supplied. Well aware that refusal could shorten his life, Cantellops accepted the proverbial offer he could not refuse. A variant of that story includes Lucky Luciano and Carlo Gambino as plotters against Genovese, with Cantellops receiving a $100,000 bribe.[26]

Whichever tale is true, the end result is history. On June 4, 1958, FBN agents arrested Genovese, fellow Apalachin delegate Natale Evola, and 15 others in connection with a heroin delivery made in Manhattan three years earlier. More arrests followed, bringing the total to 53 or 67, by various published accounts. Carmine Galante and John Ormento slipped through the dragnet, remaining at large. One month after the initial raids, on July 7, a federal grand jury indicted Genovese and 36 others on charges of conspiracy to import, receive, conceal, possess, sell and distribute heroin. Aside from Genovese, the list included Apalachin visitors Natale Evola, Carmine Galante, and John Ormento—the last two nowhere to be found when raiders made their sweep of New York City and environs.[27]

Galante and Ormento were still at large when Genovese and 15 codefendants went to trial before Judge Alexander Bicks in Manhattan, on January 5, 1959. Their trial lasted 14 weeks, but jurors required only 12 hours to convict 15 of the accused on April 3, acquitting only defendant Louis Fiano, who was already imprisoned on federal narcotics charges. Judge Bicks pronounced sentence for the convicted defendants on April 17: 15 years for Vito Genovese, plus a $20,000 fine and revocation of his previous $150,000 bond; 20 years for Lucchese Family *caporegime* Salvatore Santora; 15 years and a $20,000 fine for Joseph DiPalermo, with no bond pending appeal; 12 years for brother Charles DiPalermo, with his bond increased from $15,000 to $20,000; 14 years for Daniel Lessa; 12 years for brother Nicholas Lessa; 12 years for Rocco Mazzie; 10 years for Natale Evola, with a $20,000 fine and an increase of his bond from $35,000 to $50,000 pending appeal; 10 years each for Mafia associates Alfredo Aviles and Benjamin Rodriguez; eight years for Carmine Pollizzano; seven years for brother Ralph Polizzano, following expiration of a previous ongoing sentence; seven years for Vincent "The Chin" Gigante, with leniency secured by a flurry of supportive letters from neighbors in Greenwich

Village; and five years each for Charles Barcellona and Jean Capece (a single mother and the lone female defendant).[28]

Confusion surrounds the fate of key state witness Nelson Cantellops. While several sources report that Governor Nelson Rockefeller commuted his five-year sentence after the Genovese trial, Cantellops was still in custody on July 30, 1960, when *The New York Times* reported his beating by another inmate at Manhattan's City Prison. Meanwhile, in Atlanta's federal prison, where Vito Genovese and the rest were sent to serve their time, inmates reportedly boycotted service of cantaloupe at mealtime.[29]

Four days before Genovese's case went to the jury — on March 30, 1959 — FBN agents nabbed fugitives John Ormento and Nicholas "Big Nose" Tolentino at an apartment on Gun Hill Road, in the Bronx. Their arrest followed the February 27 fatal beating of septuagenarian Bronx resident Dr. John Jackson, a heroin-processing chemist and scheduled witness at another pending trial. Detectives from the NYPD suspected local contractor David Giampa of involvement in that case and had placed him under surveillance, which found him delivering food and clean laundry to Ormento's hideout. Investigation of the former fugitives continued, prompting the arrest of Canadian mobsters Giuseppe Cotroni and René Robert in Montreal on July 9, 1959. A federal grand jury voted new indictments on May 6, 1960, listing Ormento, Cotroni, Robert, and 26 others as members of a syndicate that had imported heroin worth more than $1 million ($7.7 million today) over the past five years. Ormento and 20 codefendants faced trial on November 21, 1960, but a mistrial was declared in May 1961. At a second trial, jurors covicted Ormento and 12 others on June 25, 1962. Two weeks later, on July 10, their judge imposed sentences totaling 276 years and fined each defendant $20,000. A federal appellate court denied their appeals on June 13, 1963.[30]

Fugitive Carmine Galante was there for the unhappy finish with Big John Ormento. Arrested by feds and New Jersey state troopers on June 3, 1959, while driving on the Garden State Parkway, he posted $100,000 bond, then surrendered peacefully on May 17, 1960, when fresh indictments added him to the list of plotters who, with Ormento, had smuggled heroin into the United States and Canada. Convicted with Ormento and 11 others on June 25, 1962, Galante received a 20-year sentence on July 11. He joined Vito Genovese and company in the Atlanta lockup, remaining there until January 1974, when parole unleashed him once again upon society.[31]

While those dramas unfolded, Don Vito Genovese continued to run his family from prison, transmitting orders to a junta that included Thomas Eboli, Jerry Catena, Michele Miranda, Anthony "Tony Bender" Strollo and Philip "Benny Squint" Lombardo. A series of appeals ensued, spiced up by charges that a key prosecution witness had been offered cash to recant his testimony in April 1960. The U.S. Supreme Court refused to hear Genovese's first appeal in May 1960, but changed its mind and ordered a new bail hearing in October 1963. That bid for temporary freedom was derailed, but Genovese filed another motion — this one to vacate his sentence — in September 1965. Denied at the district level, that motion wound its leisurely way to the U.S. Court of Appeals for the Second Circuit, where it was denied on May 26, 1967, despite the best efforts of celebrity defense attorney Edward Bennett Williams. Defeated at last, Don Vito Genovese died in prison on St. Valentine's Day 1969.[32]

Conspiracy

While prosecutors in various jurisdictions pursued individual Apalachin delegates with a mixed bag of charges, a special federal grand jury was created in December 1957 to investigate the gathering itself. On December 11 the panel questioned Vito Genovese, Michele Miranda, John Ormento, Joseph Riccobono, Natale Evola, and Joseph Profaci — who broke down during interrogation and was rushed to Lower Manhattan's Downtown Hospital, there diagnosed with a "posible peptic ulcer." Profaci returned for a second grilling on December 19, and was followed to the witness chair by Anthony Guarnieri, while James LaDucca and Carmine Galante failed to appear as scheduled. California's Frank DeSimone also skipped his hearing date, on May 7, 1958, an oversight that cost him a six-month sentence for contempt and $1,500 fine on February 10, 1959. Rosario Mancuso and the Valenti brothers faced the panel on June 12, 1958, but said nothing of substance.[33]

On May 13, 1959, the grand jury indicted 27 Apalachin delegates on charges of conspiracy to obstruct justice by refusing to disclose the purpose of their meeting at Joe Barbara's estate. Three were also charged with perjury, for lying to the panel when they testified. The indictment — kept under seal for another eight days— named 36 other attendees as unindicted co-conspirators. At 6 A.M. on May 21, federal agents launched a series of coordinated raids in nine states, bagging 21 of the indicted mafiosi. Those jailed included Joseph Bonanno, Russell Bufalino, Ignatius Cannone, Paul Castellano, Frank DeSimone, Natale Evola, Louis LaRasso, Carmine Lombardozzi, Antonio Magaddino, Joseph Magliocco (obstruction and perjury), Frank Majuri, Michele Miranda, John Montana, John Ormento, James Osticco, Joseph Profaci (obstruction and perjury), Anthony Riela, Angelo Sciandra, Simone Scozzari, and Pasquale Turrrigiano (obstruction and perjury). Still at large, but found over the next two weeks, were Joseph Civello, Frank Cucchiara, John DeMarco, and John Scalish. Missing when the trap closed and remaining on the lam until the case was finally resolved were Salvatore Falcone, Joseph Ida (back in Italy), James LaDucca, and Antonio Magaddino.[34]

The indicted delegates and their attorneys fought the charges tooth and nail. On September 21, 1959, a collective motion asked Judge Irving Kaufman to suppress any evidence obtained from the testimony of four defendants and three co-conspirators before New York's State Investigation Commission in August 1958. They further asked for a change of venue or a long postponement until media obsession with the case subsided. Kaufman ordered a hearing to determine whether any feds induced the commission to hold its inquiry, then rejected the defense's conspiracy theory on September 30, after questioning chief federal prosecutor Milton Wessel and three members of the state commission. As to moving or delaying the trial, Kaufman said, "Trying this case in a less cosmopolitan community would probably result in a greater concentration of publicity in the minds of prospective jurors and no city or community has been suggested where the publicity has been or would be substantially less than in New York. Trying it at a later time would not, in the circumstances of this case, substantially aid the defendants." Should any questions remain, Judge Kaufman issued another ruling on October 7, upholding the principal of collaboration between state and federal investigators.[35]

Trial of 23 accused conspirators convened before Judge Kaufman in Manhattan, on October 26, 1959. Missing from court was Joe Bonanno, whose case was severed from the rest after he suffered an eleventh-hour bout of angina. Three days were consumed with jury selection, while prosecutor Wessel predicted a 14-month trial. His opening statement, delivered on October 29, was almost plaintive. "The conspiracy has been successful," Wessel warned the jury. "I tell you that frankly and fairly at the beginning. The government will not be able to show what was going on at that meeting." The day closed with news that John DeMarco had suffered a heart attack.[36]

The defense replied to Wessel on October 30, with counsel Maurice Nessen leading for the battery of 16 lawyers. Representing Paul Castellano and Carmine Lombardozzi, Nessen struck at the root of the government's case, explaining that the federal grand jury the defendants were accused of stonewalling had in fact disbanded during 1956, months before the Apalachin meeting. How, he asked, could his clients conspire to obstruct a panel that no longer existed? Henry Lavine, representing hospitalized John DeMarco, took another tack, condemning the indictments as invalid since the feds did not contend that Apalachin's visitors convened to plot a crime. Maurice Edelbaum — defending Russell Bufalino, Frank Cucchiara and Natale Evola — played the same theme, describing his clients as legitimate businessmen accused of no specific offense.[37]

Testimony began on November 2, with Sergeant Croswell's description of the Barbara raid and its aftermath. The day's only witness, pale and drawn from a year of successive surgeries, Croswell detailed the events on November 14, 1957, from his perspective, inserting a previously unmentioned bribe attempt from John Montana. As Croswell now recalled it, "He told me that if I let him go back to get his car, he might be able to do something for me." After Croswell left the stand, Judge Kaufman announced the severance of John DeMarco's case, leaving 21 accused mafiosi on trial.[38]

Illness struck next at the jury, forcing brief postponement on November 4, while three defense attorneys argued for a mistrial. They complained specifically of newspaper coverage lauding Sergeant Croswell as an "urbane crime buster" (*New York Times,* November 3) and as a praiseworthy "Man in the News" (*New York Herald Tribune,* same day). Also cited was another *Times* piece published on the same date, whose sub-headline referred to an implied bribe offer. Milton Wessel defended the articles as "true and unbiased accounts of what goes on here." Judge Kaufman, rejecting the motion, agreed that all fell "in the realm of good reporting" and contained "nothing of a prejudicial nature." Jurors, while not sequestered, were admonished daily to shun any media reporting of the case, and Kaufman was prepared to take them at their word.[39]

Sergeant Croswell returned for cross-examination on November 5, challenged by lawyer Henry Singer, representing Joe Profaci. At issue was the timing of the Apalachin raid — and, more specifically, the 40-minute window between 12:40 and 1:20 P.M., when Milton Wessel claimed the 21 defendants had observed police outside, then plotted their conspiracy to frustrate any questioning before they fled. On cross, Singer dissected Croswell's timeline of events, eliciting admission of additional stops on his way from the state police barracks to Barbara's estate, suggesting that Croswell could not have reached Joe the Barber's property before 1:00 P.M. The implication: there was less time for his client and the others to "conspire" before they bolted to their cars or ran into the woods.[40]

The defense scored a victory of sorts on Monday, November 9, when Judge Kaufman granted a closed hearing on the Apalachin raid's legitimacy. At stake was the very case itself, if Kaufman found that Croswell and company lacked probable cause to detain and question any of Barbara's guests in the first place. That hearing was delayed for seven days, however, with trial testimony continuing in the meantime.[41]

Among the witnesses called through that critical in-between week were Trooper Vincent Vasisko, who essentially repeated Croswell's story of the raid; Treasury Agent Arthur Rustin, who described his ride-along with Croswell and Vasisko and their questioning of unindicted co-conspirator

Joseph Magaddino; State Police Lieutenant Kenneth Weidenborner, sergeants Joseph Benanati and Walder Kennedy and troopers Howard Eyck, Richard Geer and Joseph Smith, all describing their service on the Apalachin road-block; Helen Shaw, sales manager for the Utica Hotel, reporting a reservation booked by fugitive defendant James LaDucca; Helen Schroeder, manager of the Parkway Motel in Vestal, who logged a phone call to LaDucca's home on the day of the raid; John Salko, Jr., manager of the Arlington Hotel in Bing-hamton, who identified registration cards signed by unindicted co-conspir-ators Vito Genovese and John LaRocca; Palmer Correlea, a businessman who met Joe Barbara, Sr., Russell Bufalino, and James Osticco at Endicott's airport on October 29, 1957; Treasury Agent Kenneth Brown, Jr., who met and detained John Montana in the woods near Barbara's estate; and Marguerite Russell, Joe Barbara's maid, who saw her boss dining with Montana and "five or six other men" on November 14.[42]

Judge Kaufman convened the closed hearing as scheduled, on November 16, then delayed his ruling for a further two weeks, while testimony continued before the trial jury. Prosecution witnesses during the interim included NYPD Patrolman Bertram Scott, who grilled Carmine Lombardozzi nine days after the raid and logged his claim of an ill-prepared "hunting trip," sans guns or outdoor clothing; NYPD Lieutenant William Cuneen, with detectives Martin Rogoff and Tracy Smith, who quizzed other defendants pursuant to "an undis-closed New York police investigation"; FBI Agent William Vericker, who ques-tioned Natale Evola five days after the raid; NYPD Detective Thomas Shore, Jr., who questioned unindicted co-conspirator Anthony Guarnieri in January 1958; Binghamton meat vendor John Simek, who itemized Barbara's menu for the gathering; FBI Agent James Mee, with further details of the grocery order; and fellow agent Edward Leahy, who related co-conspirator Joseph Falcone's observation that women were excluded from the meeting. Prosecu-tors also read aloud prior statements taken from defendants Pasquale Turri-giano ("Everybody was well-dressed that day. Everybody had a shirt and tie on.") and Ignatius Cannone (claiming he visited Barbara's home with a plea for draught beer equipment), plus unindicted co-conspirator Emanuel Zicari's claim that he visited Apalachin "to get the fresh air."[43]

Judge Kaufman delivered his long-awaited ruling on December 2, upholding the Apalachin raid's legitimacy and rejecting pleas to strike all law enforcement testimony from the record. "The evidence presented in this case," he said, "establishes that the officers who had stopped the automobiles leaving Barbara's estate did so in the belief that a crime might have been com-mitted, that they had reasonable grounds for such a belief, and that the cir-cumstances of the situation were such that an immediate stoppage and investigation was rendered absolutely necessary." None of those detained had been falsely arrested, said Kaufman, since all were released without booking or charges after they provided exculpatory statements. Avoiding any mention of the "rough" handling Sergeant Croswell bragged about to journalists two years earlier, Kaufman found the police action "altogether proper."[44]

Perhaps inevitably, politics became a factor in the Apalachin trial. On December 3, Robert Kennedy testified as a prosecution witness, recounting Joe Profaci's July 1958 testimony before the McClellan Committee. On cross-examination, Henry Singer raised the specter of political motivation, sparking the following exchange:

> *Singer*: You are actually engaged in furthering your brother's ambitions to get the Presidential nomination, isn't that right?
> *Kennedy*: Now you want me to get into what I've been doing?
> *Judge Kaufman*: Isn't the Government going to object to that?
> *Milton Wessel*: I object, Your Honor, yes.
> *Judge Kaufman*: I sustain the objection.
> *Singer*: You appreciate don't you that by appearing here today there would be some publicity concerning your appearance which might benefit your brother in his search for the nomination?
> *Wessel*: Objection.
> *Judge Kaufman*: Sustained.
> *Kennedy*: Mr. Singer, I want to answer that. That did not enter my head. Mr. Singer, it did not enter my head at all.[45]

Wessel concluded presentation of his case on December 7, 1959, and Judge Kaufman surprised prosecutors two days later, directing a verdict of acquittal for defendant Frank Cucchiara on grounds that the government had demonstrated no involvement on his part in any hypothetical conspiracy. While Cucchiara thus had grounds to celebrate, his codefendants were less fortunate. Kaufman denied directed verdicts of acquittal for the others charged, likewise refusing to strike police testimony from the record on grounds suggested by Maurice Edelbaum, that the Apalachin raid had resulted from illegal wiretapping. The defense rested its case on December 10, after calling Paul Fitzpatrick, former chairman of the New York State Democratic Party, as a character witness on John Montana's behalf. None of the 20 accused testified in their own defense.[46]

Defense summations began on December 14, hewing to the theme of racist persecution. "All these men are Italian," Maurice Edelbaum told the jury. "Is that why they are here in this courtroom?" Colleague Remo Allio played the same refrain: "It is not yet a crime to be born in Italy. Don't forget that. I had hoped the days of [executed 1920s anarchists] Sacco and Vanzetti were gone forever." Attorney Moses Kove called the Apalachin raid "a police-state action — that's all it was. The police state of Nazi Germany and the blood purges of Soviet Russia started with troopers knocking at doors and asking citizens, 'What are you doing here?'" Maurice Nessen accused the prosecution of fabricating a conspiracy and thereby "creating a Frankenstein that stretches across the land." Henry Singer accused Sergeant Croswell of "conning" the federal grand jury, while contending that the prosecution had illegally suppressed exculpatory evidence.[47]

Milton Wessel had the last word, firing back on December 16 that "these defendants have tried to put Sergeant Croswell on trial. Sergeant Croswell is a great cop, and we have to be proud of him." As for alleged bigotry, he declared, "Whether these men were Italians, Jews or Greeks has nothing to do with the evidence." The Apalachin gathering, Wessel insisted, was "an organized nonsocial meeting" with "something unlawful about it." He simply could not explain *what.* The defendants, he charged, had been guilty of "lying, evasion, perjury and contempt" before various investigative bodies spanning the past two years.[48]

Judge Kaufman charged the jury on December 17, reminding members of the panel that they must ignore the dearth of defense testimony. The defendants "are not required to establish their innocence," Kaufman said, before turning to allegations of racism. "I am pained that racial issues were raised," he declared, cautioning jurors to deliberate "without sympathy or prejudice. Do not render a verdict because of race or creed."[49]

The panel debated evidence until 11 P.M. on the 17th, then returned at 9:30 the next morning to resume deliberation. At 5:10 P.M. on December 18, they returned a unanimous verdict: guilty as charged for all 20 remaining defendants. According to *The New York Times,* Natale Evola and John Montana faced the panel teary-eyed, while others slumped, glowered, or "chewed gum furiously." Judge Kaufman scheduled sentencing for January 13, then thanked the jury for delivering "a most intelligent verdict," for which "the community and the nation owe you a deep debt of gratitude for your courage and your fortitude and the patience and the perseverance and the time which you have taken in reaching your verdict." Kaufman found their efforts "heartwarming," particularly inasmuch as "decent, law-abiding citizens of this country expect that the laws of our country will be observed, and in this connection they expect that when authority and grand juries conduct investigations that they will not be defied nor sneered at by any people who consider themselves above the law."[50]

At sentencing on January 13, 1960, Kaufman gave free rein to his contempt for the defendants. After comparing their court-ordered probation reports to a "tale of horrors," he sentenced the 20 as follows:

• Russell Bufalino—"A man devoid of conscience; one who poses as a legitimate businessman; everything in the record indicates that society would be better off if he is segregated"; five years in prison and a $10,000 fine.

• Paul Castellano—"Marked with anti-social patterns; willingly spent one year in jail in order not to answer any questions, even though given immunity"; five years.

• Joseph Civello—"A high-ranking criminal who cloaked himself with the façade of legitimate business"; five years.

• Natale Evola—"A most important member of the underworld"; five years, consecutive with his 1958 federal narcotics sentence.

• Carmine Lombardozzi—"An important member of loan-shark and gambling rackets in Brooklyn and an associate of premier criminals for most of his life"; five years and $10,000.

• Joseph Magliocco—"A member of the criminal hierarchy and elite; he was arrested in Chicago [sic; actually Cleveland] at a similar meeting thirty years ago [sic; 1928]"; five years and $10,000.

• Frank Majuri—"A bootlegger and gambler who would do anything for a fast dollar"; five years.

• Michele Miranda—"Elected to serve sixteen months in civil jail rather than betray his loyalty to the criminal elements; a close friend of the top dogs of the underworld"; five years and $10,000.

• John Ormento—"Has several narcotics convictions; a veteran criminal with nothing but contempt for constituted authority"; five years and $10,000.

• James Osticco—"A strong-arm man and associate of high-ranking members of the underworld"; five years and $10,000.

• Joseph Profaci—"Has tried to present himself as a much-maligned and humble man, when he is in fact a notorious member of the underworld; the perfect example of the trinity of crime, business and politics that threatens the economy of the country"; five years and $10,000.

• John Scalish—"Feels that everybody has a price, including public officials; a high liver, contemptuous of society"; five years and $10,000.

• Angelo Sciandra—"An important man in the underworld since 1946; has attempted to cloak himself in legitimate business; tried to invade the union field by using force and violence"; five years and $10,000.

• Simone Scozzari—"Has made a mockery of the law since he arrived in this country as a stowaway in 1923"; five yeas and $10,000.

• Pasquale Turrigiano—"Had two prior convictions for illegally manufacturing alcohol; a man with little respect for law-abiding citizens": five years.

• Frank DeSimone—"Hostile and arrogant toward law enforcement and his bar associates; lived with individuals of ill repute and after Apalachin resided in the home of such an individual"; four years.

• Louis LaRasso—"A person devoid of emotion, whose first loyalty was to the underworld"; four years.

• John Montana —"Apparently an important factor in the political life of [Buffalo]; was apparently leading a double life, which was exposed at Apalachin; respected on the one hand, some law enforcement agencies suspected him of being a power in the underworld; his presence at Apalachin confirmed that suspicion"; four years.

• Anthony Riela —"Shrewd, cunning and conniving"; four years.

• Ignatius Cannone —"A rather intelligent fellow who played a minor role in the underworld; loyal to the criminal element and could be trusted by the underworld"; three years.[51]

While Milton Wessel resigned his post at the Justice Department to enter private practice with a prestigious Manhattan law firm and Attorney General William Rogers hailed the Apalachin jury's "landmark" verdict, the defendants regrouped to file their collective appeal.[52] Given the climate of the times, they seemed unlikely to succeed. A final option, if the courts rejected then, still lay in executive clemency.

But first, they would require a friendly president.

· 11 ·

Electing Giovanni

At first glance, John Fitzgerald Kennedy was an unlikely candidate for Mafia support in any White House race. He was best-known to most Americans outside his native Massachusetts as a member of the Mob-hunting McClellan Committee, which his often-caustic brother Robert served as chief counsel. Between them, they had angered many ranking members of the underworld, including Chicago's Sam Giancana (whom Robert Kennedy chastised for giggling like a "little girl") and Teamsters union leader Jimmy Hoffa (whose hatred of the Kennedys was legendary). Why would any self-respecting mafioso lift a finger to help JFK attain the Oval Office?

The answer to that question lies with his father, Joseph Kennedy.

Papa Joe

Boston born in 1888, Joseph Patrick Kennedy, Sr., was the son of an Irish ward boss and saloon owner. He attended Harvard University, and in 1914 married the eldest daughter of Boston Mayor John "Honey Fitz" Fitzgerald, thereby merging two of the city's most prominent Irish-American clans. Their union produced nine children, but never kept Joseph from the beds of other women, including celebrity lovers from Hollywood.[1]

Prohibition's advent was a golden opportunity for Joseph Kennedy, as for the Mob. He made a fortune smuggling liquor into the United States, and he was known to his former Harvard classmates as "our chief bootlegger." One customer recalled, "He arranged for his agents to have the stuff sent in right on the beach at Plymouth. It came ashore the way the Pilgrims did." His supporters included Mayor Fitzgerald, who claimed "the distinction of appointing more saloonkeepers and bartenders to public office than any previous mayor." Aside from Harvard students and alumni, Kennedy's customers included William Randolph Hearst and Hearst's mistress Marion Davies, who welcomed Joseph to their California castle at San Simeon. Buying high-quality

Scotch at $45 per case, diluting and rebottling it, then selling it stateside for $85 per case, Kennedy banked an illicit fortune. In 1925 *Fortune* magazine pegged his net worth at $2 million — the equivalent of $25 million today.[2]

And in the process, he made many shady friends. Author T.J. English stands alone in naming Kennedy as a full-fledged partner in the 1920s "Seven Group" of leading East Coast rum-runners, but Kennedy certainly knew most or all of the combination's members— and many more besides. His verified partners in crime included Frank Costello, Owney Madden, and Big Bill Dwyer in New York; Danny Walsh in Providence, Rhode Island; Moe Dalitz in Cleveland; and Al Capone in Chicago. Biographer Ted Schwartz contends that Kennedy thrived at a rarified level of bootlegging "without violence to outsiders," but some of the tales from those days are hair-raising. One claims that Meyer Lansky's gang hijacked a Kennedy shipment in 1927, killing 11 of Papa Joe's men in the process, while another says that Kennedy recruited Chicago's "Diamond Joe" Esposito to resolve "a near fatal scrape" with Detroit's Purple Gang. Yet another alleges that Kennedy's goons hijacked shipments of booze in Chicago, bombing one off the Capone gang's trucks.[3]

Whatever the details of his Prohibition-era activities, Kennedy was ideally placed to cash in on repeal in 1933. Going legit as the owner of Somerset Importers, managed by bootlegging partner Ted O'Leary, Kennedy acquired a virtual monopoly on U.S. sales of Gordon's gin and two of the big five Scotch whiskey brands, Dewar's and Haig & Haig. Soon, Somerset was bringing Kennedy an average yearly profit of $250,000 ($3.17 million today). Some of that money went to Hollywood, earning Kennedy another $5 million ($64.1 million today); more supported the presidential aspirations of Franklin Roosevelt, purchasing Kennedy's appointment as first chairman of the Securities and Exchange Commission in 1934 (ironically, it was assigned to nab shady stock manipulators), chairmanship of the fledgling Maritime Commission in 1936, and finally appointment as U.S. ambassador to the United Kingdom in 1938. In London, Kennedy displayed embarrassing pro–Nazi sympathies that led to his forced resignation in 1940.[4]

With his own presidential ambitions scuttled, Kennedy began grooming his eldest son for the White House. That dream, in turn, was cut short with Joseph Jr.'s death in August 1944, when an experimental bomb exploded prematurely aboard his B-17 Flying Fortress en route to occupied France. Second son John proved more durable, emerging as a decorated naval hero for his exploits in the Solomon Islands. Thus celebrated, JFK won election to the House of Representatives in 1946, and to the U.S. Senate in 1952. There, his brother Bobby served as assistant counsel for longtime family friend Joseph McCarthy's Red-hunting Permanent Subcommittee on Investigations, moving on after McCarthy's formal censure (which JFK failed to support) to join his brother on the McClellan Committee, grilling labor racketeers and Apalachin delegates.[5]

All concerned missed the Kefauver hearings, wherein Papa Joe was mentioned only once, and briefly, in October 1950, by Chicago mobster Joe Fusco. Formerly in charge of the Outfit's whiskey business, Fusco recalled the 1944 appearance of Miami mobster Thomas Cassara in the Windy City, traveling "as a missionary man" for Somerset Importers. Cassara's murder in Chicago, on June 30, 1946, remains unsolved today. Still, much was overlooked: Kennedy's partnership in the Mob's race track at Hialeah, Florida; his 1945 purchase of Chicago's Merchandise Mart, where syndicate gambling and prostitution flourished; and his frequent visits to Nevada, where he was a favored guest in Las Vegas and at Lake Tahoe's Cal-Neva Lodge. Joe's friendship with J. Edgar Hoover probably helped him to cover his tracks, but apprehensions lingered. Multiple acquaintances recall the bitter quarrel between father and son when Bobby Kennedy announced his plan to join the McClellan Committee. For perhaps the first time in his life, Bobby defied his father, spurning Joseph's demands that he drop the comimttee post for fear of "stirring up a hornet's nest" that would hobble brother John's presidential ambitions. A ferocious agrument ensued — "the worst we ever witnessed," according to sister Jean Kennedy Smith — but Bobby stood his ground and forged ahead. JFK prep-school classmate and campaign activist Lem Billings recalled that "the old man saw this as dangerous, not the sort of thing or the sort of people to mess around with. He felt Bobby was being awfully naïve." Another observer agreed that Papa Joe deemed Bobby "frightfully naïve about the physical and political risks."[6]

And in the end, he was correct.

"Winning Is What Counts"

That slogan was a favorite of Papa Joe's, and it epitomized his handling of son John's presidential campaign.[7] From start to finish, Kennedy Senior sought aid from the Mob and its allies in politics, laying the groundwork for a victory at any cost.

Joe Kennedy directed and dominated every step of his second son's political career. A year before his first congressional campaign, JFK told best friend Paul "Red" Fay, "I can feel Pappy's eyes on the back of my neck. Dad is ready right now and can't understand why Johnny boy isn't 'all engines ahead full.'" When the *Boston Post* failed to support John's run for the Senate in 1952, Papa Joe helped out by "loaning" the publisher $500,000. As JFK later confided to associates, "We had to buy that fucking paper, or I'd have been licked." Four years later, after John failed to secure the Democratic Party's vice-presidential nomination, Joseph persuaded Senate majority leader Lyndon Johnson to put JFK on the Foreign Relations Committee. As LBJ later recalled, "I kept picturing old Joe Kennedy sitting there with all that power and wealth feeling indebted to me for the rest of his life, and I sure liked that feeling." Four years later, Johnson got the nod as JFK's running mate, succeeding him as president in 1963.[8]

Joe Kennedy began the final groundwork for John's presidential race in 1958, prompting former first lady Eleanor Roosevelt to note that he "has been spending oodles of money all over the country and probably has a representative in every state by now." Bobby Kennedy left his post with the McClellan Committee to serve as John's campaign manager. Meanwhile, as author Richard Whalen observed, "Jack's campaign had two separate and distinct sides. On display before the voters was the candidate, surrounded by clean-cut, youthful volunteer workers, the total effect being one of wholesome amateurism. At work on the hidden side of the campaign were the professional politicians whom Joe had quietly recruited. In his hotel suite and other private meeting places, they sat with their hats on and cigars aglow, a hard-eyed, cynical band, brainstorming strategy."[9]

Nor were they simply politicians.

From the outset, people "in the know" assumed the Mob would throw its weight behind Republican contender Richard Nixon in the 1960 presidential race. Bankrolled by gangsters and their allies since his first congressional campaign in 1946, pledged to depose Fidel Castro and restore Mob rule in Cuba, as vice president, Nixon also commiserated with Teamster boss Jimmy Hoffa over his "persecution" by McClellan and the Kennedys. Longstanding corruption aside, Nixon's greatest selling point to mobsters in the wake of the McClellan hearings was the simple fact that he was not a Kennedy. Hoffa, Carlos Marcello, and other underworld denizens joined eccentric billionaire Howard Hughes to keep Nixon's campaign supplied with covert infusions of cash — $500,000 ($3.7 million today) from Marcello alone, in one suitcase.[10]

Joe Kennedy, for his part, tried to turn the tide. First, he sought to placate angry Teamsters, telling union international Vice President Harold Gibbons, "I don't think there's much of a war going on between the Kennedys and Hoffa. I hardly hear the name Hoffa in our house any more." Failing on that front, Joe persuaded JFK to phone Hoffa personally, proposing a truce, but a witness to that call on Hoffa's end — Teamster thug Joe Franco of Detroit — later described Hoffa's response as a blistering attack on brother Bobby. Next, Papa Joe approached Meyer Lansky partner Vincent "Jimmy Blue Eyes" Alo in his quest for syndicate support, but Alo rebuffed him with the observation that "I wasn't in the habit of interfering with elections."[11]

Never one to take no for an answer, Papa Joe shifted his focus to Chicago, where the Outfit had forged enduring ties to the city's political bosses. Kennedy had helped install Richard J. Daley as the Windy City's mayor in 1955, and now he wanted a return on his original investment. That included Daley's pledge to win support for JFK from Illinois delegates to the 1960 Democratic Convention, and to facilitate negotiations with current Outfit boss Sam Giancana. As Vincent Alo recalled, "Even that early they knew that Chicago would make all the difference. I don't know how they knew it. This was before computers." However Joe Kennedy made his calculations, he possessed unbounded confidence. In December 1959 he told son John, "I'm willing to bet one million dollars today with the gamblers in Las Vegas that you'll win the nomination and election."[12]

Days later, in January 1960, JFK himself was in Vegas, partying with mobbed-up entertainer Frank Sinatra and his "rat pack" at the Sands casino, during the shooting of their film *Ocean's 11*. As entourage member Sammy Davis, Jr., later wrote, "We got caught up completely in the Kennedy optimism and it was an exciting time for all of us, especially Frank. It was very much Sinatra's baby, and he played it to the hilt." Old Blue Eyes recorded a variation of his 1959 "High Hopes" single as a JFK campaign anthem, pulled political strings for the Kennedy camp in his native New Jersey, and arranged Papa Joe's first known meeting with Sam Giancana. While author Stephen Fox says that Sinatra forged the Kennedy-Giancana link "on his own," Vincent Alo said that the Kennedys "went to Sinatra" specifically, after Alo and Lansky declined to furnish the desired introduction. A published claim by author

Vincent "Jimmy Blue Eyes" Alo rejected campaign overtures from Joseph Kennedy (National Archives).

T.J. English that the Kennedys did not approach Sinatra until April 1960 clearly is erroneous.[13]

Whoever hatched the plot, it would have fateful consequences.

February 1, 1960, found JFK addressing Nevada's state legislature in Carson City. This was followed by a lavish reception that left Governor Grant Sawyer "enchanted" by Kennedy, sparking "a long and lasting friendship." A week later, back at the Sands for another Sinatra soirée, while waiting for "four wild girls to entertain him," John Kennedy met 26-year-old Judith Campbell, who within a month became one of his several secret lovers. Their affair

Frank Sinatra, shown with actress Ava Gardner, campaigned for JFK and provided introductions to the Chicago Outfit (Library of Congress).

spanned two years, during which time Campbell also shared her bed Sam Giancana. At the same Vegas party, Kennedy brother-in-law Peter Lawford drew Sammy Davis, Jr., aside and showed him a satchel containing $1 million in cash, confiding, "It's a gift from the hotel owners for Jack's campaign." While it remains unclear if JFK ever met Giancana personally, Papa Joe held secret meetings with Chicago's reigning godfather throughout 1960 — in California, at Tahoe's Cal-Neva Lodge, at Giancana's home in West Palm Beach, Florida, and elsewhere.[14]

The first test of Joe Kennedy's new Mob alliance came in May 1960, with West Virginia's primary election. JFK faced Minnesota rival Hubert Humphrey in the Mountain State, where Teamsters and Ku Klux Klansmen alike fanned the flames of anti-Catholic prejudice to defeat Boston's favorite son. Pro-Kennedy mobsters countered that tide with aid from Frank Sinatra crony Paul "Skinny" D'Amato, front man for the syndicate's 500 Club in Atlantic City. D'Amato agreed to help if the Kennedys permitted mafioso Joe Adonis to return from Italy, a favor that Papa Joe swiftly approved. D'Amato later admitted doling out $50,000 in bribes across West Virginia, but that estimate was almost certainly conservative. Whatever the amount, it prompted

Humphrey to complain that "I don't think elections should be bought. I can't afford to run through this state with a little black bag and a checkbook." Meanwhile, statewide, thugs put the arm on bars with Mob-owned jukeboxes, requiring them to stock and play Sinatra's "High Hopes" campaign song. The net result: a win for JFK.[15]

When the Democratic National Convention opened in Los Angeles on July 11, 1960, Kennedy had more than half the votes required to ensure nomination. He had won nine primaries—not seven, as often reported—and while New Jersey's delegates remained "unpledged at large," the Mob had not been idle in the Garden State. Challenged in L.A. by Lyndon Johnson, whom he privately despised—"mean, bitter, vicious, an animal in many ways"— JFK took his father's advice by naming LBJ to be his running mate. While liberal supporters were dismayed, Papa Joe advised, "Don't worry, Jack. In two weeks they'll be saying it's the smartest thing you ever did." Kennedy secured first-ballot nomination, with Mayor Daley delivering 59½ of Illinois's 69 votes. Joe Kennedy and Frank Sinatra heard the news together, with Marion Davies and others in her Hollywood mansion. Observers recall that Sinatra "went wild, jumping up and down," shouting, "We're on our way to the White House!"[16]

And so they were, but not without continuing chicanery. Days before the November election, brother Edward "Ted" Kennedy bet $25,000 on John to win, at Sam Giancana's Cal-Neva Lodge. November 4 found JFK scheduled to address a crowd at the Chicago Stadium, with Mayor Daley anxious to secure media coverage. "Get me a network," he ordered his press secretary. The gofer ran to Papa Joe at the Merchandise Mart and left with a check for $125,000. Kennedy's speech aired nationwide.[17]

After the fact, John Kennedy tried to conceal his father's role in the campaign, telling one journalist, "He's really had less to do with my campaign than any of the other members of my family." That story would not fly, though. Back on September 4, 1960, asked if he was keeping track of the campaign, JFK had told the *Boston Herald*, "I read the papers." And in fact, he spent most of the autumn in virtual seclusion, at the family compound in Hyannis Port.[18]

Too Close to Call

Sixty-nine million Americans voted for their next president on November 8, 1960. From daybreak to dusk, the balloting was marked by glaring fraud in various locations, amply documented by reporters and observers on both sides.

In sparsely-populated New Mexico, county sheriffs and local *patrons* doled out cash to Hispanic voters within sight of the polls, sometimes accompanying them into the voting booths for what author Edmund Kallina, Jr., dubbed "informal and highly irregular voting procedures." Far-off Hawaii produced complaints of burly thugs advising Asian-Americans how to vote, thus avoiding any "unpleasantness for you and your family." Kennedy votes from the Westside ghetto of Las Vegas outnumbered registered voters. Similar reports emerged from Missouri, New Jersey, Pennsylvania, and South Carolina.[19]

In Texas, home of JFK running mate Lyndon Johnson, poll-watchers reported that "the stuffing of ballot boxes reached a new high"— no mean achievement in a state where pundits quipped that voters never lost their right to cast a ballot, even when they died. At least 100,000 Nixon ballots were disqualified on suspect grounds, while tens of thousands more were simply "lost." In Fanin County, 4,895 registered voters cast 6,138 ballots, 75 percent of them for JFK. Angelina County, with 86 verified voters, produced 147 ballots for Kennedy and 24 for Nixon. Despite such anomalies, the state's all-Democratic election board rejected calls for a recount and certified Kennedy as the winner.[20]

Still, Chicago was the crucial battleground. Mob-dominated wards cast 80 percent of their ballots for Kennedy, by fair means or foul. One election judge fled her polling place in tears, rushing to church where she confessed her "mortal sin" in confidence. After the fact, *New York Herald Tribune* reporter Earl Mazo investigated Chicago's election. In one local cemetery, he found names of long-dead voters who had risen from the grave to cast their Democratic ballots. One house, allegedly the home of 56 Kennedy voters, had been razed long before the election. The Republican National Committee filed a lawsuit challenging Chicago's tallies, but the case was dismissed by Circuit Court Judge Thomas Kluczynski, a Democrat close to Mayor Daley. In a futile rejoinder, the *Chicago Tribune* editorialized that "the election of November 8 was characterized by such gross and palpable fraud as to justify the conclusion that [Nixon] was deprived of victory." And barely so, at that. Even with Giancana's aid, Kennedy carried only nine of 102 Illinois counties, winning the state by .2 percent of votes cast. Nevada's margin was 1.3 percent, Michigan's 1 percent, Missouri's .6 percent, and so on. Nationwide, the Democratic edge of 113,000 votes over Nixon amounted to a mere one-fifth of one percent for all the ballots cast.[21]

But still, it was enough.

Some in the Mob's orbit were bitter; others, jubilant. Sam Giancana, in his pillow talk with Judith Campbell, said, "Listen honey, if it wasn't for me your boyfriend wouldn't even be in the White House." Skinny D'Amato had another take, crediting Frank Sinatra. "Frank won Kennedy the election," he declared. "All the guys knew it."[22]

And in the time-honored tradition of politics, those who had helped expected rewards.

Absolved

On November 28, 1960 — eight days after Kentucky Senator Thruston Morton, chairman of the Republican National Committee, grudgingly conceded JFK's victory — the United States Court of Appeals for the Second Circuit announced its ruling on the Apalachin case. The appeal from Russell Bufalino and his 19 codefendants challenged the original conspiracy indictment and its list of 29 "overt acts" used to prove a plot extending from November 1957 to the date of the indictment's issuance in May of 1959. Chief Judge Edward Lumbard, an ardent civil libertarian, chaired the panel that also included circuit judges Charles Clark and Henry Friendly.[23]

Judge Lumbard began by noting a glaring hole in the government's case: "The indictment did not allege what the November 14, 1957, gathering at Apalachin was about, and the government stated at the beginning of the trial that it could present no evidence of its purpose. There is nothing in the record of the trial to show that any violation of federal or state law took place or was planned at the gathering, although federal grand juries in the Southern and Western Districts of New York on 20 occasions over the following year and one-half, and a variety of other federal and state officials on numerous other occasions, questioned many of these present about the Apalachin gathering and the surrounding circumstances."[24]

Despite that paucity of knowledge, Lumbard noted,

> The government contends that the November 14 gathering was planned in advance; that when those present became aware that law-enforcement officers had discovered the assemblage they thought there might be an investigation and immediately agreed to give false, fictitious and evasive accounts of the circumstances of the gathering to official inquiries including formal proceedings calling for sworn testimony; and that when some were summoned before federal grand juries inquiring into the nature of the gathering, they testified falsely pursuant to the agreement. The government's claim was that "the participants gave false and evasive accounts as to the planning and purpose of the meeting and the circumstances and reasons for their presence, all of which were basically similar in that they were calculated to explain away the meeting as a mere coincidental gathering."[25]

Furthermore

> The government claimed that the conspiracy was formed between 12:40 P.M. on November 14, when Barbara's wife saw the officers' unmarked car in the driveway, and 1:20 P.M. when a mass exodus from Barbara's home began. The court

charged the jury that in order to find that any defendant was a member of the conspiracy it would have to conclude that he "willingly entered" the conspiracy sometime before midnight on November 14, at which time the officers completed their questioning of the alleged conspirators at the state police barracks at Vestal. The government's proof of the agreement consisted entirely of testimony by state and federal officers regarding unsworn statements made by the conspirators on November 14 and on numerous occasions thereafter and of excerpts from official records of sworn statements made after November 14.... The government's theory is that the similarity of the statements, insofar as "they all deny planning and seek to concoct a picture of accidental and coincidental presence at Barbara's," and insofar as most of them explain the visits as motivated by concern for Barbara's illness, can be accounted for only if there was an agreement on November 14, 1957.[26]

Lumbard and the other judges rejected that contention, finding that:

The fact that none of those present admitted that he was asked to attend a meeting for other than social purposes and that at least some of those present must have lied, does not warrant a jury's conclusion that any or all lies were told pursuant to an agreement made on November 14. There is nothing in the record or in common experience to suggest that it is not just as likely that each one present decided for himself that it would be wiser not to discuss all that he knew. Indeed, the pervasive innuendo throughout this case that this was a gathering of bad people for an evil purpose would seem to us to rebut any possible argument that only as a result of group action would any individual lie. Even an otherwise law abiding citizen who is stopped and interrogated by police, and who is given no reason for his detention and questioning, may feel it his right to give as little information as possible and even perhaps to respond evasively if he believes he might thereby be earlier rid of police inquiry. That others may at times go to the brink of truth, or beyond, is likely, particularly when, as may have been true in the present case, they know that the existing law does not require them to give a truthful account to police officers.[27]

With that in mind, Lumbard declared, "We therefore conclude that there was insufficient evidence for the jury to find the defendants had, on November 14, entered into an agreement to commit perjury. We conclude also that there was not sufficient evidence for the jury to find that the defendants knew or should have known on November 14 that they would be called to testify under oath concerning the Apalachin gathering."[28]

As Lumbard explained,

The indictment charged a conspiracy to commit perjury and obstruct justice by giving false and evasive testimony. Evidence of the same intent or knowledge would be required to convict conspirators as to convict those charged with the substantive offense.... The essence of perjury is that the untruthful testimony be given under oath.... Falsehoods given before non-judicial inquiries are not encompassed within the federal obstruction of justice statute. Thus, even had the government proved that an agreement had been entered into, it would further have had to prove that the conspirators intended to lie under oath or that they envisaged proceedings where they would be called upon to testify under oath. This the government failed to do. There was no direct evidence that those present at Barbara's foresaw or should have foreseen a formal investigation of the meeting. Nor was there any circumstantial proof to support such a finding since there was no evidence that the meeting was called for an illegal purpose. Without evidence that the meeting was unlawful, the presence of state troopers in Barbara's driveway, and the fact that the troopers then parked their car off the road, probably to observe or stop cars as they left, would not suggest to those present that a more formal investigation should be feared. Nor does the mass exodus from the Barbara place in response to the police curiosity show more than that those leaving did not care to subject themselves to further police scrutiny.[29]

Judge Clark, in his concurring opinion, went even further than Lumbard. He wrote:

I agree with the decision and opinion herein, but believe it desirable to point out what seems to me an even more basic failure of proof than the two so fully delineated by Chief Judge Lumbard. Perhaps the most curious feature of this strange case is the fact that after all these years there is not a shred of legal evidence that the Apalachin gathering was illegal or even improper in either purpose or fact. For 13 years prior to the meeting as a modern Inspector Javert, State Trooper Croswell pursued Barbara, Sr., in all ways possible (including tapping of his telephone) and got no evidence of illegality, although he did get wind of the meeting if not of its purpose. After it occurred on November 14, 1957, there were no less than 133 examinations of those present (as the government reports in its brief) by various state and federal officials, including 27 instances before federal grand juries and 29 by the FBI. The results were fruitless, as is highlighted by the government's frank admission at the outset of the trial that it would not be able to show what was going on at the meeting. The only suggestion, outside of an innuendo not here provable that the defendants were evil, is the bizarre nature of the gathering itself. But that gets us nowhere; common experience does not suggest that plotting to commit crime is done in convention assembled, or even the converse, also suggested here, namely, plotting to desist from crime. It must be taken, therefore, that for aught we can know the gathering was innocent.

On this basis the defendants would appear to be under no duty to explain their actions, and this the prosecution freely admits, saying in its brief that "the government has never taken the position that the defendants were guilty of wrongdoing by merely failing to reveal what occurred at the Apalachin meeting." This being admitted it is difficult to see how a defendant commits a wrong if he endeavors to preserve his privacy and individual freedom by misleading answers not perjurious in character. True, there might arise circumstances where a defendant's concealment would raise questions of propriety, as where he was concealing an actual crime. But under the circumstances here present, where no crime is indicated, some proof of illegality in the actions concealed would seem an essential to any conviction on either a substantive or a conspiracy count. For otherwise it would seem that a citizen's privacy is subject to invasion at any time on the mere suspicion of any police officer, federal, state, or local, and the presumption of innocence has no potency at the police level.

From its inception this case was given unusual and disturbing publicity in newspapers, journals, and magazines; and this unfortunate feature has persisted up to this date, with even the prosecutors indulging in highly colored accounts while the case has been pending on appeal. Much of this has been in terms of a crisis in law administration seemingly demonstrated by an unexplained gathering of arch criminals and of a general satisfaction that somehow they have now met their just desserts of long imprisonment. This is vastly unfortunate; not only does it go beyond the judicial record necessary for its support, but it suggests that the administration of the criminal law is in such dire straits that crash methods have become a necessity. But it seems we should have known better, and a prosecution framed on such a doubtful basis should never have been initiated or allowed to proceed so far. For in America we still respect the dignity of the individual, and even an unsavory character is not to be imprisoned except on definite proof of specific crime. And nothing in present criminal law administration suggests or justifies sharp relaxation of traditional standards.

Chief Judge LUMBARD and Judge FRIENDLY authorize me to state that they agree with the writer that the publication by former special prosecutors of accounts and comments regarding this case and the appellants, while this appeal was pending, was improper.[30]

Accordingly, the convictions of all 20 defendants were reversed and remanded to the trial court with an order to dismiss all charges.[31] The Apalachin delegates had won their freedom without aid from John Kennedy — who would soon present them with a rude surprise.

Double-Crossed

While Giancana and Sinatra basked in the reflected glory of the president-elect, Chicago Outfit elder statesman Murray Humphreys waited for the other shoe to drop. Throughout the long campaign he had reviled Papa Joe as a "four-flusher," telling anyone who'd listen that he would not trust the elder Kennedy "as far as I could throw a piano." The second shoe fell 10 days after the election, with the announcement that JFK was "giving serious consideration" to appointing brother Bobby as attorney general of the United States. The Senate Judiciary Committee approved that appointment without objection one week before the president's inauguration.[32]

The choice of Robert Kennedy was neither John's nor Bobby's; it came down to Papa Joe. The president-elect opposed it, but he lacked the courage to defy his father. Instead, JFK asked advisor Clark Clifford and Senator George Smathers of Georgia, a longtime family friend, to change Joe's mind.

The patriarch thanked both men for sharing their views, then told them flatly, "Bobby is going to be attorney general." Joe's motive for the controversial demand? At one point, he told John, describing Bobby, "He's a lawyer, he's savvy, he knows all the political ins and outs and he can protect you." Later, growing more emotional as JFK persisted in his frail resistance, Joseph raged, "By God, he deserves to be attorney general, and by God, that's what he's going to be! Do you understand that?" Conditioned by a life of browbeating, the president-to-be responded meekly, "Yes, sir."[33]

Whatever Joseph's reasons, some historians believe he sealed the fate of both sons at a single stroke.

The double-cross, once under way, cut wide and deep. Papa Joe's first broken campaign promise involved Joe Adonis. Despite his assurance to Skinny DiAmato that repatriation of Adonis was "no problem," it never happened. The former boss of Brooklyn died in Italy, still pining for America, on November 26, 1971. Meanwhile, Attorney General Kennedy repaid the architect of his brother's West Virginia primary landslide by investigating Skinny D'Amato on tax-evasion charges. D'Amato avoided prison, but the IRS closed his 500 Club in Atlantic City.[34]

Next on the Kennedy hit list was Nixon supporter Carlos Marcello, in New Orleans. Kidnapped from a Crescent City street corner on April 4, 1961, Marcello was flown to Guatemala, falsely listed by Marcello as the nation of his birth. (He had, in fact, been born in Tunisia to Sicilian immigrants in transit.) Guatemalan authorities wanted no part of him, either. They jailed Marcello for traveling on a false passport, then deported him to a jungle village in El Salvador, where Salvadoran soldiers grilled him for five days, then left him on a mountaintop near the Honduran border. Still dressed in the suit he had worn from New Orleans, Marcello walked 17

Murray Humphreys warned fellow mobsters that he would not trust Joe Kennedy "as far as I could throw a piano" (National Archives).

miles to another village, breaking two ribs in a fall while en route, then made his tortuous way to the coast. Pilot David Ferrie, a sometime Mafia wingman and associate of New Orleans political activist Lee Harvey Oswald, flew Marcello back to Louisiana — where feds met him with an $835,396 tax lien and charges of entering the United States illegally.[35]

New Orleans mafioso Carlos Marcello was deported by the Kennedys in 1961 but returned to seek vengeance (**National Archives**).

Not even sycophantic Frank Sinatra could escape the heat. Cautioned by brother Bobby and J. Edgar Hoover in early 1962, JFK brusquely severed all ties with the crooner — and with Judith Campbell, who since 1960 had been spending equal time in bed with Kennedy and Momo Giancana. The rejection stunned Sinatra, who had recently added a presidential wing and helipad to his home at Palm Springs, California. The new construction stood idle, and JFK spent his next Palm Springs vacation with Sinatra rival Bing Crosby (himself a longtime friend of Cleveland mobster Moe Dalitz). The Kennedy split also soured relations between Sinatra and Giancana, but the pair reconciled in time to reap more profits from Nevada gaming.[36]

Tackling the Mob was not a one-man operation. After procuring Harry Anslinger's files on the Mafia, Robert Kennedy confronted J. Edgar Hoover at FBI headquarters, demanding that the bureau join his fight against organized crime. Although embittered and resistant to the end, Hoover dared not defy the White House openly. Ordered by Bobby to "go into it like they went into the Communist Party," Hoover did precisely that, installing hundreds of illegal bugs and wiretaps nationwide. At the same time, he launched a slow war of nerves against Camelot's leaders, needling the president and his attorney general with classified reports on Judith Campbell, Giancana, and the CIA's collusion with mafiosi in the ongoing campaign to depose Fidel Castro.[37]

That effort was another aspect of the Kennedy double-cross that remains nearly inexplicable today. Why would mobsters who supported JFK's election, then suffered the wrath of his brother at Justice, agree to join in the illegal federal war against Cuba? Clearly, some hoped Kennedy would succeed where Eisenhower and Nixon had failed, returning Fulgencio Batista or someone like him to power in Havana, whereupon the Mob's casinos would reopen and their looting of the island nation would resume. The most ambitious of those dreams was dashed two weeks after Carlos Marcello's abduction, with the abortive Bay of Pigs invasion. Plots against Castro continued thereafter, but none would bear fruit. By 1962 furious right-wing Cuban exiles had joined mafiosi, CIA leaders, and southern segregationists in the growing company of Kennedy-haters.[38]

For all the opposition and explicit criticism of his tactics, though, the new attorney general got results. Eisenhower's Justice Department had indicted only 49 mobsters in 1960, convicting 45. Bobby Kennedy indicted 121 in 1961 (with 73 convicted), 350 in 1962 (138 convicted), and 615 in 1963 (288 convicted). At the same time, IRS man-hours spent on organized crime matters increased from 8,836 in 1961 to 96,182 in 1963. Whether the bulk of those cases were solid, or amounted to shady harassment as some civil libertarians contended, the Mob was running for cover.[39]

But its leaders would not suffer in silence.

Dallas and Beyond

Reactions from the Mafia against JFK's regime in Washington were logged even before the president's inauguration, growing ever more insidious as Bobby's drive against the Mob continued. Ranging from vague complaints of harassment to death threats, all were duly logged — and then ignored by leaders of the FBI, who failed to notify the Secret Service.

Sam Giancana had more reason to be angry than most mobsters, after all that he had done for Kennedy. As G-men dogged his steps, Giancana told associates, "I never thought it would get this fucking rough. When they put the brother in there, we were going to see some fireworks, but I never knew it was going to be like this. This is murder." In part, he blamed Sinatra, fuming, "Eatin' out of the palm of his hand, that's what Frank told me. Jack's eatin' out of his hand. Bullshit, that's what it is. One minute he says he's talked to Robert and the next minute he says he hasn't talked to him. So he never did talk to him. It's a lot of shit. Why lie to me? I haven't got that coming." Strangest of all, Giancana continued working with the Kennedys to murder Castro, even while complaining to his fellow mafiosi, "Here I am, helping my government, helping my country, and that little son of a bitch is breaking my balls." JFK, unconcerned, told Judith Campbell during one of their last trysts, "Don't worry. Sam works for us."[40]

But others did not.

This is what other mobsters were saying:

• Stefano Magaddino, from Buffalo: "They know everything under the sun. They know who's back of it, they know *amici,* they know *capodecina,* they know there's a commission."[41]

• Peter Magaddino, from Niagara Falls, New York: "He [Bobby Kennedy] should drop dead. They should kill the whole family, the mother and the father, too."[42]

• Willie Weisberg, in Philadelphia, to Angelo Bruno: "With Kennedy, a guy should take a knife, like one of them other guys, and stab and kill the bastard, where he is now. Somebody should kill the bastard. I mean it. This is true. Honest to God. It's about time to go. But I tell you something. I hope I get a week's notice. I'll kill. Right in the fucking White House."[43]

Nor were all the threats simply expressions of hatred for one or both Kennedy brothers. Two high-ranking mafiosi and two close Mob associates claimed knowledge of specific murder plans. First out of the gate with a plot was Teamster boss Jimmy Hoffa, in August 1962. Meeting Louisiana union business agent Edward Grady Partin, Sr., at Teamsters headquarters in Washington, D.C., Hoffa declared, "I've got to do something about that son of a bitch Bobby Kennedy. He's got to go." Hoffa questioned Partin as to the availability of firearms silencers and plastic explosives, asking Partin to bring a bomb to Nashville, Tennessee, where Hoffa faced trial for receiving illegal kickbacks. In a later conversation with Partin, Hoffa debated "the possible use of a lone gunman equipped with a rifle with a telescopic sight ... an assassin without any identifiable connection to the Teamster organization or to Hoffa himself." Hoffa suggested "the advisability of having the assassination committed somewhere in the South," where right-wing racists could be blamed. More specifically, Hoffa cited "the potential desirability of having Robert Kennedy shot while riding in a convertible." As Partin later told Congress, "Hoffa had believed that having the Attorney General murdered would be the most effective way of ending the federal government's intensive investigation of the Teamsters and organized crime."[44]

Carlos Marcello's hatred of the Kennedy brothers rivaled Hoffa's, but he had a different take on how to solve the problem. In September 1962, meeting with private investigator Edward Becker and associate Carl Roppolo, Marcello pronounced a Sicilian curse on Robert Kennedy: "*Livarsi na petra di la scarpa*" (Take the stone out of my shoe). He quickly added, "Don't worry about that little Bobby son of a bitch. He's going to be taken care of." When Becker opined that killing Bobby would only bring more heat down on the Mob,

Marcello replied, "No, I'm not talkin' about that. You know what they say in Sicily: If you want to kill a dog, you don't cut off the tail, you cut off the head. That dog will keep biting you if you only cut off its tail. But if the dog's head is cut off, the dog will die, tail and all." Elaborating further, Don Carlos said he planned to have "a nut" set up to take the blame for JFK's murder, "the way they do it in Sicily."[45]

Days later, in Miami Beach, Santo Trafficante, Jr., met Cuban exile leader José Alemán at the Scott Byron Motel to discuss a pending $1.5 million Teamster loan. As they talked, Trafficante turned his thoughts to JFK, saying, "Have you seen how his brother is hitting Hoffa, a man who is a worker, who is not a millionaire, a friend of the blue collars? He doesn't know that this kind of encounter is very delicate. Mark my words, this man Kennedy is in trouble and he will get what is coming to him." When Alemán voiced his belief that JFK would win re-election in 1964, Trafficante replied, "No, José. Kennedy's not going to make it to the election. He is going to be hit."[46]

Two months later, on November 9, police informer William Somerset recorded his conversation with one Joseph Milteer, a Georgia resident affiliated with the Ku Klux Klan and other extreme racist groups, who also did business with the Marcello Family. The tape captured Milteer's description of an active plot "to assassinate the president with a high-powered rifle from a tall building." Milteer added that authorities "will pick somebody up within hours afterward ... just to throw the public off," explaining that the crime had been choreographed to "drop the responsibility right into the lap of the Communists ... or Castro." Milteer said that "this conspiracy originated in New Orleans, and probably some in Miami," powered by "a lot of money ... from men who could afford to contribute." Secret Service agents, learning of the threat, canceled JFK's motorcade tour of Miami on November 18 — and sent him on to Dallas.[47]

The rest is history. JFK *was* slain by rifle fire, while riding in an open car. A "lone nut" with alleged ties to Cuba *was* jailed within hours — then murdered two days later by a second "lone nut," before dozens of policemen and a television audience of millions. Both "lone nuts" had lengthy histories of Mafia and CIA associations, all of which were somehow overlooked by LBJ's blue-ribbon Warren Commission. Celebrity lawyer Percy Foreman, representing Jack Ruby at his trial for killing Lee Harvey Oswald, had formerly served as counsel on Joseph Civello's appeal of his Apalachin conviction. Four years later, Foreman would squeeze a dubious confession out of Martin Luther King's alleged "lone nut" assassin, James Earl Ray.

Upon receiving news of JFK's death, Santo Trafficante, Jr., convened a celebratory banquet at Tampa's International Inn. "Isn't that something," he gloated. "They killed the son of a bitch. The son of a bitch is dead." To attor-

Chicago mobster Jack Ruby murders JFK assassination suspect Lee Harvey Oswald before police and a national audience (**Library of Congress**).

ney Frank Ragano, Trafficante said, "This is like lifting a load of stones off my shoulders." In Washington, a jubilant Jimmy Hoffa told friends, "Bobby Kennedy is just another lawyer now."[48]

He was correct. Although the younger Kennedy remained in office as attorney general for another nine months, his true power was gone. FBI Director J. Edgar Hoover ignored him henceforth, reporting directly to close friend and Washington neighbor Lyndon Johnson — who fired Kennedy in early September 1964. Kennedy left Justice convinced that his brother had been slain by "the guy from New Orleans," but lacked the authority — or personal resolve — to file a charge against Marcello. He chose a different path, winning election to the U.S. Senate from New York in November 1964, then campaigning for the presidency four years later. On June 5, 1968 — moments after winning California's vital primary election — Bobby Kennedy was executed in Los Angeles by another "lone nut" gunman with Mob connections, under circumstances indicating that convicted killer Sirhan Sirhan did not fire the fatal shots at all.[49]

Joe Kennedy was not available to witness the results of his Faustian bargain with the Mafia and its subsequent betrayal. A massive stroke left him immobilized and incoherent on December 19, 1961. It is impossible to know what he perceived of the disasters that ensued, before his death at Hyannis Port on November 18, 1969.[50]

· 12 ·

The Roundup

Regardless of the wealth and power they accumulate, mobsters cannot escape the ravages of time. Two of those arrested by police at Apalachin in November 1957 died before the charges filed against their cohorts were dismissed: Salvatore Tornabe on December 30, 1957, and host Joe Barbara, Sr., on June 17, 1959.[1] The rest would follow in due time.

Giuseppe "Fat Joe" Magliocco joined in Joe Bonanno's plot against rival New York City godfathers (National Archives).

Apalachin delegate Joseph Profaci, AKA "Don Peppino," aggravated members of his New York family by taxing each mafioso $25 per month in accordance with ancient Sicilian tradition. That "tithe," amounting to $50,000 per month, was earmarked for support of imprisoned gang members' dependents, but most stuck to Profaci's fingers. The volatile Gallo brothers rebelled against Profaci in February 1961, sparking a bloody internecine war. The conflict continued beyond Profaci's death, from liver cancer, on June 7, 1962.[2]

Giuseppe "Fat Joe" Magliocco survived a kidnapping by the Gallos in February 1961 and succeeded Profaci as boss of the family 16 months later. Joe Gallo's conviction on extortion charges, with a 10-year sentence, quelled the brothers' insurrection, but Magliocco soon found himself embroiled in another gang war, backing Joe Bonanno's plot to kill fellow commission members Carlo Gambino, Tommy Lucchese and Stefano Mag-addino. Magliocco trusted underboss Joseph Colombo, Sr., to handle the details, but Colombo tipped off the targets instead. Called to account for his treachery, Magliocco confessed, paid a $50,000 fine, and retired from Mafia affairs. A heart attack killed him on December 28, 1963, leaving Colombo in charge of the former Profaci Family. Police exhumed Fat Joe's corpse in 1969 to investigate rumors that he had been poisoned, but no trace of toxins was found.[3]

Buffalo underboss John Montana was the next to go. After surviving state investigations of the Apalachin gathering, Montana was embarrassed once again during October 1963 by testimony in the U.S. Senate. Informer Joe Valachi and a Buffalo detective seemed to think Montana was retired, while claiming that his taxis dominated public transport in the city. Montana suffered a heart attack on March 18, 1964, and died soon after his admission to Buffalo General Hospital.[4]

Gambino Family underboss Joseph Biondo—alias "Joe Bandy," "Joe the Blonde," and "Little Rabbit"—missed his chance to explain Albert Anastasia's execution at Apalachin. He died of natural causes in New York City at age 69, on June 10, 1966.[5]

Suspected Apalachin delegate Gaetano "Tommy Brown" Lucchese ruled his family without a hitch for nearly a decade after the ill-fated sit-down. In 1962 his daughter married Carlo Gambino's eldest son, bringing Lucchese a $30,000 cash prize and a share of Don Carlo's lucrative airport rackets. Joe Bonanno's abortive rebellion against the Mafia commission made Lucchese even richer, as the victors divided Bonanno's domain. A brain tumor ended his reign on July 13, 1967, followed by a funeral that drew politicians, judges, and racketeers in equal numbers.[6]

Frank DeSimone maintained his command of L.A.'s "Mickey Mouse Mafia" despite exposure of his gangland ties at Apalachin. Primary rival Mickey Cohen drew a second federal prison term for income tax evasion in 1961, and was crippled by a jailhouse beating while in custody. Joe Bonanno added DeSimone to his prospective hit list in 1963, and while no murder was attempted, revelation of the plot inspired a brooding paranoia that curtailed DeSimone's social outings. A heart attack ended his worries forever on August 4, 1967.[7]

Presumptive Apalachin delegate Joseph "Sox" Lanza held sway over New York's Fulton Fish Market despite his wartime extortion conviction and a 1957 arrest for parole violation. He commanded the waterfront until his death from natural causes at age 64, on October 11, 1968.[8]

Salvatore Chiri maintained his role as *consigliere* of the Genovese Family until November 1968, when he died from natural causes at Fort Lee, New Jersey.[9]

Imprisoned for his 1959 narcotics conviction, Chiri's lord and master ultimately did more harm to the Cosa Nostra than any other Apalachin delegate. Believing that fellow convict-mafioso Joseph "Joe Cargo" Valachi had broken his oath of *omertà*, Genovese schemed to have him killed. Valachi, learning of the plot, murdered the wrong man on suspicion of stalking him, then turned federal informant to escape execution. His testimony before the McClellan Committee offered few details not aired by Abe Reles in 1940 and contained many inaccuracies— Joe Bonanno likened it to "asking a new convert to Catholicism in New Guinea to explain the inner workings of Vatican City"— but it still drew international attention to the Mafia. Genovese died in federal prison at age 71, on February 14, 1969.[10]

Mafioso Joseph Valachi turned informer after Vito Genovese plotted to kill him in prison (National Archives).

Dallas mafioso Joseph Civello received a five-year conspiracy sentence in 1959 for attending the Apalachin conference, but celebrity attorney Percy Foreman — who once boasted that his fee alone was punishment enough for any crime — won a reversal of that verdict on appeal in 1960. One of Civello's underlings, former Chicago mobster Jack Ruby, also hired Foreman to appeal his capital conviction for killing alleged JFK assassin Lee Harvey Oswald in 1963. Subsequent investigation revealed that Civello underboss Joseph Campisi dined with Ruby at Campisi's Egyptian Restaurant the night before Oswald's slaying, and that Campisi was Ruby's first jailhouse visitor after the shooting. Overlooked by both the Warren Commission and New Orleans District Attorrney Jim Garrison's subsequent probe of the JFK murder, Civello died in Dallas from natural causes on January 17, 1970.[11]

Joe Bonanno's brother-in-law and *caporegime*, Gaspar DiGregorio, played a key role in Bonanno's plot against the Mafia commission and the subsequent "Banana War." Aspiring to promotion as Bonanno's *consigliere*, DiGregorio saw his hopes dashed when Bonanno's son filled that post. Feeling cheated, DiGregorio arranged an ambush for Salvatore Bonanno and his closest friends in Brooklyn, on January 28, 1966, but the intended targets escaped. The war sputtered on until summer 1968, when a heart attack forced Bonanno's retirement and Paul Sciacca assumed command of the family, sidelining DiGregorio. The traitorous *caporegime* died from lung cancer at St. John's Hospital in Smithtown, New York, on June 11, 1970.[12]

Antonio Magaddino, brother and *consigliere* to Buffalo's reigning Mafia boss, served the family until April 1971, when he died from natural causes in Niagara Falls, New York, two months shy of his 74th birthday.[13]

Barbara Family member Emanuel Zicari logged no more arrests after the Apalachin sitdown. He died from natural causes in Endicott, New York, at age 70, in July 1970.[14]

Pennsylvania mafioso William Medico, suspected but never confirmed as an Apalachin delegate, shuffled off the mortal coil in September 1972, at age 63. Federal records contain no details of the date, location or circumstances.[15]

Authorities never clarified Salvatore Falcone's Mafia affiliation, listing him simply as a soldier of the Barbara or Magaddino Family. In any case, he lived to see retirement in Miami, Florida, and died there at age 81, in October 1972.[16]

Luigi Greco's attendance at Apalachin remains unconfirmed, but the Canadian mafioso definitely welcomed Joe Bonanno's son to Montreal in November 1966, presumably to iron out details of collaboration between their two families on various illicit enterprises. Police surprised them and detained both bosses, with several subordinates, after confiscating three illegal handguns. Bonanno and his New York crew were shipped home after posting bail, but no one supposed that the Manhattan-Montreal link had been severed. On December 3, 1972, while renovating a pizzeria with brother Antonio, Greco doused a mop with kerosene to clean the floor, and somehow sparked a flash-fire that left him critically burned. He died four days later at Sacre-Coeur Hospital and was treated to a full-dress gangland funeral, complete with a teary-eyed mobster singing "Ave Maria."[17]

James Colletti retained control Denver's Cosa Nostra family after Apalachin and avoided any hint of guilt by association when business partner Joe Bonanno plotted to kill rival commission members in 1963. Coletti died from natural causes in Englewood, Colorado, at age 81, in March 1973.[18]

Joseph Rosato, a member of the Gambino Family and brother-in-law to Tommy Lucchese, retired to enjoy his golden years in Florida. He died in Miami, at age 69, in April 1973.[19]

Following Vito Genovese's narcotics conviction, *consigliere* Michele Miranda served with Thomas Eboli and Gerardo Catena on a three-man mini-commission assigned to run the family in Don Vito's absence. In October 1965, NYPD officers arrested parolees Miranda and Eboli for consorting with known criminals—each other—but both were freed within a week. A year later, on September 22, 1966, raiders nabbed Miranda and 12 other mafiosi at La Stella Restaurant in Queens, compelling the 13 to post $100,000 bond apiece on new consorting charges that were later dismissed. Plagued by diabetes in his later years, Miranda retired from active family affairs in 1972 and died in Boca Raton, Florida, on September 16, 1973. He was 80 years old.[20]

Bonanno Family *caporegime* Natale "Joe Diamond" Evola was convicted with Vito Genovese and 13 other defendants on drug-trafficking charges in 1959, but emerged from prison to briefly lead the family in 1968, before Paul Sciacca replaced him. Cancer claimed Evola's life at age 66, on August 28, 1973.[21]

FBN agents missed Giovanni Ormento when they busted Vito Genovese's heroin-smuggling ring in July 1958, but they persevered to arrest him with two other drug-trafficking mafiosi on April 1, 1959. Convicted on that charge—his third narcotics conviction since 1937—Ormento shuffled off to federal prison and died there in March 1974, at age 61.[22]

Buffalo boss Stefano Magaddino left a suit of clothes at Apalachin but escaped the dragnet that corralled his fellow mafiosi. Some mobsters blamed him for choosing Joe Barbara's estate over a safer meeting place in Sam Giancana's Chicago, and police blamed that anger for the hand grenade someone pitched through Magaddino's kitchen window in 1958. The pineapple was a dud, and Magaddino lived peaceably until November 1968, when federal agents arrested Stefano and son Peter on interstate gambling charges. Jurors acquitted Peter in May 1971, while Stefano's indictment was quashed three years later, on grounds that the G-men had placed illegal wiretaps on his telephones. By then, Don Stefano had only two months to live. A heart attack killed him on July 19, 1974, leaving his family divided between hostile factions.[23]

Frank Zito, the Chicago Outfit's man in Springfield, Illinois, remained in harness for nearly three decades after Apalachin. He died in Springfield from natural causes at age 81, in August 1974.[24]

Stefano LaSalle remained in place as underboss for Tommy Lucchese and successor Carmine Tramunti until his formal retirement in 1972. LaSalle died in Brooklyn from natural causes in December 1974, a few days short of his 91st birthday.[25]

Joseph Riccobono, *consigliere* of the Gambino Family and owner of multiple Brooklyn dress shops, pursued his various illicit and legitimate activities until May 1975, when he died on Staten Island at age 81.[26]

Sam Giancana gloated over his role in John Kennedy's 1960 presidential election, but he soon had cause to regret that support. Posted near the top of Attorney General Robert Kennedy's Mafia hit list, Giancana endured FBI harassment that finally drove him to sue the bureau, winning a judgment that required federal agents to remain at least one foursome behind Giancana while he was golfing. The surveillance was particularly irksome since Giancana regarded himself as a sterling American patriot, deeply immersed with Tampa boss Santo Trafficante, Jr., in the CIA's plots to kill Cuban dictator Fidel Castro in the early 1960s. Giancana's high profile, including the FBI lawsuit, prompted "retired" boss Tony Accardo to replace Giancana with Joseph "Joey Doves" Aiuppa in 1966, dispatching Giancana to exile in Mexico. Mexican authorities expelled Giancana in 1974, and the following year saw him slapped with a subpoena to testify before the U.S. Senate's Select Committee to Study Governmental Operations with Respect to Intelligence Activities. Before he could testify, an unknown gunman executed Giancana in the basement kitchen of his home in Oak Park, Illinois, on June 19, 1975. He was shot once in the back of the head, and six more times around his mouth — a sign of punishment for an informer.[27]

New England mafioso Frank "The Cheeseman" Cucchiara passed more peacefully, dying in Belmont, Massachusetts from natural causes at age 80 in January 1976.[28]

Cleveland's John Scalish holds dubious honors as the Forest City's longest-serving Mafia boss. Anointed in 1944, he reigned for nearly 19 years after his brief embarrassment at Apalachin, presiding over a stable empire. On May 26, 1976, Scalish died during heart surgery, at age 62. His failure to name a successor left a power vacuum in Cleveland, sparking a brutal war between would-be bosses James "Blackie" Licavoli and John Nardi, ending with Nardi's murder by car-bomb on May 17, 1977.[29]

After Apalachin, Carlo Gambino emerged as the dominant boss among New York's five Mafia families. His power was enhanced by absorption of Joe Bonanno's rackets during the "Banana War" of 1966–68, and some observers believe that Gambino orchestrated the public shooting of flamboyant boss Joseph Colombo, Sr., in June 1971, over Colombo's embarrassment of La Cosa Nostra through the antics of his Italian-American Civil Rights League. Before a heart attack ended his life on October 15, 1976, Gambino named brother-in-law Paul Castellano as his successor, bypassing longtime underboss Aniello Dellacroce. That unpopular decision paved the way for Castellano's subsequent assassination and the rise of "Teflon Don," John Gotti, Sr.[30]

Another long-serving boss, Detroit's Joseph Zerilli, enjoyed peace and prosperity for nearly four decades, from 1936 until his death from natural causes on October 30, 1977. Until that day, Zerilli remained active in rackets nationwide, and claimed his family's share of the Las Vegas skim from old friend and longtime business partner Moe Dalitz.[31]

Suspected Apalachin delegate John Colletti remained an active member of the Texas-based Civella Family until May 1978, when death overtook him in Lafayette, Louisiana, at age 72.[32]

California mafioso Joseph Xavier Cerrito slipped through the police net at Apalachin, despite his registration at a nearby hotel, and returned safely to San Jose. He died in nearby Los Gatos at age 67, from natural causes, in September 1978.[33]

Lucchese Family member Carmine "Gribbs" Tramunti left his business card at Apalachin in November 1957, but escaped the dragnet. Ten years later, he became the family's boss by default, when Tommy Lucchese died with his hand-picked successor — Anthony "Tony Ducks" Corallo — imprisoned on a bribery charge. While serving as interim boss, Tramunti won acquittal on charges stemming from a multi-million-dollar stock swindle, then became embroiled in the French Connection heroin-smuggling case. That caper earned Tramunti a 15-year sentence, despite his insistence that he had been framed. "I may be a mobster and may have done bad things," he insisted, "but I am not a drug dealer." Tramunti died from natural causes while serving his sentence, on October 15, 1978.[34]

Internet author Thom Jones names Pasquale "Patsy" Mancuso as an Apalachin delegate, stating that he was among those interviewed by state police on the night of November 14–15, 1957, but Jones cites no evidence to prove it and no other source confirms the allegation. In any case, Mancuso died at age 70 in January 1979, at Corona, in New York's Borough of Queens.[35]

Presumed delegate Carmine "Lilo" Galante, identified by Joe Barbara's housekeeper as a guest at the estate during the sit-down, escaped from state police but was less fortunate with agents of the FBN. Galante and John Ormento eluded the federal sweep that jailed Vito Genovese and 16 codefendants in July 1958, but authorities persisted, capturing Galante in New Jersey on June 3, 1959. Formally indicted in May 1960 and convicted two years later, Galante received a 20-year sentence in federal prison. Some Mob-watchers believe that Frank Costello and Meyer Lansky engineered Galante's downfall, despite his long record of smuggling and selling narcotics. Perhaps in retaliation, Galante reached out from prison to have Costello's mausoleum dynamited in 1973. Paroled the following year, Galante assumed command of the Bonanno Family when boss Phillip "Rusty" Rastelli was jailed for extortion in August 1978. Fighting charges of parole violation from October 1977 through March 1979, Galante sought to augument his family ranks with imported Sicilians — dubbed "zips" — who served as the spearhead for Galante's bid to recapture control of New York's heroin trade. In reckless

Carmine Galante (at right) was slain with two companions in 1979 after boasting that "no one will ever kill me; they wouldn't dare" (National Archives).

arrogance, Galante told associates, "No one will ever kill me, they wouldn't dare." Gunmen proved him wrong on July 12, 1979, when they blasted Galante with shotguns at Joe and Mary's Italian-American Restaurant in Bushwick, Brooklyn. The fusillade also killed bodyguard Leonard Coppola and restaurant owner Giuseppe Turano, a relative of Galante's.[36]

Multiple sources name Montreal mafioso Giuseppe Cotroni as one of those who slipped past New York State Police at Apalachin. Authorities could never prove it, but the FBN pursued Cotroni with a vengeance, sending Agent Patrick Biase to infiltrate Cotroni's heroin network with smuggler-turned-informant Eddie Smith in 1959. Cotroni met the pair, with cohort René Robert, and agreed to sell them two kilos of smack for $14,000. That deal earned Cotroni a 10-year sentence in November 1959, while Robert was slapped with eight years. In May 1960 Cotroni received another seven-year term for trading $3.75 million worth of stolen bonds, that sentence to be served consecutively with his drug term. Paroled in April 1971, Cotroni allegedly returned to a full-time life of crime, but he avoided any further charges prior to his death from natural causes in September 1979.[37]

Magaddino *caporegime* Rosario Carlisi rode out the turmoil that disturbed his family after Apalachin, remaining loyal to boss Stefano Magaddino while dissidents schemed against him. In June 1970 police in Buffalo arrested Carlisi while he shared lunch with Rochester mafiosi Frank Valenti and Joseph Fino, but all three were soon released without charges. Carlisi died in Buffalo from natural causes at age 70, in April 1980.[38]

Gabriel Mannarino, known to friends as "Kelly," continued as a *caporegime* then underboss of Pittsburgh's LaRocca Family after Apalachin, profiting from far-flung enterprises that included New Kensington's Ken Iron and Steel Company, plus nightclubs in that city and in Miami Beach, Florida. He died from natural causes in July 1980, at age 64.[39]

Named by three sources (but never confirmed) as Sicily's delegate to Apalachin, Giuseppe Settacase was overheard discussing the embarrassment on wiretaps monitored by FBI agents and officers of the Royal Canadian Mounted Police. As boss of Agrigento's Mafia family and a member of Sicily's first Mafia commission, Settacase continued to profit from global drug-trafficking until March 23, 1981, when he was shot and killed near his home. The crime remains officially unsolved, though police blame members of the rival Cuntrera-Caruana Mafia clan, based in Siculiana.[40]

Former Bonanno Family underboss Frank Garofalo "retired" to Sicily in 1956, but subsequently attended the heroin confab at Palermo's Grand Hotel et Des Palmes in October 1957. A month later, he had motel reservations in Apalachin, but police missed their chance to nab him. Safely back in Sicily, Garofolo died at age 83, in January 1982.[41]

Another mafioso who slipped through the net while leaving a motel registration behind was Alfred Angelicola of New Jersey. He avoided any further headlines until May 1970, when prosecutors charged Joseph Zicarelli and four Hudson County cohorts with bribing Mayor John Ralph Armellino of West New York to protect their illegal gambling operations. A *New York Times* report linked Angelicola to the conspiracy, but he was not among those convicted and sentenced to prison in April 1971. Angelicola died from natural causes at Fair Lawn, New Jersey, in April 1982, at age 68.[42]

John Vitale of St. Louis was another possible guest at the Barbara sitdown, representing the St. Louis family. A decade after Apalachin, the U.S. Department of Justice identified him as the family's *consigliere*, "representing the national cartel in St. Louis." Four years later, the *St. Louis Globe-Democrat* named Vitale as second in command to local boss Anthony Giordano. Giordano died from cancer in August 1980, two months before FBI agents stopped Vitale at Lambert-St. Louis International Airport, carrying $36,000 in cash. By 1981 he was reportedly employed as an FBI informant, feeding data to the feds on dissidents within his family. Heart disease claimed Vitale's life on

June 5, 1982, at Faith Hospital in Creve Coeur, Missouri. He was 73 years old.[43]

Missouri authorities charged Nicholas Civella with two counts of tax evasion in 1959, but they achieved little: he paid a $150 fine in one case, while the other was dismissed. On June 13, 1960, Civella and brother Carl claimed dubious honors as two of 11 persons banned from setting foot in Nevada casinos. Despite that ban, in 1974 he registered at the Dunes hotel-casino in Las Vegas under a pseudonym, where his VIP handling by hotel managers prompted punitive state action against the resort. A year later, Kansas City jurors convicted Civella on gambling charges. Marathon appeals delayed his imprisonment until 1977, and a cancer diagnosis won him early release in 1978. During November of that year, Civella tried to bribe a federal prison official, seeking transfer of his inmate nephew to a Texas lockup. Convicted on that charge in July 1980, Civella received a four-year sentence. November 1981 brought new indictments, charging Civella and 10 other defendants with skimming cash from the Tropicana resort in Las Vegas. A recurrence of his cancer saved Civella from that trial, but he could not beat the disease. Released from custody on March 1, 1983, Civella died at the Menorah Medical Center in Overland Park, Kansas, on March 12.[44]

A federal narcotics indictment encouraged Philadelphia mafioso Joseph Ida to retire and leave America for his native Sicily in 1959. The U.S. consulate in Italy reported his death from natural causes at age 90, in March 1984.[45]

Pittsburgh boss John LaRocca was the next to go, still in charge of the Steel City's rackets when he died from natural causes at age 83, on December 3, 1984.[46]

Joseph Filardo, described in various accounts as a soldier or *caporegime* of Nick Civella's Missouri family, outlived his boss by 29 months. He died in Kansas City from natural causes, days short of his 87th birthday in August 1985.[47]

Returning home from Apalachin, New Jersey *consigliere* Frank Majuri found himself demoted to the rank of *caporegime* by new boss Nicholas Delmore. He filled that post dependably, while clinging to his façade as "labor foreman" for C.F. Brown & Company in Linden, and was reinstated as *consigliere* in 1964, when Delmore died and was replaced by Simone "Sam the Plumber" DeCavalcante. Majuri's fortunes took another downturn in 1976, when DeCavalcante passed the reins to Giovanni "John the Eagle" Riggi. Replaced as *consigliere* by Stefano "Steve the Truck Driver" Vitabile, Majuri ran his Newark crew in peace until October 1985, when he died from natural causes at age 84.[48]

Paul Castellano's elevation to serve as head of the Gambino Family in 1976 angered many mafiosi loyal to longtime underboss Aniello Dellacroce.

Paul Castellano was murdered on orders from rival John Gotti (National Archives).

Those dissidents were further aggravated by Castellano's ban on drug-dealing, under penalty of death. The crowning insult came with Dellacroce's death on December 2, 1985. Castellano not only missed his underboss's funeral — a sign of grave disrespect — but also named his personal bodyguard, brutish Tommy Bilotti, to fill Dellacroce's post as second in command of the family. Two weeks later, on December 16, a hit team organized by *caporegime* John Gotti, Sr., executed Castellano and Bilotti outside a Manhattan steak house. Gotti then assumed control of the family and ruled until April 1992, when federal jurors convicted him on multiple racketeering charges, including the Castellano-Bilotti murders.[49]

Santo Trafficante, Jr., lost his lucrative Cuban investments in 1959, when Fidel Castro unseated Fulgencio Batista and closed Havana's Mob-owned casinos. Briefly detained in a Cuban prison, the Tampa boss received visits from Dallas mobster Jack Ruby before Castro's police deported Trafficante to the United States. By September 1960, Trafficante was immersed in CIA plots to assassinate Castro, along with Chicago's Sam Giancana and other mafiosi. The bungled Bay of Pigs invasion, coupled with federal prosecutions of high-ranking mobsters from 1961 to 1963, embittered Trafficante against President Kennedy and his attorney general brother. In 1963, as JFK began his campaign for reelection, Trafficante told Cuban-exile associate José Alemán, "Mark my word, this man Kennedy is in trouble, and he will get what is coming to him.

Kennedy's not going to make it to the election. He is going to be hit." When questioned about that statement in September 1978 by the House Select Committee on Assassinations, Trafficante claimed that he only meant JFK would be "hit by a lot of Republican votes" in November 1964. That disingenuous comment failed to pacify conspiracy theorists, and Trafficante himself acknowledged a plot to kill the president, shortly before his own death in 1987. Speaking to longtime Mob attorney Frank Ragano, Trafficante said, "I think Carlos [Marcello] fucked up in getting rid of John — maybe it should have been Bobby. We shouldn't have killed John. We should have killed Bobby." Trafficante died at a hospital in Houston, Texas, on March 17, 1987. He was 72 years old.[50]

Barbara Family *caporegime* Angelo Sciandra continued his Mafia duties for three decades after Apalachin, maintaining various dress shops and clothing factories as legitimate fronts in Pennsylvania and New York. He died in Pittson from natural causes at age 63, in April 1987.[51]

New England mafioso Filippo Buccola departed the U.S. for his Sicilian homeland in 1954, ceding command of his family to Raymond Patriarca, but FBN agents asserted that he returned in November 1957 for the Apalachin gathering. Their only evidence, never produced in any court, allegedly involved wiretap recordings that contained a reference to the meeting two weeks in advance. Some versions of the story further claim that Harry Anslinger's agents tipped New York State Police to the gathering, thus deserving credit for the raid that followed. Be that as it may, Buccola eluded authorities — if, in fact, he attended the meeting — and made his way safely back to Sicily. He reportedly died there in 1987, at age 101, specific date unknown.[52]

As with several other Apalachin delegates, Pasquale Turrigiano confused reporters who could never decide if he served the Barbara or Magaddino Family. A grocery store in Endicott, New York, served as his legitimate cover until his Turrigiano's death from natural causes at age 81, on April 13, 1988.[53]

Joseph Valachi's testimony in 1963 prompted long-running surveillance of Lucchese Family *consigliere* Vincent Rao. In January 1965 a federal grand jury granted Rao immunity from prosecution in a bid to force his testimony against boss Tommy Lucchese, then charged him with perjury on March 18, when his answers failed to satisfy the panel. Convicted on November 17, 1967, Rao received a five-year sentence, thereby scuttling media reports that he had been tapped to replace Lucchese as boss. Rao emerged from prison to regain his post as *consigliere* under Carmine Tramunti, and he outlived Lucchese's successor, retiring to Florida in 1973. He died in the Sunshine State at age 90, on September 25, 1988.[54]

Barbara Family *caporegime* Anthony Guarnieri flew under law enforcement's radar after Apalachin until 1988, when undercover officers in Broward

County, Florida, arrested him with two other defendants—Anthony Pelosi and Stanley Reppucci — on charges of trafficking in marijuana and counterfeit watches. A separate case in New York charged Guarnieri with manufacturing firearms silencers. Guarnieri pled guilty on two counts in Florida and received a two-year sentence, later matched by a concurrent term in New York. Guarnieri died in custody at age 79, on August 12, 1990.[55]

After the abortive Apalachin meeting, New Jersey boss Nicholas Delmore promoted Louis LaRasso to serve as underboss, while demoting Frank Majuri to *caporegime.* Successor Simone DeCavalcante retained LaRasso as his second in command, but did not know the feds had wired their offices for sound. In 1969 DeCavalcante and LaRasso were among the 55 defendants charged with running a $20 million gambling empire. Both were convicted and sentenced to prison. Following parole and DeCavalcante's retirement in the 1970s, LaRasso was demoted to a soldier's rank by new boss Giovanni Riggi. He fared even worse with successor John D'Amato, and relatives reported LaRasso missing when he failed to appear for his 65th birthday party in November 1991. As the story was later pieced together by police, D'Amato suspected LaRasso of plotting a hostile takeover and moved to eliminate the threat. Triggerman-turned-acting boss Vincent Palermo confessed to LaRasso's murder in 2001. Two years later, jurors convicted *consigliere* Stefano Vitabile and two *caporegimes*— Philip Abramo and Giuseppe Schifilliti — on various charges including LaRasso's murder, but an appellate court reversed that verdict and the resultant life sentences in September 2008.[56]

Like his brother Salvatore, Joseph Falcone baffled police with his Cosa Nostra family affiliation. Observers documented meetings with Stefano Magaddino, but other reports still name Falcone as a member of the Barbara Family. The early 1960s found him under investigation for illegal gambling in Utica, but he dropped out of sight for four years, leaving brother Salvatore to take the heat (case dismissed on appeal). Joseph Falcone died in Utica from natural causes, at age 90, in March 1992.[57]

Bonanno Family *caporegime* Anthony Riela survived the "Banana War" and remained active in Mob affairs into the 1980s, operating two motels in Newark, New Jersey, as quasi-legitimate fronts. He died from natural causes on June 21, 1992, at age 94.[58]

Carmine "The Doctor" Lombardozzi never rose above the rank of *caporegime,* but he managed most of the Gambino Family's loan-sharking and stock market rackets, earning a reputation as the "King of Wall Street" and the "Italian Meyer Lansky." Aside from his jail terms for contempt served in the aftermath of Apalachin, Lombardozzi faced multiple charges over the next three decades. In April 1964 he was indicted with his lawyer on charges of conspiring to obstruct a federal investigation (he was acquitted in September 1970). He was sentenced to jail on a new contempt charge in December 1964, and a brawl with police left him briefly detained in April 1965. Six months later, prosecutors jailed Lombardozzi as a scofflaw for failure to pay 102 parking tickets, but a judge dismissed that charge in November 1965. December 1967 saw The Doctor charged with perjury; he was convicted in September 1968. A month before that guilty verdict, Lombardozzi was accused of stealing brokerage checks worth $50,000; he received a two-year sentence for that crime in June 1970, trailing a March 1969 one-year sentence for perjury before a Brooklyn grand jury. A hung jury spared Lombardozzi from conviction on tax-evasion charges in September 1970. This was followed by abortive perjury charges in November 1975 and another dead-end tax case in April 1981. Lombardozzi died from natural causes at age 79, on September 5, 1992.[59]

College-educated mafioso Frank Balistrieri graduated to serve as boss of the Milwaukee family when father-in-law John Aloito retired in 1961. Balistrieri's gangland nicknames—"Mr. Slick" and "Mad Bomber"—illustrate his management style and reputation for literally explosive violence. A 1967 tax-evasion charge sent him to prison for two years. He was released in 1971, and his power was undiminished. In March 1974 Balistrieri met with Kansas City mobsters Nicholas Civella and Carl DeLuna in Las Vegas, orchestrating a $62.75 million Teamster loan to front man Allen Glick, earmarked for purchase of the Fremont and Stardust hotel-casinos. Both joints were thoroughly skimmed until September 1983, when federal prosecutors indicted Balistrieri, his two sons, and various codefendants on multiple felony charges. Before facing trial in that case, Balistrieri and his sons were convicted of extortion in a separate indictment, with "Mr. Slick" receiving a 13-year sentence. Convicted of the Vegas skim in September 1985, Balistrieri drew a concurrent 10-year sentence three months later. He died in prison from natural causes on February 7, 1993. The Mad Bomber was 74.[60]

James LaDucca, Stefano Magaddino's son-in-law and loyal *caporegime*, was indicted in February 1961 for obstructing justice by evading hearings on the Apalachin conference. He hid out for a month, then surrendered to police in Niagara Falls and ultimately beat the charge in court. After a long and lucrative career outside the law, LaDucca died from natural causes at age 80, in September 1993.[61]

Apalachin delegate Sam Monachino seemed to lead a charmed life in Utica, New York, and environs. He had yet to log a criminal indictment at his death, on December 8, 1993, at age 96.[62]

Rosario "Russell" Bufalino succeeded Joe Barbara, Sr., as boss of the family in 1959. Some other Cosa Nostra leaders blamed him personally for promoting the November 1957 meeting at Barbara's estate instead of at Sam

Giancana's secure Chicago preserve, but their antipathy did not obstruct Bufalino's rise to prominence within the Mob. The McClellan Committee later named Bufalino as "one of the most ruthless and powerful leaders of the Mafia in the United States." Allegations of his participation in the plot to kill President Kennedy remain unsubstantiated, but many lesser deaths have been laid at his doorstep. Flamboyant Pennsylvania congressman Daniel Flood weathered multiple investigations of his ties to Bufalino before censure on a bribery charge forced his resignation in January 1980. The final straw was Flood's procurement of a $3.9 million military contract for Medico Industries of Plains Township, Pennsylvania, run by Bufalino *caporegime* Philip Medico, brother of reputed Apalachin delegate William Medico. In 1977 federal prosecutors charged Bufalino with extorting $25,000 from a dealer in stolen diamonds who testified for the state against him. Convicted in August 1978, Bufalino received a four-year sentence. Following release from prison, Bufalino was indicted and convicted once again — this time for plotting to kill the witness who turned on him in 1977. That charge carried a 10-year sentence. He got parole in May 1989. Laboring under constant surveillance, Bufalino named Billy D'Elia as his successor and subsequently died from natural causes at age 90 on February 25, 1994.[63]

While his descendants remain active in Pittsburgh's underworld, few traces remain of unconfirmed Apalachin delegate Louis Pagnotti. He died in Scranton, Pennsylvania, on November 13, 1996, at age 87. The rest is silence.[64]

Another mafioso left in limbo by reporters, alternately labeled as a member of the Barbara or Magaddino Family, Pasquale "Patsy" Monachino, died in Rochester, New York, at age 90, on October 14, 1998.[65]

Six months later, another "Patsy" died in Rochester. Apalachin delegate and Barbara Family soldier Pasquale Sciortino was 84 when he made his final exit on May 1, 1999.[66]

Only one source names New Orleans restaurateur Joseph Marcello as an Apalachin delegate, representing brother Carlos, but several name him as Mafia underboss of the Big Easy. No evidence thus far produced has placed him at the Barbara estate or anywhere nearby. Joseph outlived his infamous elder brother by six years, dying from natural causes in Metairie, Louisiana, on June 15, 1999. He was 75 years old.[67]

Magaddino Family *caporegime* Samuel Lagattuta moved west in his declining years, after a long career in New York and New Jersey. He died in Las Vegas, Nevada, at age 89, on April 3, 2000.[68]

Gerardo Catena shrugged off Joe Valachi's public identification of him as a high-ranking Genovese Family member, but police were watching. On October 29, 1965, they nabbed Catena and six cohorts at a restaurant in Little Italy, engaged in what *The New York Times* called a "Little Apalachin" gathering. A grand jury jailed Catena for contempt when he refused to testify in March 1970, despite a grant of immunity from prosecution. Stubbornly silent, Catena sat in prison until August 19, 1975, when he was freed by order of the New Jersey Supreme Court. While that ordeal enhanced his reputation with the Mob, it left him in poor health at age 73. Catena soon decamped for Florida and died there, at Punta Gorda, on April 23, 2000.[69]

Three Internet sources name Detroit *caporegime* Anthony Giacalone as a "probable" Apalachin delegate, but no solid evidence confirms his presence at the meeting. More substantial indicators link Giacalone to the disappearance of Teamster ex-president Jimmy Hoffa, who left home for a meeting with "Tony Jack" and New Jersey mafioso Anthony Provenzano on July 30, 1975. Shortly after 2:00 P.M. that day, Hoffa phoned home from the Machus Red Fox Restaurant in Bloomfield Township, Michigan, reporting that the two mobsters were late for their luncheon. Soon afterward, a passing trucker saw Hoffa leave the restaurant's parking lot in a car later traced to Joe Giacalone, Anthony's son. Hoffa was never seen again, and while hairs found in the car matched Hoffa's DNA when they were tested in 2001, no one has yet been charged with his murder. Meanwhile, Tony Giacalone was convicted of tax fraud in 1976 and spent 10 years in prison, then went back inside for parole violations in March 1987. He was released once again in March 1990. He faced yet another indictment — on charges of extortion, racketeering and conspiracy — when heart failure and complications from kidney disease claimed his life on February 23, 2001.[70]

On the same day that Tony Jack died in Detroit, former Rochester mafioso and confirmed Apalachin delegate Constenze Valenti died at age 75, in Victor, New York. His friends — and the U.S. Social Security Administration — knew him as "Stanley."[71]

After Joseph Colombo, Sr., squealed on Joe Bonanno's plot to decimate the Mafia's ruling commission in 1963, that body ordered Bonanno and compliant ally Giuseppe Magliocco to present themselves for questioning. Magliocco complied, escaping execution with a $50,000 fine and forced retirement, but Bonanno declined to surrender. In October 1964 he was allegedly abducted from a New York City street, perhaps by soldiers of the Magaddino Family in Buffalo. Dubbed the "Banana Split" by newspapers, his disappearance may have been a staged event or some form of house arrest imposed by Bonanno's rivals. He remained invisible until 1968, when he ended the two-year "Banana War" by announcing his retirement to Tucson, Arizona. There, a spate of bombings targeted Bonanno's family, promoting rumors of a new gang war, but police later blamed the explosions on hoodlums hired by an over-zealous FBI agent. Bonanno published a self-serving memoir, titled *A Man of Honor*, in 1983, and son Salvatore followed suit with his own autobiography, *Bound by Honor*, in 2000. Journalist Mike Wallace interviewed both Bonannos in April 2002, on television's *60 Minutes*, but Joe was running out of time. Heart failure killed him in Tucson at age 97, on May 11, 2002.[72]

Rochester mafioso Frank Valenti outlived his brother Costenze by two years and nine months. Retired from Mafia affairs to Florida, he died from natural causes at West Palm Beach, at age 92, on November 3, 2003.[73]

San Francisco underboss James Lanza graduated to command of the local family in July 1961, when Immigration officers deported boss Mike Abati to his native Italy. One of history's longest-lived mafiosi, he ruled the local Cosa Nostra until February 14, 2006, when he finally died from natural causes at age 103. A newspaper obituary described Lanza as a restaurateur, winemaker, wholesaler of specialty Italian food products, and a "pioneer in Fisherman's Wharf."[74]

Michael Genovese shared command of the Pittsburgh family with Gabriel Mannarino and Joseph "Jo Jo" Pecora in 1978, after failing health forced boss John LaRocca's retirement. Pecora soon went off to prison, and with Mannarino's death in 1980, Genovese stood alone at the helm. He steered the family into wholesale narcotics trafficking, and held the reins despite intensive federal scrutiny until October 31, 2006, when he died from natural causes at age 87 in Gibsonia, Pennsylvania.[75]

Joseph Campisi continued as underboss to Joe Civello in Dallas, until Civello retired to Florida in 1968. A known associate of mobster Jack Ruby who dined with Ruby the night before Ruby shot Lee Harvey Oswald, Campisi ruled an increasingly unruly Texas underworld until August 23, 2007, when he died from natural causes in Beaumont, at age 83.[76]

New York State Police found Joseph Zammuto's motel reservation in November 1957, but the Chicago Outfit's representative from Rockford, Illinois, slipped through their net. Eleven years later, in December 1968, a federal grand jury grilled Zammuto and 11 cohorts on their gambling activities in northern Illinois, but no indictments resulted. Confusion surrounds his final days. The Social Security Death Index lists his demise as occurring in Roscoe, Illinois, at age 74, in May 1974, while an article published in the *Rockford Register Star* 10 years later (March 4, 1984) announced Zammuto's retirement in favor of successor Frank Buscemi. That strange contradiction stands unresolved.[77]

The last confirmed Apalachin delegate to die, as of press time for this book, was Ignatius Cannone of the former Barbara Family. He was 85 when he died of natural causes on January 21, 2011, 64 years after his first arrest on a charge of disorderly conduct.[78]

Two other Apalachin participants were still living at completion of this manuscript. Aniello Migliore, a Lucchese soldier linked to the Barbara meet by a car crash in Binghamton, New York, the day after Sergeant Croswell's raid, ultimately graduated to the top ranks of the family. March 1986 saw him indicted with other mafiosi and union officials on charges of construction bid rigging. Convicted in May 1988, Migliore received a 100-year sentence, overturned on appeal in August 1991. Drive-by gunmen critically wounded him with a shotgun blast on April 3, 1992, during a friend's birthday party in Westbury, Long Island, but Migliore survived that attack and returned to full duty. In 2006, Mob-watchers named Migliore as one of three mafiosi directing the family — with Joseph DiNapoli and Matthew Madonna — after boss Steven "Wonderboy" Crea pled guilty to racketeering charges, receiving a sentence of two to six years in prison.[79]

The other Apalachin survivor, Joseph Barbara, Jr., quickly tired of scrutiny from journalists and law enforcement. Soon after his father's death, Joe Jr. accepted an invitation from Detroit boss Peter Licavoli and relocated to Motor City. There, with father-in-law Pietro Vitale and Pietro's brother Paul, Barbara organized Tri-County Sanitation, undercutting competition in the garbage-hauling trade through an arrangement with the Teamsters that let Barbara and company hire non-union drivers at cut-rate wages. In 1968 Barbara faced rape and extortion charges involving the wife of jailed associate Peter Lazaros. He beat the rape charge at trial in 1970, but received a 7-to-20-year term for extortion. Back on the street by 1979, Barbara was slapped with a new indicment for racketeering that brought him a four-year sentence in October 1980, plus another year for violating terms of his parole. Today he is considered an inactive member of Detroit's Mafia family.[80]

Two confirmed Apalachin delegates vanished from the public record on Italian soil. Bonanno Family *caporegime* Giovanni Bonventre had moved home to Sicily in 1950, returning to the U.S. for the Barbara convention, but escaped after the roundup. Our last word of him comes from May 1971, when Italian authorities banished Bonventre and 14 other mafiosi to Filicudi, a three-mile-long island in the Aeolian archipelago, located in the Tyrrhenian Sea off Sicily's northern coastline.[81] Immigration authorities deported Los Angeles underboss Simone Scozzari to Rome on June 13, 1962, and he reportedly made his way back to Palermo, where we lose his trail.[82]

Six confirmed Apalachin delegates and four suspected attendees remain as elusive in death as they were in life, with no information on their fates available at press time for this book. Death records of the U.S. Social Security Administration contain no listings for known meeting participants Dominick D'Agostino (born December 7, 1889), Bartolo Guccia (December 26, 1891), Rosario Mancuso (January 29, 1907), Dominick Olivetto (January 6, 1907), James Osticco (April 22, 1913), or Armand Rava (January 7, 1911). One Web site claims that Osticco died from natural causes on June 15, 1990, but its dates for other gangland passings are frequently mistaken and the site offers no corroboration. Likewise, no records were discovered during research for this book concerning suspected delegates Vincenzo Colletti, Charles Montana, Antonio Polina, or Salavatore Trivalino (though one unsourced Web site claims that Trivalino "died peacefully in 1990").[83]

Conversely, *too many* death records exist for people by the names of four other confirmed or suspected Apalachin delegates. The Social Security Death Index contains no listing for a Dominick Alaimo born in January 1910, but three others, born between March 1916 and November 1920, died between October 1975 and March 2002. One Web site's claim that Alaimo died on August 10, 1985, also fails to match federal records.[84]

John DeMarco, 54 years old in 1957, has no record, but five others of that name are listed, born between December 1901 and June 1916, their deaths recorded between February 1970 and March 2007.[85]

Alleged Chicago *caporegime* Frank Ferarro, named as an Apalachin delegate on one Internet list, is otherwise untraceable — but eight Illinois residents bearing that name were born between March 1896 and April 1926. All died between November 1961 and May 2003.[86]

Two Internet lists of Apalachin visitors name Iowa mafioso Louis "Lew Farrell" Fratto, though his presence at the meeting remains unconfirmed. Mob historian Allan May writes that Fratto died in Madison, Wisconsin, on November 24, 1967, while awaiting trial on fraud and murder charges, but if so, the event escaped federal notice. According to the Social Security Death Index, no Lewis Fratto has ever died in the United States — but two Louis Farrells, born in July 1912 and April 1928, died in Illinois during November 1980 and May 1992, respectively.[87]

Thus ends the record of the mafiosi who who gathered in November 1957 to plot the future course of their "honored society." As with all mortals, they have passed — or will pass, in due time. As for the criminal society they served, despite predictions of its dissolution spanning nearly half a century, it still persists. In spite of state and federal prosecutions, internecine wars, and deadly competition from a host of new arrivals — Russians and Jamaicans, Japanese and Chinese, Cubans and Colombians — reports of the death of *La Cosa Nostra* have been exaggerated to the point of hopeful fantasy.

The Mafia endures.

Chapter Notes

Chapter 1

1. Hess, pp. 2–3; The American Mafia, http://onewal.com/maf-chr1.html (accessed Feb. 1, 2011).
2. Dickie, pp. 55–61; Peterson, p. 451.
3. "Mafia," New World Encyclopedia, http://www.newworldencyclopedia.org/entry/Mafia (accessed Feb. 3, 2011); Paoli, p. 24; Lupo, p. 49.
4. Dickie, pp. 26–33.
5. Behan, pp. 9–12.
6. "Raffaele Agnello," The American Mafia, http://onewal.com/w-agnell.html; "Joseph Macheca," The American Mafia, http://onewal.com/w-machec.html (both accessed Feb. 1, 2011).
7. Ibid.; Hunt and Sheldon, "America's First Mafia War."
8. Hunt and Sheldon.
9. "Giuseppe Esposito," The American Mafia, http://onewal.com/w-esposi.html; "Giuseppe Provenzano," The American Mafia, http://onewal.com/w-proven.html#giuseppe (both accessed Feb. 1, 2011).
10. "David C. Hennessy," The American Mafia, http://onewal.com/p-hennes.html (accessed Feb. 1, 2011).
11. "Chronology," The American Mafia, http://onewal.com/maf-chr1.html (accessed Feb. 1, 2011).
12. Persico, "Vendetta in New Orleans."
13. "Chronology," American Mafia, http://www.onewal.com/maf-chr1.html; "San Francisco crime family," Wikipedia, http://en.wikipedia.org/wiki/San_Francisco_crime_family#Francesco_Lanza (accessed Feb. 3, 2011); *The New York Times,* Jan. 2, 1892, pg. 1.
14. *The New York Times,* Nov. 11, 1890; May 5, 1891; and June 22, 1891.
15. "Chronology," American Mafia; "Patriarca crime family," Wikipedia, http://en.wikipedia.org/wiki/Patriarca_crime_family#Early_years (accessed Feb. 3, 2011).
16. *The New York Times,* March 6 and April 1, 1893.
17. *The New York Times,* June 20, 1893; "Trafficante crime family," Wikipedia, http://en.wikipedia.org/wiki/Trafficante_crime_family (accessed Feb. 4, 2011).
18. "Jim Colosimo," The American Mafia, http://www.onewal.com/w-colosi.html (accessed Feb. 3, 2011); "Unione Siciliane," Wikipedia, http://en.wikipedia.org/wiki/Unione_Siciliane (accessed Feb. 1, 2011).
19. "The Story of Italian Immigration," The American Immigration Law Foundation, http://www.ailf.org/awards/benefit2004/ahp04essay.asp (accessed Feb. 3, 2011).
20. *The New York Times,* March 28, 1891.
21. *The New York Times,* Oct. 22, 1888 and March 27, 1889; American Mafia, http://onewal.com/maf-chr1.html (accessed Feb. 1, 2011).
22. *The New York Times,* April 23, 1891.

23. The American Mafia, http://onewal.com/maf-chr1.html (accessed Feb. 1, 2011); "Morello crime family," Wikipedia, "'Clutch Hand Confusion," American Mafia, http://www.onewal.com/a005/f_clutchhandp02.html (accessed Feb. 4, 2011).

24. *The New York Times,* May 16, 1893.

25. *The New York Times,* May 22, 1893.

26. "The War between New York Gang Chiefs," Herbert Asbury.com, http://herbertasbury.com/BilltheButchertheGangsters/PaulKellyMonkEastman/tabid/199/Default.aspx (accessed Feb. 4, 2011).

27. *The New York Times,* May 23, 1894.

28. *The New York Times,* Dec. 21, 1894.

29. *The New York Times,* Jan. 17, 1896.

30. *The New York Times,* May 10, 1896.

31. *The New York Times,* Jan. 18, 1898.

32. "Ignazio Lupo," The American Mafia, http://onewal.com/w-lupo.html; "Giuseppe Balsamo," The American Mafia, http://onewal.com/w-balsam.html (both accessed Feb. 1, 2011).

Chapter 2

1. "The Black Hand," Gangrule.com, http://www.gangrule.com/gangs/the-black-hand (accessed Feb. 23, 2011).

2. *The New York Times,* March 5 and 26, 1910; Feb. 17, 1915.

3. *The New York Times,* Jan. 8, 1905.

4. *The New York Times,* April 12, 1908.

5. *The New York Times,* July 18, 1909.

6. "The Black Hand," Gangrule.com.

7. *The New York Times,* Jan. 8, 1905.

8. *The New York Times,* Sept. 13–14, 1905.

9. *The New York Times,* Sept. 26, 1905.

10. *The New York Times,* Nov. 10, 1905.

11. *The New York Times,* March 3, 1906.

12. *The New York Times,* Nov. 24, 1906.

13. *The New York Times,* Dec. 14, 1907.

14. *The New York Times,* March 25, 1908.

15. *The New York Times,* Sept. 10, 1908.

16. *The New York Times,* May 15, 1909.

17. *The New York Times,* Nov. 21, 1909.

18. *The New York Times,* Dec. 10, 1910.

19. *The New York Times,* July 19 and 25, 1911.

20. *The New York Times,* Aug. 1, 1915.

21. "Charles Matranga," The American Mafia, http://onewal.com/w-matran.html (accessed Feb. 233, 2011); *The New York Times,* June 18, 1908; July 14, 1910; April 26, 1909; July 3, 1911.

22. Maclean, pp. 59–60; "Angelo Genna," The American Mafia, http://onewal.com/w-genna.html (accessed Feb. 23, 2011).

23. Lombardo, pp. 396–7.

24. *The New York Times,* Nov. 20, 1907; Feb. 28, 1908; Maclean, p. 60.

25. *The New York Times,* June 20, 1909 and April 4, 1909; "Crime Bosses of Detroit," The American Mafia, http://onewal.com/maf-b-de.html (accessed Feb. 23, 2011); "Giovanni Vitale," Mafia Wiki, http://mafia.wikia.com/wiki/Giovanni_Vitale (accessed March 4, 2011).

26. "Crime Bosses of Cleveland," The American Mafia, http://onewal.com/maf-b-cl.html (accessed Feb. 23, 2011); "Cleveland Family," La Cosa Nostra Database, http://www.lacndb.com/php/Info.php?name=Family%20-%20Cleveland%20Family (accessed March 4, 2011).

27. *The New York Times,* June 9, 10, 13, 16, 18 and 19, 1909; Jan. 20 and 30, 1910.

28. *The New York Times,* Feb. 13, 1910; March 17, 1910; Aug. 9, 1912; June 8, 1913; Jan. 7, 1915.

29. "St. Louis Family," Rick Porrello's American Mafia, http://www.americanmafia.com/

Cities/St_Louis.html (accessed March 4, 2011); *The New York Times,* April 4, 1910; Dec. 24, 1910; May 1, 1914.

30. "Kansas City," Rick Porrello's American Mafia, http://www.americanmafia.com/cities/kansas_city.html (accessed March 4, 2011); "Patrolman Joseph Raimo," Officer Down Memorial Page, http://www.odmp.org/officer/10969-patrolman-joseph-raimo (accessed March 4, 2011); "Crime Bosses of Kansas City," The American Mafia, http://onewal.com/maf-b-kc.html (accessed Feb. 23, 2011).

31. *The New York Times,* Aug. 15, 1906; Jan. 19, 1908; March 17, 1909.

32. *The New York Times,* Aug. 31, 1904; Nov. 5, 1905; Feb. 23, 1908; June 14, 1909; Aug. 7, 1909; Jan. 4, 1912; May 24, 1914.

33. "New England Crime Bosses," The American Mafia, http://www.onewal.com/maf-b-ne.html (accessed March 4, 2011).

34. "Crime Bosses of Scranton/Pittson," The American Mafia, http://onewal.com/maf-b-sc.html (accessed Feb. 23, 2011); *The New York Times,* April 26, 1903.

35. "Salvatore Sabella," The American Mafia, http://onewal.com/w-sabell.html (accessed Feb. 23, 2011).

36. "Crime Bosses of Pittsburgh," The American Mafia, http://onewal.com/maf-b-pi.html (accessed Feb. 23, 2011).

37. *The New York Times,* Jan. 15, 1905; May 23, 1905; Jan. 26, 1906; Feb. 25, 1906; May 12, 1907; Aug. 4, 11 and 12, 1907; Sept. 23, 1907; Dec. 10, 1907; Jan. 11, 1908; Feb. 6, 1908; Jan. 20, 1909; April 11, 1910.

38. *The New York Times,* Aug. 21, 1904; April 30, 1906; Feb. 9, 1907; Jan. 20, 1908; May 7 and 11, 1908.

39. The American Mafia, http://onewal.com/maf-chr2.html (accessed Feb. 23, 2011); "LoMonte Brothers," The American Mafia, http://onewal.com/maf-b-ny.html (accessed Feb. 23, 2011).

40. The American Mafia, http://onewal.com/maf-chr2.html; "Joe Catania," The American Mafia, http://www.onewal.com/w-catani.html (accessed March 5, 2011).

41. "New York City Police Department," Bomb Technician Memorial Foundation, http://www.rspservices.com/petrosino.htm (accessed March 5, 2011); "Lt. Joseph Petrosino Murder," GangRule.com, http://www.gangrule.com/events/petrosino-murder-1909 (accessed March 5, 2011); *The New York Times,* Oct. 18, 1905; Dec. 20, 1906; Jan. 25, 1908.

42. "Lt. Joseph Petrosino Murder," GangRule.com.

43. The American Mafia, http://onewal.com/maf-chr2.html; *The New York Times,* Oct. 25, 1906; Dec. 28 and 30, 1906; April 30, 1907; April 2, 1908; Sept. 13, 1913.

44. The American Mafia, http://onewal.com/maf-chr2.html; "Lt. Joseph Petrosino Murder," GangRule.com.

45. "Lt. Joseph Petrosino Murder," GangRule.com; *The New York Times,* March 14, 1909; May 2 and 13, 1909; June 10 and 11, 1909; Aug. 7, 1909; Aug. 19, 1913; Sept. 12, 1913.

46. *The New York Times,* Sept. 24, 1911; Sept. 15, 1910; April 15, 1909; May 18 and 19, 1909; June 11 and 30, 1909; July 10 and 17, 1909; Sept. 8, 1909; Jan. 23, 1910; Oct. 10, 1910; Dec. 13, 1910; March 3, 1911; April 7, 1911; Sept. 4, 1911; Dec. 31, 1911; April 15, 1912; Feb. 28, 1913; March 22, 1913; Oct. 5 and 13, 1913; Dec. 13, 1913; Nov. 13 and 23, 1914; Sept. 10, 1915.

47. "Crime Bosses of Buffalo/Niagara Falls," The American Mafia, http://onewal.com/maf-b-bu.html (accessed Feb. 23, 2011).

48. The American Mafia, http://onewal.com/maf-chr2.html; *The New York Times,* April 18, 1903; May 8, 1903; Nov. 13, 16 and 22, 1909; Feb. 20, 1910; April 3, 1910; Dec. 31, 1911.

49. "Giuseppe Masseria," The American Mafia, http://www.onewal.com/w-masser.html (accessed March 7, 2011); *The New York Times,* May 9, 1922.

50. "The Struggle for Control," GangRule.com, http://www.gangrule.com/events/struggle-for-control-1914-1918 (accessed Feb. 23, 2011); *The New York Times,* May 24, 1914.

51. "The Struggle for Control," GangRule.com; "LoMonte Brothers," The American Mafia, http://www.onewal.com/w-lomont.html (accessed Oct. 26, 2011.)

52. "The Struggle for Control," GangRule.com.

53. Ibid.; *The New York Times,* Nov. 28, 1917; Dec. 1, 1917.

Chapter 3

1. Thomas Slaughter, *The Whiskey Rebellion: Frontier Epilogue to the American Revolution* (New York: Oxford University Press, 1986); John L. Merrill, "The Bible and the American Temperance Movement: Text, context and pretext," *Harvard Theological Review* 81 (1988): 147; Jed Dannenbaum, "The Origins of Temperance Activism and Militancy among American Women," *Journal of Social History* 14 (1981): 235–36.

2. Merz, pp. 14, 20, 26–7, 40–1.

3. *The New York Times,* Dec. 19, 1917; David Pietrusza, *1920: The Year of Six Presidents* (New York: Carroll & Graf, 2007), p. 160.

4. Charles Towne, *The Rise and Fall of Prohibition: The Human Side of What the Eighteenth Amendment Has Done to the United States* (New York: Macmillan, 1923), pp. 159–162; Deborah Blum, "The Chemist's War: The little-told story of how the U.S. government poisoned alcohol during Prohibition with deadly consequences," *Slate,* http://www.slate.com/id/2245188 (accessed March 10, 2011).

5. Newton, p. 24; Helmer and Mattix, pp. 65, 292–303.

6. Newton, pp. 16–17.

7. "Sylvestro Carolla," The American Mafia, http://onewal.com/w-caroll.html (accessed March 8, 2011).

8. "Crime Bosses of Los Angeles," American Mafia, http://www.onewal.com/maf-b-la.html.

9. "Crime Bosses of Cleveland," American Mafia, http://www.onewal.com/maf-b-cl.html; Newton, pp. 32–41.

10. "Crime Bosses of Kansas City," American Mafia, http://www.onewal.com/maf-b-kc.html.

11. "Crime Bosses of Detroit," The American Mafia, http://onewal.com/maf-b-de.html (accessed March 8, 2011).

12. "Crime Bosses of New England," American Mafia, http://www.onewal.com/maf-b-ne.html.

13. "Crime Bosses of Pittsburgh," American Mafia; "Crime Bosses of Scranton/Pittston," American Mafia, http://www.onewal.com/maf-b-pi.html; http://www.onewal.com/maf-b-sc.html.

14. "Crime Bosses of Philadelphia," American Mafia, http://www.onewal.com/maf-b-ph.html.

15. "Stefano Magaddino," The American Mafia, http://www.onewal.com/w-magadd.html (accessed March 12, 2011); Allan May, "Waxey Gordon's Half Century of Crime," *Crime Magazine,* http://crimemagazine.com/waxey-gordon%e2%80%99s-half-century-crime?page=1 (accessed March 12, 2001); "Abner Zwillman," FBI File No. 62-36085.

16. Maclean, pp. 71–2, 121.

17. "Crime Bosses of Chicago," American Mafia, http://wwwlonewal.com/maf-b-ch.html.

18. Messick and Goldblatt, p. 58; Helmer and Mattix, pp. 83, 86.

19. Helmer and Mattix, pp. 86–9, 99, 118–23.

20. Ibid., pp. 102–5, 114, 122; The American Mafia, http://onewal.com/maf-chr3.html.

21. Maclean, p. 69; Hammer, pp. 69–80.

22. Hammer, pp. 69–80.

23. *The New York Times,* Oct. 11, 1928; Dec. 30, 1920; May 9, 1922; Aug. 10 and 12, 1922.

24. "Salvatore Maranzano," The American Mafia, http://www.onewal.com/w-maranz.html (accessed March 8, 2011).

25. Peterson, pp. 156–7.

26. Jack McPhaul, *Johnny Torrio: The First of the Gang Lords* (New York: Arlington House, 1970), pp. 235–6.

27. Maclean, pp. 155–6; Messick and Goldblatt, pp. 105–6; Peterson, pp. 158–9.

28. Ibid.; *The New York Times,* May 16, 1929.

29. Raab, *Five Families,* pp. 26–34; Newton, p. 46.

30. Ibid.; The American Mafia, http://onewal.com/maf-chr3.html.

31. Raab, pp. 26–34; *The New York Times,* Feb. 23, 1931.

32. Helmer and Mattix, p. 168.

33. Raab, pp. 26–34.

34. Ibid.

35. Messick and Goldblatt, pp. 106–12.

Chapter 4

1. Hammer, pp. 117–19; Newton, pp. 51–2; Helmer and Mattix, p. 175.

2. Messick and Goldblatt, pp. 127–32.

3. Hammer, pp. 150–3; Messick and Goldblatt, pp. 125–7; Newton, pp. 73–4.

4. Hammer, pp. 125–30; Messick and Goldblatt, pp. 115–17.

5. Newton, pp. 59–60.

6. Ibid., pp. 62–6; Hammer, pp. 130–3; Messick and Goldblatt, pp. 119–25.

7. Messick and Goldblatt, p. 137; Hammer, pp. 149–50.

8. *The New York Times,* July 24, 1930; Dec. 20, 1930; March 13, 1931; Oct. 18, 1931; Jan. 15, 1933; June 28, 1933.

9. *The New York Times,* Nov. 21, 1930; Sept. 5, 1931; Nov. 26, 1931; April 26, 1932; May 22, 1932; Dec. 22, 1932; Feb. 4, 1933.

10. Raab, pp. 87–8; "A Brief History of the FBI," Federal Bureau of Investigation, http://www.fbi.gov/about-us/history/brief-history (accessed March 18, 2011).

11. Whitehead, pp. 83–4; Messick, pp. 83–4; Summers, pp. 259–60; Lowenthal, pp. 19–20.

12. Summers, p. 260; Nash, p. 86.

13. Deloach, p. 298; Davis, p. 96.

14. Ungar, pp. 392–3; Gentry, pp. 327–9; Summers, pp. 275–85.

15. Messick, pp. 144–8; Hack, p. 285; Summers, pp. 265, 267, 272–6; Gentry, p. 329.

16. Raab, p. 90; Fox, *Blood and Power,* pp. 139–46; *The New York Times,* Aug. 26–27, 1939.

17. Hammer, pp. 140–2; Newton, pp. 92–3.

18. Allan May, "The Guileless Gangster," *Crime Magazine,* http://crimemagazine.com/guileless-gangster (accessed March 19, 2011).

19. Ibid.; Folsom, "The Big Pardon"; Gentry, pp. 334–5.

20. Fox, pp. 158–60; Allan May, "The Wexler/Gordon Story," Rick Porrello's American Mafia, http://www.americanmafia.com/Allan_May_7-12-99.html (accessed March 19, 2011); *The New York Times,* July 4, 1933.

21. Hammer, pp. 153–63; Messick and Goldblatt, pp. 137–8.

23. *The New York Times,* April 3, 1936; April 12, 17 and 18, 1936; May 12 and 29, 1936; June 8 and 19, 1936; Hammer, pp. 171–4.

24. *The New York Times,* July 12, 1936; Nov. 13, 1936; Nov. 21, 1937; Feb. 17, 1938; April 15, 1938; Aug. 25, 1939; Dec. 21, 1939; Jan. 3, 1940; March 2, 1940; April 6, 1940.

25. *The New York Times,* Feb. 3, 1940; March 24, 1940; April 14, 1940; May 16, 1940; June 4, 1940; Sept. 17, 1940.

26. *The New York Times,* May 9, 1940; Sept. 12 and 13, 1940; "Murder Inc: The Trials," Museum of Learning, http://www.museumstuff.com/learn/topics/Murder_Inc.::sub::The_Trials (accessed March 19, 2011).

27. *The New York Times,* Sept. 23, 1941; Nov. 13–14, 1941; Dec. 8, 1945; Feb. 21, 1942; Raab, p. 73.

28. Hammer, pp. 203–4.

29. Ibid., pp. 204–7.

30. Ibid.; Raab, pp. 76–8; *The New York Times,* Nov. 12, 1942; Jan. 13 and 30, 1943.

31. Hammer, pp. 207–9.

32. Ibid., pp. 212–17; *The New York Times,* Nov. 25, 1944; June 3, 1945; June 11, 1946.

33. Jones, "Lucky's Luck."

34. Ibid.

35. *The New York Times,* Oct. 31, 1945; Nov. 1, 4, 15 and 17, 1945; Dec. 21–22, 1945; Feb. 7, 1946; April 7, 1946; Nov. 25, 1964.

36. Allan May, "Havana Conference — 1946," *Crime Magazine,* http://crimemagazine.com/havana-conference-%E2%80%93-1946 (accessed March 20, 2011).

37. Ibid.

38. Ibid.

39. Ibid.

40. Ibid.; Charles Siragusa, *The Trail of the Poppy* (Englewood Cliffs, N.J.: Prentice-Hall, 1966), pp. 181–9.

41. Newton, pp. 120–4.

42. May, "Havana Conference."

43. *The New York Times,* Feb. 22–23, 1947; March 20, 1947; April 13, 1947; May 15, 1947.

44. Gentry, pp. 330–3; Deloach, p. 303.

45. "Bugsy Siegel and the Flamingo Hotel," Online Nevada Encyclopedia, http://www.on-linenevada.org/Bugsy_Siegel_and_the_Flamingo_Hotel (accessed March 20, 2011).

46. Hammer, pp. 224–5.

Chapter 5

1. *The New York Times,* Dec. 22, 1948; Sept. 21–23, 1949; Oct. 24, 1949; Dec. 3, 1949; Jan. 15, 1950.

2. *The New York Times,* Feb. 3, 1949; Aug. 16, 1949; Oct. 20, 1949; Dec. 23, 1949; Jan. 17, 1950.

3. "Carey Estes Kefauver," Biographical Directory of the United States Congress, http://bioguide.congress.gov/scripts/biodisplay.pl?index=K000044 (accessed March 22, 2011).

4. Newton, pp. 140–1.

5. Ibid., p. 141.

6. Ibid.; Frank Shanty, *Organized Crime: From Trafficking to Terrorism.* (Santa Barbara, CA: ABC-CLIO, 2008), p. 22; Fox, p. 337; Summers, p. 263.

7. Denton and Morris, pp. 118–21.

8. Kefauver, *First Interim Report,* p. 2; *Second Interim Report,* pp. 2–3; *Third Interim Report,* pp. 145, 147.

9. Kefauver, *Final Report,* pp. 6–12, 88–95.

10. Ibid., pp. 88–95.

11. Ibid., pp. 96–98; "Contempt," New Criminologist, http://www.newcriminologist.com/article.asp?nid=754 (accessed March 21, 2011).

12. The American Mafia, http://www.onewal.com/maf-chr5.html (accessed March 21, 2011).

13. *The New York Times,* Dec. 14, 1952; "Investigations: After Kefauver," *Time* (April 9, 1951), http://www.time.com/time/magazine/article/0,9171,814574,00.html (accessed March 21, 2011); "Investigations: Texas Pleasure Dome," *Time* (July 9, 1951), http://www.time.com/time/magazine/article/0,9171,806096,00.html (accessed March 21, 2011); David Humphrey, "Prostitution," The Handbook of Texas Online, http://www.tshaonline.org/handbook/online/articles/jbp01 (accessed March 26, 2011).

14. "Investigations: After Kefauver"; *The New York Times,* March 28–31, 1951; Sept. 9, 1953.

15. "Investigations: After Kefauver"; *The New York Times,* Dec. 13, 1951; May 17, 1953; Dec. 20, 1952; Sept. 30, 1953; March 11, 1954; April 15 and 26, 1954; Nov. 21, 1954; May 3 and 24, 1955; June 4, 1955; Sept. 20, 1955.

16. *The New York Times,* May 20, 22, 29 and 30, 1951; Feb. 17, 18 and 21, 1953; April 3 and 25, 1953; June 3, 16, 17 and 25, 1953; Aug. 6, 1953; Dec. 18, 1953; Jan. 4, 1956.

17. "Investigations: After Kefauver"; *The New York Times,* March 12, 1953; May 14 and 18, 1954; Dec. 2, 1954.

18. *The New York Times,* Nov. 22, 1952; Dec. 10, 1952; March 3, 11 and 13, 1953; Aug. 26, 1953; May 19, 1955; Dec. 14, 1957.

19. *The New York Times,* Jan. 2, 1955; Joe Allen, "RFK and Hollywood Mythmaking," Counterpunch, http://www.counterpunch.com/allen12022006.html (accessed March 26, 2011).

20. Fox, pp. 321–3; *The New York Times,* June 2, 3, 8, 29 and 30, 1956.

21. *The New York Times,* Jan. 17–31, 1957; Feb. 7, 17, 18, 20, 27 and 28, 1957; May 26, 1957; Nov. 1, 1957; Dec. 7, 1957; Feb. 21, 1958; Feb. 28, 1959.

22. Fox, pp. 321, 323; *The New York Times,* Sept. 5, 1957; Jan. 11, 12, 23, and 28, 1958; Feb. 1 and 7, 1958; March 21, 1958; July 16, 18, 20 and 22, 1958; Oct. 25, 1959.

23. Fox, pp. 323, 325–6.

Chapter 6

1. The American Mafia, http://www.onewal.com/maf-chr5.html (accessed March 21, 2011); Fox, p. 327.

2. The American Mafia, http://www.onewal.com/maf-chr5.html; Jon Hopwood, "Albert Anastasia: 'Lord High Executioner' of Murder, Inc.," Yahoo! Contributor Network, http://www.associatedcontent.com/article/1328898/albert_anastasia_lord_high_executioner.html?cat=37 (accessed March 28, 2011).

3. Raab, p. 102; Davis, pp. 74–5.

4. Newton, pp. 169–70.

5. Ibid., p. 170.

6. *The New York Times,* May 3–10 and 23, 1957; June 12, 1957.

7. *The New York Times,* June 18, 1957; Aug. 20–24, 1957; Sept. 17 and 19, 1957.

8. Davis, p. 103; Raab, p. 110.

9. Joe Bonanno, *A Man of Honor* (New York: St. Martin's, 1983), pp. 196–201.

10. *The New York Times,* Jan. 2, 1968; Gaia Servadio, *Mafioso: A History of the Mafia from Its Origins to the Present Day,* (London: Secker & Warburg, 1976), p. 189.

11. Raab, pp, 112–13.

12. Diego Gambetta, *The Sicilian Mafia* (Cambridge, MA: Harvard University Press, 1996), pp. 112–16.

13. Raab, p. 113.

14. Davis, pp. 75–84; *The New York Times,* Dec. 12, 1957.

15. Newton, p. 170.

16. Ibid., pp. 170–1; Raab, p. 116; *The New York Times,* Oct. 26–27, 1957.

17. *The New York Times,* Oct. 30, 1957; Nov. 2, 1957.

18. Raab, p. 116.

19. Newton, p. 170.

Chapter 7

1. Fox, p. 327; The American Mafia, http://www.onewal.com/maf-chr5.html (accessed March 21, 2011).

2. Kelly, "How America Met the Mob"; "Mob Meeting at Apalachin: The Big Barbeque," Gangsters Inc., http://gangstersinc.ning.com/profiles/blogs/mob-meeting-at-apalachin-the (accessed Jan. 19, 2011); "The Apalachin Meeting," *Ovi Magazine*; Hudson.

3. "Apalachin, New York," Wikipedia, http://en.wikipedia.org/wiki/Apalachin,_New_York (accessed March 5, 2011); La Sorte, "The Mob on the Nob"; Kelly.

4. U.S. Census Bureau; Hafer.

5. "Joseph Barbara," American Mafia; "Joseph Barbara (mobster)," Wikipedia, http://en.wikipedia.org/wiki/Joseph_Barbara_(mobster) (accessed Jan. 9, 2011); Hafer; *The New York Times,* Nov. 17, 1957.

6. "John Sciandra," Wikipedia, http://en.wikipedia.org/wiki/John_Sciandra (accessed April 23, 2011); "Joseph Barbara (mobster)"; Hafer; Kelly.

7. Hafer; "Joseph Barbara (mobster)"; Kelly.

8. "Joseph Barbara (mobster)."

9. "Apalachin Meeting," Wikipedia, http://en.wikipedia.org/wiki/Apalachin_Meeting (accessed Jan. 8, 2011); Hafer.

10. "Apalachin Meeting," Wikipedia.

11. Ibid.; "French Connection," Wikipedia, http://en.wikipedia.org/wiki/French_Connection (accessed April 24, 2011).

12. "Apalachin Meeting," Wikipedia; "Labor Slugger Wars," Wikipedia, http://en.wikipedia.org/wiki/Labor_Slugger_Wars (accessed April 24, 2011); "Tommy Lucchese," Wikipedia, http://en.wikipedia.org/wiki/Tommy_Lucchese (accessed April 24, 2011).

13. *The New York Times,* Nov. 16, 1957; Jan. 10, 1958; "Apalachin Meeting," Wikipedia; Hafer; La Sorte, "Attendee Profiles at the 1957 Apalachin Mob Confab"; "Mobsters at the Apalachin Mob Meeting"; "Mob Meeting at Apalachin: The Big Barbeque."

14. *The New York Times,* Nov. 16, 1957; Hafer; La Sorte, "Attendee Profiles"; "Mobsters at the Apalachin Mob Meeting"; "Mob Meeting at Apalachin: The Big Barbeque."

15. "Apalachin Meeting," Wikipedia; "Salvatore Trivalino," Mafia Wiki, http://mafia.wikia.com/wiki/Salvatore_Trivalino, (accessed April 20, 2011); La Sorte, "The Mob on the Nob"; *United States Department of Justice, et al., Petitioners v. Reporters Committee for Freedom of the Press, et al.* No. 87-1379 In the Supreme Court of the United States, October Term, 1987; "Nomenclature of the Assassination Cabal," http://scribblguy.50megs.com/torbitt45.htm (accessed April 20, 2011).

16. *The New York Times,* Nov. 16, 1957; "Apalachin Meeting," Wikipedia; Hafer; La Sorte, "Attendee Profiles"; La Sorte, "The Mob on the Nob"; "Mob Meeting at Apalachin: The Big Barbeque"; "Mobsters at the Apalachin Mob Meeting."

17. *The New York Times,* Nov. 16, 1957; "Apalachin Meeting," Wikipedia; Hafer; La Sorte, "Attendee Profiles"; La Sorte, "The Mob on the Nob"; "Mob Meeting at Apalachin: The Big Barbeque"; "Mobsters at the Apalachin Mob Meeting"; "Joseph Biondo," Wikipedia, http://en.wikipedia.org/wiki/Joseph_Biondo (accessed Jan. 9, 2011); "Aniello Migliore," Wikipedia, http://en.wikipedia.org/wiki/Aniello_Migliore (accessed Jan. 9, 2011).

18. *The New York Times,* Nov. 16, 1957; "Apalachin Meeting," Wikipedia; Hafer; La Sorte, "Attendee Profiles"; La Sorte, "The Mob on the Nob"; "Mob Meeting at Apalachin: The Big Barbeque"; "Mobsters at the Apalachin Mob Meeting."

19. *The New York Times,* Nov. 16, 1957; "Apalachin Meeting," Wikipedia; Hafer; La Sorte, "Attendee Profiles"; La Sorte, "The Mob on the Nob"; "Mob Meeting at Apalachin: The Big Barbeque"; "Mobsters at the Apalachin Mob Meeting."

20. *The New York Times,* Nov. 16, 1957; "Apalachin Meeting," Wikipedia; Hafer; La Sorte, "Attendee Profiles"; La Sorte, "The Mob on the Nob"; "Mob Meeting at Apalachin: The Big Barbeque"; "Mobsters at the Apalachin Mob Meeting"; "Joe Profaci," Wikipedia, http://en.wikipedia.org/wiki/Joseph_Profaci (accessed Jan. 9, 2011); "Joseph Magliocco," Wikipedia, http://en.wikipedia.org/wiki/Joseph_Magliocco (accessed Jan. 9, 2011).

21. *The New York Times,* Nov. 16, 1957; "Apalachin Meeting," Wikipedia; Hafer; La Sorte, "Attendee Profiles"; La Sorte, "The Mob on the Nob"; "Mob Meeting at Apalachin: The Big Barbeque"; "Mobsters at the Apalachin Mob Meeting"; "Stefano Magaddino," Wikipedia, http://en.wikipedia.org/wiki/Stefano_Magaddino (accessed Jan. 9, 2011); "John C. Montana," Wikipedia, http://en.wikipedia.org/wiki/John_C._Montana (accessed Jan. 9, 2011).

22. *The New York Times,* Nov. 16, 1957; "Apalachin Meeting," Wikipedia; Hafer; La Sorte, "Attendee Profiles"; La Sorte, "The Mob on the Nob"; "Mob Meeting at Apalachin: The Big Barbeque"; "Mobsters at the Apalachin Mob Meeting"; "Antonio Magaddino," La Cosa Nostra Database, http://www.lacndb.com/php/Info.php?name=Antonio%20Magaddino (accessed April 20, 2011); "Rosario Carlisi," La Cosa Nostra Database, http://lacndb.com/Info.php?name=Rosario%20Carlisi (April 2, 2011).

23. *The New York Times,* Nov. 16, 1957; "Apalachin Meeting," Wikipedia; Hafer; La Sorte, "Attendee Profiles"; La Sorte, "The Mob on the Nob"; "Mob Meeting at Apalachin: The Big Barbeque"; "Mobsters at the Apalachin Mob Meeting"; "DeCavalcante Crime Family," Wikipedia, http://en.wikipedia.org/wiki/DeCavalcante_crime_family#Beginnings (accessed April 25, 2011).

24. *The New York Times,* Nov. 16, 1957; "Apalachin Meeting," Wikipedia; Hafer; La Sorte, "Attendee Profiles"; La Sorte, "The Mob on the Nob"; "Mob Meeting at Apalachin: The Big Barbeque"; "Mobsters at the Apalachin Mob Meeting."

25. *The New York Times,* Nov. 16, 1957; "Apalachin Meeting," Wikipedia; Hafer; La Sorte, "Attendee Profiles"; La Sorte, "The Mob on the Nob"; "Mob Meeting at Apalachin: The Big Barbeque"; "Mobsters at the Apalachin Mob Meeting"; "John Sebastian Larocca," Wikipedia, http://en.wikipedia.org/wiki/John_Sebastian_LaRocca (accessed Jan. 9, 2011); "Michael James Genovese," Wikipedia, http://en.wikipedia.org/wiki/Michael_Genovese (accessed Jan. 9, 2011); *The Morning Call* (Allentown, PA), Nov. 1, 1988.

26. *The New York Times,* Nov. 16, 1957; "Apalachin Meeting," Wikipedia; Hafer; La Sorte, "Attendee Profiles"; La Sorte, "The Mob on the Nob"; "Mob Meeting at Apalachin: The Big Barbeque"; "Mobsters at the Apalachin Mob Meeting."

27. Newton, p. 71; *The New York Times,* Nov. 16, 1957; "Apalachin Meeting," Wikipedia; Hafer; La Sorte, "Attendee Profiles"; La Sorte, "The Mob on the Nob"; "Mob Meeting at Apalachin: The Big Barbeque"; "Mobsters at the Apalachin Mob Meeting"; "John T. Scalish," Wikipedia, http://en.wikipedia.org/wiki/John_T._Scalish (accessed Jan. 9, 2011).

28. "Apalachin Meeting," Wikipedia; Hafer; "Mobsters at the Apalachin Mob Meeting"; La Sorte, "The Mob on the Nob"; "Mob Meeting at Apalachin: The Big Barbeque"; "Joseph Zerilli," Wikipedia, http://en.wikipedia.org/wiki/Joseph_Zerilli (accessed Jan. 9, 2011).

29. "Apalachin Meeting," Wikipedia; La Sorte, "The Mob on the Nob"; "Mob Meeting at Apalachin: The Big Barbeque"; "Sam Giancana," Wikipedia, http://en.wikipedia.org/wiki/Salvatore_Giancana (accessed Jan. 9, 2011); "The Chicago Outfit," La Cosa Nostra, http://mafiasite.8m.com/chicago.htm (accessed April 20, 2011).

30. *The New York Times,* Nov. 16, 1957; "Apalachin Meeting," Wikipedia; Hafer; La Sorte, "Attendee Profiles"; La Sorte, "The Mob on the Nob"; "Mob Meeting at Apalachin: The Big Barbeque"; "Mobsters at the Apalachin Mob Meeting"; "Frank Zito," Wikipedia, http://en.wikipedia.org/wiki/Frank_Zito (accessed Jan. 9, 2011); "The Rockford Family," http://members.fortunecity.com/sosdie/mob/family/rockford/rockford.htm (accessed April 26, 2011).

31. "Apalachin Meeting," Wikipedia; La Sorte, "The Mob on the Nob"; "Mob Meeting at Apalachin: The Big Barbeque"; "Milwaukee crime family," Wikipedia, http://en.wikipedia.org/wiki/Milwaukee_crime_family (accessed April 26, 2011); "Frank Balistrieri," Wikipedia, http://en.wikipedia.org/wiki/Frank_Balistrieri (accessed Jan. 9, 2011).

32. "Apalachin Meeting," Wikipedia; La Sorte, "The Mob on the Nob"; "John Vitale," Mafia Wiki, http://mafia.wikia.com/wiki/John_Vitale (accessed April 20, 2011).

33. *The New York Times,* Nov. 16, 1957; "Apalachin Meeting," Wikipedia; Hafer; La Sorte, "Attendee Profiles"; La Sorte, "The Mob on the Nob"; "Mob Meeting at Apalachin: The Big Barbeque"; "Mobsters at the Apalachin Mob Meeting"; "Nicholas Civella," Wikipedia, http://en.wikipedia.org/wiki/Nicholas_Civella (accessed Jan. 9, 2011).

34. "Apalachin Meeting," Wikipedia; "Louis Fratto," Wikipedia, http://en.wikipedia.org/wiki/Louis_Fratto (accessed Jan. 9, 2011).

35. *The New York Times,* Nov. 16, 1957; "Apalachin Meeting," Wikipedia; Hafer; La Sorte, "Attendee Profiles"; La Sorte, "The Mob on the Nob"; "Mob Meeting at Apalachin: The Big Barbeque"; "Mobsters at the Apalachin Mob Meeting"; "Santo Trafficante, Jr.," Wikipedia, http://en.wikipedia.org/wiki/Santo_Trafficante_Jr. (accessed Jan. 9, 2011).

36. La Sorte, "The Mob on the Nob"; "Carlos Marcello," Wikipedia, http://en.wikipedia.org/wiki/Carlos_Marcello (accessed April 26, 2011).

37. *The New York Times,* Nov. 16, 1957; "Apalachin Meeting," Wikipedia; Hafer; La Sorte, "Attendee Profiles"; La Sorte, "The Mob on the Nob"; "Mob Meeting at Apalachin: The Big Barbeque"; "Mobsters at the Apalachin Mob Meeting"; "Dallas crime family," Wikipedia, http://en.wikipedia.org/wiki/Dallas_crime_family (accessed April 27, 2011); "Joseph Civello," Wikipedia, http://en.wikipedia.org/wiki/Joseph_Civello (accessed Jan. 9, 2011); "Joseph Campisi," Wikipedia, http://en.wikipedia.org/wiki/Joseph_Campisi (accessed Jan. 9, 2011).

38. *The New York Times,* Nov. 16, 1957; "Apalachin Meeting," Wikipedia; Hafer; La Sorte, "Attendee Profiles"; La Sorte, "The Mob on the Nob"; "Mob Meeting at Apalachin: The Big Barbeque"; "Mobsters at the Apalachin Mob Meeting"; Mario Machi, Allan May and Charlie Molino, "Denver, Colorado," Rick Porrello's American Mafia, http://www.americanmafia.com/Cities/Denver.html (accessed April 27, 2011).

39. *The New York Times,* Nov. 16, 1957; "Apalachin Meeting," Wikipedia; Hafer; La Sorte,

"Attendee Profiles"; La Sorte, "The Mob on the Nob"; "Mob Meeting at Apalachin: The Big Barbeque"; "Mobsters at the Apalachin Mob Meeting"; "Frank DeSimone," Wikipedia, http://en.wikipedia.org/wiki/Frank_DeSimone (accessed Jan. 9, 2011); "Simone Scozzari," Wikipedia, http://en.wikipedia.org/wiki/Simone_Scozzari (accessed Jan. 9, 2011).

40. "Apalachin Meeting," Wikipedia; Hafer; La Sorte, "Attendee Profiles"; La Sorte, "The Mob on the Nob"; "Mob Meeting at Apalachin: The Big Barbeque"; "Mobsters at the Apalachin Mob Meeting"; "San Francisco crime family," Wikipedia, http://en.wikipedia.org/wiki/San_Francisco_crime_family (accessed April 27, 2011).

41. "Apalachin Meeting," Wikipedia; La Sorte, "Attendee Profiles"; La Sorte, "The Mob on the Nob; "Mob Meeting at Apalachin: The Big Barbeque"; Jay Ambler, "San Jose, CA," Rick Porrello's American Mafia, http://www.americanmafia.com/Cities/San_Jose.html (accessed April 27, 2011); "Joseph Cerrito," Mafia Wiki, http://mafia.wikia.com/wiki/Joseph_Cerrito (accessed April 27, 2011).

42. "Apalachin Meeting," Wikipedia; La Sorte, "The Mob on the Nob"; "Mob Meeting at Apalachin: The Big Barbeque"; "Giuseppe Cotroni," Mafia Wiki, http://mafia.wikia.com/wiki/Giuseppe_Cotroni (accessed April 9, 2011).

43. "Apalachin Meeting," Wikipedia; La Sorte, "The Mob on the Nob"; "Mob Meeting at Apalachin: The Big Barbeque"; "Giuseppe Settecase," La Cosa Nostra Database, http://www.lacndb.com/php/Si_Info.php?name=Giuseppe%20Settecase (accessed April 9, 2011).

Chapter 8

1. "Weather History for Apalachin, New York," The Old Farmer's Almanac, http://www.almanac.com/weather/history/NY/Apalachin/1957-11-13 (accessed April 30, 2011).

2. The New York Times, Nov. 3, 1959; Kelly.

3. Social Security Death Index; "The Apalachin Meeting," Ovi Magazine; "Mob Meeting at Apalachin: The Big Barbecue."

4. "The Apalachin Meeting," Ovi Magazine; Hafer; Kelly; "Mob Meeting at Apalachin: The Big Barbecue."

5. "The Apalachin Meeting," Ovi Magazine; "Apalachin Meeting," Wikipedia; Hudson; "Mob Meeting at Apalachin: The Big Barbecue."

6. "The Apalachin Meeting," Ovi Magazine; Hafer; Kelly; "Mob Meeting at Apalachin: The Big Barbecue."

7. Hafer; Kelly; "Mob Meeting at Apalachin: The Big Barbecue."

8. "Weather History for Apalachin, New York"; Kelly.

9. Kelly; The New York Times, Nov. 15, 1957.

10. Hudson; "Apalachin Meeting," Wikipedia; Kelly; La Sorte, "Mob on the Nob"; Hafer.

11. Hafer; Hudson.

12. Kelly; The New York Times, Nov. 15, 1957.

13. "The Apalachin Meeting," Ovi Magazine; Hafer; Tuohy.

14. The New York Times, Nov. 15, 1957; Kelly; Hudson.

15. The New York Times, Nov. 16, 1957; "Apalachin Meeting," Wikipedia.

16. The New York Times, Nov. 15–16, 1957; Jan. 10, 1958.

17. The New York Times, Nov. 16, 1957.

18. Bonanno, A Man of Honor, pp. 215–16; Kelly.

19. Kelly.

20. The New York Times, Jan. 10, 1958; "Apalachin Meeting," Wikipedia; Hafer; La Sorte, "Mob on the Nob"; "Mob Meeting at Apalachin: The Big Barbecue."

21. The New York Times, Nov. 16, 1957; "Apalachin Meeting," Wikipedia; Hafer; La Sorte, "Mob on the Nob"; "Mob Meeting at Apalachin: The Big Barbecue."

22. The New York Times, Nov. 16, 1957.

23. Hudson; Kelly; "Mob Meeting at Apalachin: The Big Barbecue."

24. Hudson; Kelly.

25. English, Paddy Whacked, pp. 276–7; Davis, p. 91.

26. Davis, p. 91.

27. Ibid., pp. 91–2.
28. Messick, pp. 168–9; La Sorte, "Mob on the Nob"; Tuohy.

Chapter 9

1. Kelly.
2. Bonanno, *A Man of Honor,* p. 208; Hudson.
3. Tuohy.
4. Peter Maas, *The Valachi Papers* (New York: Harper Paperbacks, 2003), p. 238.
5. Thom Jones, "Death in the Afternoon," Mob Corner, http://realdealmafia.com/mob corner_galante2.html (accessed May 6, 2011); *Investigation of Improper Activities in the Labor or Management Field, Part 32* (hereafter "McClellan Report"), p. 12201.
6. *The New York Times,* Nov. 16–20, 1957; Dec. 4 and 22, 1957; Jan. 12, 1958; Nov. 14, 1958; April 5, 1959.
7. Gentry, p. 453.
8. *The New York Times,* Sept. 20, 1957; October 21, 1957.
9. Theoharis, p. 316; Gentry pp. 453–4.
10. Theoharis, p. 346; Gentry pp. 451–2; Summers, pp. 285–91.
11. Gentry, p. 454.
12. Ibid.; Theoharis, pp. 354–5.
13. Ungar, pp. 394–5; Theoharis, p. 212.
14. Gentry, p. 455; Hack, p. 303; Kessler, p. 103; Raab, pp. 120–2; Russo, p. 330; Theoharis, pp. 35–6; Ungar, pp. 393–5.
15. "Timeline of FBI History," Federal Bureau of Investigation, http://www2.fbi.gov/lib ref/historic/history/historicdates.htm (accessed May 5, 2011).
16. "A Byte Out of History: Organized Crime and 'Joe's Barbecue,'" FBI Headline Archives, http://www2.fbi.gov/page2/nov03/crime111403.htm (accessed May 5, 2011).
17. Deloach, pp. 306, 308–9.
18. "Turning Point: Using Intel to Stop the Mob," Federal Bureau of Investigation, http://www.fbi.gov/news/stories/2007/august/mobintel2_080907 (accessed May 5, 2011).
19. Turner, p. 164; Roemer, *Accardo,* pp. 403, 410; Roemer, *War of the Godfathers,* pp. 71, 130; *Congressional Record* 139 Cong Rec E 571 (March 10, 1993); FBI Files No. 92–911 (Carmine Galante) and 92–389 (Abner Zwillman).
20. Deloach, p. 303; "Turning Point: Using Intel to Stop the Mob."
21. "Sherman Anti-Trust Act," Wikipedia, http://en.wikipedia.org/wiki/Sherman_An titrust_Act (accessed May 7, 2011).
22. Theoharis, pp. 6, 46–7.
23. "Clayton Antitrust Act," Wikipedia, http://en.wikipedia.org/wiki/Clayton_An titrust_Act (accessed May 7, 2011).
24. Theoharis, pp. 6–7.
25. Gentry, p. 156.
26. Theoharis, pp. 112–13.
27. "History of the National Firearms Act," Bureau of Alcohol, Tobacco, Firearms and Explosives, http://www.atf.gov/firearms/nfa (accessed May 7, 2011).
28. U.S. Code Title 18 — Crimes and Criminal Procedure Sections 2314 and 2315.
29. U.S. Code Title 18 — Crimes and Criminal Procedure Section 1073.
30. U.S. Code Title 18 — Crimes and Criminal Procedure Section 371; Summers, p. 284.
31. *The New York Times,* Jan. 16, 1958; June 26, 1958.
32. Messick, p. 169; Overstreet, p. 371.
33. Summers, p. 284; Messick, p. 169.
34. W.C. Sullivan memo to A.H. Belmont, July 9, 1958.
35. Gentry, pp. 454–5.
36. Ibid.
37. Davis, p. 96; Nash, p. 94; Ungar, p. 393.
38. Sullivan monograph, Section 1, p. iii.

39. Ibid., p. xii.

40. Ibid., p. xiii.

41. Ibid., p. 50.

42. Sullivan monograph, Section 2, p. i.

43. Ibid., p. iii.

44. Ibid., pp. vi, 85.

45. Ibid., p. vii.

46. Sullivan monograph, Section 1, p. i.

47. Powers, p. 335.

48. *The New York Times,* Dec. 4, 20 and 31, 1957.

49. *The New York Times,* Jan. 14 and 15, 1958.

50. *The New York Times,* Jan. 21 and 25, 1958.

51. *The New York Times,* Jan. 29, 1958; Feb. 5, 7 and 26, 1958.

52. *The New York Times,* Feb. 26, 1958; March 6, 1958.

53. *The New York Times,* Oct. 16 and 25, 1958; May 6 and 18, 1959; Jan. 1, 1960; April 22, 1960.

54. *The New York Times,* Dec. 3–5, 1957.

55. *The New York Times,* Dec. 16, 19 and 30, 1957; Jan. 8, 1958.

56. *The New York Times,* Jan. 9, 1958.

57. *The New York Times,* Jan. 12, 1958.

58. *The New York Times,* Jan. 29, 1958; April 28, 1958.

59. *The New York Times,* July 11, 1958; Aug. 17 and 19, 1958; " New York state election, 1958," Wikipedia, http://en.wikipedia.org/wiki/New_York_gubernatorial_election,_1958 (accessed May 10, 2011).

60. *The New York Times,* Dec. 4, 1957.

61. *The New York Times,* Dec. 4 and 5, 1957.

62. *The New York Times,* Dec. 17, 1957; April 3, 1958; Nov. 21, 1958; March 21, 1959.

63. *The New York Times,* Nov. 24, 1957; Dec. 4, 1957.

64. *The New York Times,* Dec. 6 and 8, 1957.

65. *The New York Times,* Dec. 8, 11 and, 1957.

66. *The New York Times,* Dec. 11 and 15, 1957; Feb. 11, 1958.

67. *The New York Times,* Dec. 7, 1957.

68. *The New York Times,* Nov. 30, 1957; Dec. 4, 14 and 18, 1957.

69. *The New York Times,* Dec. 5 and 17, 1957.

70. *The New York Times,* Dec. 19 and 21, 1957; Jan. 3, 1958.

71. *The New York Times,* Jan. 7 and 8, 1958.

72. *The New York Times,* Jan. 8, 1958.

73. *The New York Times,* Jan. 8 and 9, 1958; Feb. 4, 1958; Sept. 9, 1971; *State of New Jersey, Plaintiff — respondent, v. Ray R. Louf, Joseph Zicarelli and Frank Mallamaci, Defendants — appellants,* New Jersey Superior Court, Appellate Division, Decided July 2, 1973.

74. *The New York Times,* Nov. 24, 1957; Dec. 18, 1957.

75. *United States of America v. Vito Genovese, Appellant,* 236 F.2d 757 (3rd Cir. 1956); *The New York Times,* Dec. 18, 1957.

76. *The New York Times,* Dec. 18 and 25, 1957; Jan. 3, 1958; March 11, 1958.

77. *The New York Times,* Jan. 23, 1958; Sept. 3, 1958; *Daytona Beach Morning Journal,* June 14, 1962; *The Morning Call* (Allentown, PA), Jan. 3, 2008.

78. *The New York Times,* Nov. 4, 1958; June 23, 1970; Nov. 6, 1971; *Carlo Gambino, Petitioner — appellant, v. Immigration and Naturalization Service, Respondent — appellee,* 419 F.2d 1355 (2nd Cir. 1970).

79. *United States of America, Plaintiff — Appellee, v. Joe Profaci, Also Known as Joseph Profaci and as Giuseppe Profaci, Defendant — Appellant,* 274 F.2d 289 (2nd Cir. 1960).

80. *The New York Times,* June 6, 1959; *Observer-Dispatch* (Utica, NY), Dec. 6, 1962.

81. *The New York Times,* Aug. 24, 1960; *United States of America, v. Antonio Riela, Appellant,* 337 F.2d 986 (3rd Cir. 1964).

82. *The New York Times,* July 16, 1957; Nov. 26, 1957; Dec. 10, 1957.

83. *The New York Times,* Dec. 13–15, 1957.

84. *The New York Times,* Dec. 21–22, 1957.
85. "John C. Montana," Wikipedia.
86. *The New York Times,* Jan. 10, 1958.
87. *The New York Times,* Jan. 14–15, 1958.
88. *The New York Times,* Feb. 13, 21 and 28, 1958; March 7, 1958.
89. *The New York Times,* April 1 and 30, 1958.
90. *The New York Times,* April 29, 1958; May 1, 1958.
91. *The New York Times,* Aug. 8 and 15, 1958.
92. *The New York Times,* Aug. 13–16, 1958.
93. *The New York Times,* Aug. 20–23 and 28, 1958; Sept. 4, 1958.
94. *The New York Times,* Sept. 12–13 and 23, 1958; Dec. 10, 1958.
95. *The New York Times,* Nov. 7, 1958.
96. *The New York Times,* Dec. 3, 1958; Jan. 14, 1959.
97. *The New York Times,* Jan. 15–17, 22 and 28, 1959.
98. *The New York Times,* Feb. 7, 1959; March 16, 1959.
99. *The New York Times,* March 18–19, 1959.
100. *The New York Times,* March 21, 25 and 26, 1959.
101. *The New York Times,* April 15, 1959; May 5, 8 and 15, 1959.
102. *The New York Times,* May 12, 1959; June 10, 1959.
103. *The New York Times,* June 17, 1959.
104. *The New York Times,* June 18, 26 and 30, 1959; July 18, 21, 22 and 31, 1959.
105. *The New York Times,* July 9, 1959; Aug. 1 and 22, 1959; Sept. 1, 1959; Dec. 9 and 12, 1959; March 16, 1960.
106. *The New York Times,* Aug. 13, 1959; Nov. 21, 1959.
107. *The New York Times,* Aug. 14, 15 and 21, 1959; Oct. 6, 1959.
108. *The New York Times,* Oct. 6, 1959; Nov. 28, 1959; Dec. 19, 1959.
109. *The New York Times,* Dec. 20, 1959.
110. *The New York Times,* Dec. 22 and 24, 1959; Jan. 21 and 29, 1960; Nov. 2, 1960.

Chapter 10

1. *The New York Times,* Nov. 30, 1957.
2. *The New York Times,* Sept. 25, 1958; June 17 and 23, 1958; March 14 and 29, 1959; April 2 and 28, 1959; May 30, 1959; June 18, 1959; April 18, 1960; "Apalachin: After the Raid," The Community Press Web site, Tioga County, NY, http://www.greaterowego.com/communitypress/1997/12-97/BARBARA.htm (accessed June 30, 2011).
3. *The New York Times,* April 23, 1960; "Apalachin: After the Raid."
4. *The New York Times,* July 28, 1960; Dec. 2, 1960; "Apalachin: After the Raid."
5. *The New York Times,* July 31, 1959; Internet Movie Database, http://www.imdb.com (accessed June 30, 2011).
6. *The New York Times,* Nov. 21, 23, 24, 25, 27 and 28, 1957.
7. *The New York Times,* Dec. 6, 1957; Hafer, "Mafia in Apalachin."
8. *The New York Times,* July 25, 1958; Jan. 27, 1962.
9. *The New York Times,* Feb. 13, 1958; Aug. 26, 1958; June 2, 1959.
10. *The New York Times,* March 4, 1959; Nov. 1, 1959; *United States of America v. Dominic Alaimo, Appellant,* 297 F.2d 604 (1962).
11. *The New York Times,* Sept. 27, 1959; Dec. 18 and 23, 1959; May 25, 1960.
12. *The New York Times,* May 19, 1960; July 12, 1960; March 10, 1964; Aug. 5, 1964; Dec. 1, 1964; Aug. 28, 1965; Aug. 23, 1968; Feb. 21, 1969; June 13, 1970; Nov. 20, 1975.
13. *The New York Times,* Dec. 24, 1957; April 21, 1958; May 13, 1958; June 29, 1958.
14. *Hearings Before the Select Committee on Improper Activities in the Labor or Management Field* (hereafter "McClellan Hearings").
15. Fox, pp. 19–20, 308–12; Newton, pp. 129–31, 164, 175–6.
16. McClellan Hearings, p. 12192.
17. Ibid., pp. 12201–12465.

18. Ibid., pp. 12201–19, 12251–8, 12321, 12341, 12429.
19. Ibid., pp. 12201–12465.
20. Ibid., pp. 12404–12415.
21. Ibid., pp. 12293–12318.
22. Ibid.
23. Ibid.
24. Hudson.
25. Jones, "Get 'The Right Man.'"
26. Ibid.; Tuohy, "New York Stories."
27. *The New York Times,* June 5, 1958; July 7, 9 and 10, 1958; Jones, "Get 'The Right Man.'"
28. *The New York Times,* April 3, 4 and 18, 1959; Jones, "Get 'The Right Man.'"
29. Jones, "Get 'The Right Man'"; *The New York Times,* July 30, 1960; Anthony Bruno, "The Genovese Family," truTV Crime Library, http://www.trutv.com/library/crime/gangste rs_outlaws/family_epics/genovese1/14.html (accessed July 10, 2011).
30. *The New York Times,* March 31, 1959; July 10, 1959; May 7, 1960; Nov. 22, 1960; May 16, 1961; June 26, 1962; July 11, 1962; June 14, 1963; Jones, "Get 'The Right Man.'"
31. *The New York Times,* June 4, 1959; May 18, 1960; June 26, 1962; July 11, 1962; Jones, "Get 'The Right Man.'"
32. Bruno, "The Genovese Family"; *The New York Times,* April 27, 1960; May 17, 1960; Oct. 22, 1963; *Vito Genovese, Petitioner — appellant, v. United States of America, Respondent — appellee,* 378 F.2d 748 (1967).
33. *The New York Times,* Dec. 12 and 20, 1957; May 8, 1958; June 13, 1958; Feb. 11, 1959.
34. *The New York Times,* May 22 and 23, 1959; June 5, 1959; Dec. 19, 1959.
35. *The New York Times,* Sept. 22, 1959; Oct. 1 and 8, 1959.
36. *The New York Times,* Oct. 26, 27, 29 and 30, 1959.
37. *The New York Times,* Oct. 31, 1959.
38. *The New York Times,* Nov. 3, 1959.
39. *The New York Times,* Nov. 5, 1959.
40. *The New York Times,* Nov. 6, 1959.
41. *The New York Times,* Nov. 10, 1959.
42. *The New York Times,* Nov. 10, 11, 13 and 14, 1957.
43. *The New York Times,* Nov. 17, 18, 19, 20, 24 and 26, 1959.
44. *The New York Times,* Dec. 3, 1959.
45. *The New York Times,* Dec. 4, 1959.
46. *The New York Times,* Dec. 8, 10 and 11, 1959.
47. *The New York Times,* Dec. 15 and 16, 1959.
48. *The New York Times,* Dec. 17, 1959.
49. *The New York Times,* Dec. 18, 1959.
50. *The New York Times,* Dec. 18 and 19, 1959.
51. *The New York Times,* Jan. 14, 1960.
52. *The New York Times,* Jan. 15, 1960; "The Law: The Apalachin Verdict," *Time,* Dec. 28, 1959.

Chapter 11

1. Schwartz, 21–44, 49, 75, 86, 133–4, 154–5, 159–60, 165–6, 347–8.
2. Fox, pp. 14, 20; English, *Paddy Whacked,* pp. 265, 267.
3. English, *Paddy Whacked,* pp. 266–7; Fox, p. 43; Newton, p. 23; Russo, pp. 52–3; Schwartz, p. 95; Denton and Morris, pp. 22–3; Russo, p. 361.
4. Fox, p. 55, 61; Denton and Morris, p. 186; Schwarz, pp. 97–105, 172–263.
5. Edward Renehan Jr., *The Kennedys at War, 1937–1945* (New York: Doubleday, 2002), p. 304; Robert Donovan, *PT-109: John F. Kennedy in WW II* (New York: McGraw-Hill, 1961), pp. 99–184.
6. Fox, pp. 101, 296, 315, 320–1; Denton and Morris, pp. 173, 192; Schwarz, p. 324; English, *Paddy Whacked,* p. 261.

7. Fox, p. 317.

8. Fox, pp. 318–19.

9. Ibid., pp. 330; Denton and Morris, p. 194; Russo, pp. 362–3.

10. Denton and Morris, pp. 218, 220; Scheim, pp. 299–303.

11. Russo, pp. 363, 367–8.

12. Fox, pp. 331–2; Russo, p. 368.

13. Fox, pp. 332–3; Russo, p. 368; English, *Paddy Whacked,* p. 278.

14. Denton and Morris, pp. 180–2, 369–78; Fox, p. 333.

15. English, *Paddy Whacked,* pp. 280–1; Fox, pp. 333–4; Russo, pp. 363–4; Schwarz, pp. 411–12.

16. Fox, pp. 332, 334; Denton and Morris, pp. 214–15; "1960 Presidential Election Primaries," John F. Kennedy Presidential Library and Museum, http://www.jfklibrary.org/Research/Ready-Reference/JFK-Miscellaneous-Information/Primaries-1960.aspx (accessed July 20, 2011).

17. Fox, p. 334.

18. Denton and Morris, p. 218.

19. Ibid., p. 217; Peter Carlson, "Another Race to the Finish," *The Washington Post,* Nov. 17, 2000.

20. Carlson.

21. Fox, p. 334; Denton and Morris, p. 217; Carlson; Russo, p. 401.

22. Fox, p. 335.

23. *The New York Times,* June 7, 1960; Nov. 21 and 29, 1960.

24. *United States of America, Appellee, v. Russell A. Bufalino, Ignatius Cannone, Paul C. Castellano, Joseph F. Civello, Frank A. Desimone, Natale Evola, Louis A. Larasso, Carmine Lombardozzi, Joseph Magliocco, Frank T. Majuri, Michele Miranda, John C. Montana, John Ormento, James Osticco, Joseph Profaci, Anthony P. Riela, John T. Scalish, Angelo J. Sciandra, Simone Scozzari and Pasquale Turrigiano, Defendants—Appellants,* 285 F.2d 408 (2nd Cir. 1960).

25. Ibid.

26. Ibid.

27. Ibid.

28. Ibid.

29. Ibid.

30. Ibid.

31. Ibid.

32. Russo, p. 372; *The New York Times,* Nov. 19, 1960; Jan. 14, 1961.

33. Fox, pp. 335–6; Russo, pp. 405–6.

34. Fox, p. 339; *The New York Times,* Nov. 27, 1971; Jonathan Van Meter, *The Last Good Time: Skinny D'Amato, the Notorious 500 Club, and the Rise and Fall of Atlantic City* (New York: Bloomsbury, 2003), pp. 206–7.

35. English, *Paddy Whacked,* pp. 283–4; Fox, 339–40.

36. Fox, pp. 338–9; Russo, pp. 407–8; Schwarz, p. 414.

37. Fox, pp. 336–8; Russo, pp. 424–5; Schwarz, p. 413.

38. Denton and Morris, p. 284; English, *Paddy Whacked,* p. 284; Fox, p. 341.

39. Denton and Morris, p. 239; Fox, pp. 336, 347; Russo, p. 410.

40. English, *Paddy Whacked,* p. 285; Fox, p. 341; Russo, pp. 406–8.

41. Scheim, p. 54.

42. English, *Paddy Whacked,* p. 285.

43. Scheim, p. 54.

44. Ibid., pp. 60–1.

45. Ibid., pp. 56–7; English, *Paddy Whacked,* p. 285.

46. Fox, p. 342; Scheim, p. 59.

47. Waldron, pp. 77–8.

48. Raab, p. 125; Scheim, p. 54.

49. English, *Paddy Whacked,* p. 288; Philip Melanson, *The Robert F. Kennedy Assassination* (New York, S.P.I. Books, 1991).

50. Schwarz, pp. 433–6.

Chapter 12

1. Social Security Death Index (hereafter, SSDI).

2. "Joe Profaci," Wikipedia, http://en.wikipedia.org/wiki/Joe_Profaci (accessed April 7, 2011).

3. "Joseph Magliocco," Wikipedia, http://en.wikipedia.org/wiki/Joseph_Magliocco (accessed Jan. 9, 2011).

4. "John C. Montana," Wikipedia, http://en.wikipedia.org/wiki/John_C._Montana (accessed Jan. 9, 2011).

5. "Joseph Biondo," http://en.wikipedia.org/wiki/Joseph_Biondo (accessed April 9, 2011).

6. "Tommy Lucchese," Wikipedia, http://en.wikipedia.org/wiki/Tommy_Lucchese (accessed April 9, 2011).

7. "Frank DeSimone," Wikipedia, http://en.wikipedia.org/wiki/Frank_DeSimone (accessed April 9, 2011).

8. "Joseph Lanza," Wikipedia, http://en.wikipedia.org/wiki/Joseph_Lanza (accessed April 9, 2011).

9. SSDI.

10. "Vito Genovese," Wikipedia, http://en.wikipedia.org/wiki/Vito_Genovese (accessed Jan. 9, 2011); Bonanno, *A Man of Honor,* p. 119.

11. "Joseph Civello," Wikipedia, http://en.wikipedia.org/wiki/Joseph_Civello (accessed April 9, 2011).

12. "Gaspar DiGregorio," Wikipedia, http://en.wikipedia.org/wiki/Gaspar_DiGregorio (accessed April 9, 2011).

13. SSDI.

14. Ibid.

15. Ibid.

16. Ibid.

17. "Little Joe" Shots, "Montreal Crime Family," Mafia-International.com, http://realdealmafia.com/montreal9.html (accessed April 12, 2011).

18. SSDI.

19. Ibid.

20. "Michele Miranda," Wikipedia, http://en.wikipedia.org/wiki/Michele_Miranda (accessed Jan. 9, 2011); *The New York Times,* March 3, 1969; Sept. 21, 1973.

21. "Natale Evola," Wikipedia, http://en.wikipedia.org/wiki/Natale_Evola (accessed Jan. 9, 2011).

22. SSDI; Jones, "Get 'The Right Man.'"

23. *The New York Times,* Nov. 27 and 29, 1968; May 15, 1974; May 8, 1974; July 20–21, 1974.

24. SSDI.

25. Ibid.; "Stefano LaSalle," Wikipedia, http://en.wikipedia.org/wiki/Stefano_LaSalle (accessed April 9, 2011).

26. SSDI.

27. "Sam Giancana," Wikipedia, http://en.wikipedia.org/wiki/Sam_Giancana (accessed April 9, 2011).

28. SSDI.

29. "John T. Scalish," Wikipedia, http://en.wikipedia.org/wiki/John_T._Scalish (accessed April 9, 2011).

30. "Gambino Crime Family," Wikipedia, http://en.wikipedia.org/wiki/Gambino_crime_family (accessed April 11, 2011).

31. "Crime Bosses of Detroit," American Mafia, http://www.onewal.com/maf-b-de.html; Newton, p. 231.

32. SSDI.

33. Ibid.

34. "Carmine Tramunti," La Cosa Nostra Database, http://lacndb.com/php/Info.php?name=Carmine%20Tramunti (accessed April 9, 2011).

35. Jones, "Mob Meeting at Apalachin"; SSDI.

36. *The New York Times,* June 4, 1949; May 18, 1960; July 11, 1962; Oct. 12, 1977; March 4, 1978; April 14, 1978; June 14, 1978; Feb. 28, 1979; March 8, 1979; July 13, 1979; "Carmine Galante," Wikipedia, http://en.wikipedia.org/wiki/Carmine_Galante (accessed April 9, 2011).

37. "Giuseppe Cotroni," Mafia Wiki, http://mafia.wikia.com/wiki/Giuseppe_Cotroni (accessed April 9, 2011).

38. "Rosario Carlisi," La Cosa Nostra Database, http://lacndb.com/Info.php?name= Rosario%20Carlisi (accessed April 2, 2011); SSDI.

39. "Crime Bosses of Pittsburgh," American Mafia, http://www.onewal.com/maf-b-pi.html; SSDI.

40. "Giuseppe Settecase," La Cosa Nostra Database, http://www.lacndb.com/php/Si_Info.php?name=Giuseppe%20Settecase (accessed April 9, 2011).

41. SSDI.

42. *The New York Times,* May 7, 1970; Nov. 5, 1970; March 17, 1971; April 4 and 24, 1971; SSDI.

43. Mario Machi, Allan May and Charlie Molino, "St. Louis, Mo.," Rick Porrello's American Mafia, http://www.americanmafia.com/Cities/St_Louis.html (accessed April 16, 2011); SSDI.

44. Allan May, "Nick Civella: Kansas City Chief," Rick Porrello's American Mafia, http://www.americanmafia.com/Allan_May_1-31-00.html (accessed April 12, 2011).

45. "Joseph Ida," La Cosa Nostra Database, http://lacndb.com/Info.php?name=Joseph%20Ida (accessed April 12, 2011); SSDI.

46. SSDI.

47. Ibid.

48. "Frank Majuri," Wikipedia, http://en.wikipedia.org/wiki/Frank_Majuri (accessed Jan. 9, 2011); SSDI.

49. "Paul Castellano," Wikipedia, http://en.wikipedia.org/wiki/Paul_Castellano (accessed Jan. 9, 2011).

50. "Santo Trafficante, Jr.," Wikipedia, http://en.wikipedia.org/wiki/Santo_Trafficante,_Jr. (accessed April 9, 2011); HSCA pp. 214–15; Waldron, pp. 756–7.

51. SSDI.

52. "Philip Buccola," Mafia Wiki, http://mafia.wikia.com/wiki/Philip_Buccola (accessed April 15, 2011).

53. SSDI.

54. The American Mafia, http://www.onewal.com/maf-chr5.html; SSDI.

55. *Sun-Sentinel* (Fort Lauderdale), May 27, 1988; 891 F.2d 296: *United States of America, Plaintiff— appellee, v. Stanley Reppucci, Defendant— appellant,* United States Court of Appeals, Ninth Circuit.— 891 F.2d 296; SSDI.

56. "Louis LaRasso," Wikipedia, http://en.wikipedia.org/wiki/Louis_LaRasso (accessed Jan. 9, 2011); *The New York Times,* April 20, 2001; June 5, 2003; Sept. 5, 2008.

57. Rocco LaDucca, "Utica: The Mob Files," *Observer-Dispatch* (Utica, NY), May 1–9, 2009; SSDI.

58. SSDI.

59. "Carmine Lombardozzi," Wikipedia, http://en.wikipedia.org/wiki/Carmine_Lombardozzi (accessed Jan. 9, 2011); *The New York Times,* April 24, 1964; Dec. 1 and 19, 1964; Aug. 28, 1965; Oct. 27, 1965; Nov. 13, 1965; Dec. 7, 1967; Aug. 23, 1968; Sept. 21, 1968; March 19, 1969; June 13, 1970; Sept. 27 and 30, 1970; Nov. 20, 1975; April 16, 1981.

60. "Frank Balistrieri," Wikipedia, http://en.wikipedia.org/wiki/Frank_Balistrieri (accessed April 9, 2011).

61. SSDI.

62. Ibid.

63. "Russell Bufalino," Wikipedia, http://en.wikipedia.org/wiki/Russell_Bufalino (accessed Jan. 9, 2011).

64. SSDI.

65. Ibid.

66. Ibid.
67. Ibid.
68. Ibid.
69. *The New York Times,* Oct. 30, 1965; Oct. 13, 1971; Aug. 20, 1975; SSDI.
70. Anthony Bruno, "The Disappearance of Jimmy Hoffa," truTV Crime Library, http://www.trutv.com/library/crime/notorious_murders/famous/jimmy_hoffa/1.html (accessed April 14, 2011); "Anthony Giacalone," Wikipedia, http://en.wikipedia.org/wiki/Anthony_Giacolone (accessed April 9, 2011).
71. SSDI.
72. "Joseph Bonanno," Wikipedia, http://en.wikipedia.org/wiki/Joe_Bonanno (accessed April 9, 2011).
73. SSDI.
74. Ibid.; "San Francisco crime family," Wikipedia, http://en.wikipedia.org/wiki/San_Francisco_crime_family (accessed April 14, 2011).
75. "Crime Bosses of Pittsburgh," American Mafia; SSDI.
76. SSDI.
77. "FBI Mob Files Deal with Garbage," The Chicago Syndicate, http://www.thechicagosyndicate.com/2005_12_11_archive.html (accessed April 16, 2011); SSDI.
78. SSDI.
79. "Aniello Migliore," Wikipedia, http://en.wikipedia.org/wiki/Aniello_Migliore (accessed April 9, 2011).
80. "Joseph Barbara Jr.," Mafia Wiki, http://mafia.wikia.com/wiki/Joseph_Barbara_Jr (accessed April 9, 2011).
81. "Giovanni Bonventre," Wikipedia, http://en.wikipedia.org/wiki/Giovanni_Bonventre (accessed Jan. 9, 2011).
82. "Simone Scozzari," Wikipedia, http://en.wikipedia.org/wiki/Simone_Scozzari (accessed April 9, 2011).
83. SSDI; "Bufalino Crime Family Membership," Gangster BB, http://www.gangsterbb.net/threads/ubbthreads.php?ubb=showflat&Number=597486 (accessed April 20, 2011); "Salvatore Trivalino," Mafia Wiki, http://mafia.wikia.com/wiki/Salvatore_Trivalino, (accessed April 20, 2011).
84. SSDI; "Bufalino Crime Family Membership," Gangster BB.
85. SSDI.
86. Ibid.
87. Allan May, "Louis Fratto: The Mob's Invisible Man," http://www.midwestmafia.com (accessed April 15, 2011); SSDI.

Bibliography

Books

Behan, Tom. *The Camorra*. London: Routledge, 1996.

Davis, John. *Mafia Dynasty: The Rise and Fall of the Gambino Crime Family*. New York: Harper Paperbacks, 1993.

Deloach, Cartha. *Hoover's FBI: The Inside Story by Hoover's Trusted Lieutenant*. Washington, DC: Regnery Publishing, 1997.

Denton, Sally, and Roger Morris. *The Money and the Power: The Making of Las Vegas and Its Hold on America*. New York: Knopf, 2001.

Dickie, John. *Cosa Nostra: A History of the Sicilian Mafia*. London: Coronet Books, 2004.

English, T.J. *Havana Nocturne: How the Mob Owned Cuba and Then Lost It to the Revolution*. New York: Harper Paperbacks, 2009.

_____. *Paddy Whacked: The Untold Story of the Irish American Gangster*. New York: Regan Books, 2005.

Farrell, Ronald. *The Black Book and the Mob: The Untold Story of the Control of Nevada's Casinos*. Madison: University of Wisconsin Press, 1995.

Fox, Stephen. *Blood and Power: Organized Crime in Twentieth-Century America*. New York: William Morrow, 1989.

Gentry, Curt. *J. Edgar Hoover: The Man and the Secrets*. New York: W.W. Norton, 2001.

Hack, Richard. *Puppetmaster: The Secret Life of J. Edgar Hoover*. Beverly Hills, CA: New Millennium, 2007.

Hammer, Richard. *Playboy's Illustrated History of Organized Crime*. Chicago: Playboy Press, 1975.

Helmer, William, and Rick Mattix. *Public Enemies: America's Criminal Past, 1919–1940*. New York: Checkmark, 1998.

Hess, Henner. *Mafia & Mafiosi: Origin, Power, and Myth*. London: Hurst, 1998.

Kessler, Ronald. *The Bureau: The Secret History of the FBI*. New York: St. Martin's Press, 2002.

Lupo, Salvatore. *The History of the Mafia*. New York: Columbia University Press, 2009.

Maclean, Don. *Pictorial History of the Mafia*. New York: Galahad Books, 1974.

Merz, Charles. *The Dry Decade*. Garden City, NY: Doubleday, Doran, 1930.

Messick, Hank. *John Edgar Hoover: A Critical Examination of the Director and of the Continuing Alliance between Crime, Business, and Politics*. New York: David McKay, 1972.

Messick, Hank, and Burt Goldblatt. *The Mobs and the Mafia: The Illustrated History of Organized Crime*. New York: Ballantine Books, 1972.

Moldea, Dan. *Dark Victory: Ronald Reagan, MCA, and the Mob*. New York: Viking, 1986.

Nash, Jay. *Citizen Hoover: A Critical Study of the Life and Times of J. Edgar Hoover and His FBI*. Chicago: Nelson-Hall, 1972.

Newton, Michael. *Mr. Mob: The Life and Crimes of Moe Dalitz*. Jefferson, NC: McFarland, 2007.

Overstreet, Harry, and Bonaro Overstreet. *The FBI in Our Open Society*. New York: W.W. Norton, 1969.

Paoli, Letizia. *Mafia Brotherhoods: Organized Crime, Italian Style.* New York: Oxford University Press, 2003.

Peterson, Virgil. *The Mob: 200 Years of Organized Crime in New York.* Ottawa, IL: Green Hill, 1983.

Powers, Richard. *Secrecy and Power: The Life of J. Edgar Hoover.* New York: Free Press, 1987.

Raab, Selwyn. *Five Families: The Rise, Decline, and Resurgence of America's Most Powerful Mafia Empires.* New York: Thomas Dunne Books, 2005.

Roemer, William Jr. *Accardo: The Genuine Godfather.* New York: Ivy Books, 1996.

_____. *War of the Godfathers.* New York: Ivy Books, 1991.

Russo, Gus. *The Outfit: The Role of Chicago's Underworld in the Shaping of Modern America.* New York: Bloomsbury, 2003.

Scheim, David. *Contract on America: The Mafia Murder of President John F. Kennedy.* New York: Shapolsky, 1988.

Schwarz, Ted. *Joseph P. Kennedy.* Hoboken, NJ: John Wiley & Sons, 2003.

Summers, Anthony. *Official and Confidential: The Secret Life of J. Edgar Hoover.* New York: Pocket Books, 1994.

Theoharis, Athan, ed. *The FBI: A Comprehensive Reference Guide.* New York: Checkmark Books, 2000.

Turkus, Burton, and Sid Feder. *Murder, Inc.: The Story of the Syndicate.* New York: Da Capo Press, 2003.

Turner, William. *Hoover's FBI.* New York: Thunder's Mouth Press, 1993.

Ungar, Sanford. *FBI.* New York: Little, Brown, 1976.

Waldron, Lamar. *Legacy of Secrecy.* Berkeley, CA: Counterpoint, 2009.

Whitehead, Don. *The FBI Story.* New York: Random House, 1956.

Government Publications

Federal Bureau of Investigation. *Mafia.* Internal monograph, July 9, 1958.

Final Report of the Special Committee to Investigate Organized Crime in Interstate Commerce. Washington, D.C.: U.S. Government Printing Office, 1951.

Hearings before the Select Committee on Improper Activities in the Labor or Management Field, June 30–July 3, 1958. Washington, D.C.: U.S. Government Printing Office, 1958.

House Select Committee on Assassinations. *The Final Assassinations Report.* New York: Bantam, 1979.

Second Interim Report of the Special Committee to Investigate Organized Crime in Interstate Commerce. Washington, D.C.: U.S. Government Printing Office, 1951.

Articles

Hudson, Mike. "Magaddino's Apalachin blunder led to an aftermath of murder, arrests here." *Niagara Falls Reporter,* Jan. 29, 2008.

Kelly, Jack. "How America Met the Mob." *American Heritage Magazine* Vol. 51, No. 4 (July/August 2000).

"The Law: The Apalachin Conspiracy." *Time* Vol. 74, No. 26 (Dec. 28, 1959).

Lombardo, Robert. "The Black Hand: Terror by Letter in Chicago," *Journal of Contemporary Criminal Justice* 18 (November 2002): 394–409.

The New York Times, October 1888 through December 1960.

Persico, Joseph. "Vendetta in New Orleans." *American Heritage Magazine* Vol. 24, No. 4 (July 1973).

Internet Sources

"A Look Back," American Mafia, http://www.americanmafia.com/Allan_May_9-25-00.html (accessed Jan. 9, 2011).

The American Mafia, http://www.onewal.com/maf-chr1.html.

"The Apalachin Meeting," Ovi Magazine (Nov. 14, 2009), http://www.ovimagazine.com/art/5084 (accessed Jan. 19, 2011).

Folsom, Robert. "The Big Pardon," New Criminologist, http://www.newcriminologist.com/art icle.asp?cid=103&nid=2149 (accessed, Jan. 20, 2011).

GangRule.com, http://www.gangrule.com.

Hafer, Gary. "Mafia in Apalachin." http://apalachin.net/apalachin01.htm (accessed Jan. 8, 2011).

Hunt, Thomas, and Martha Sheldon. "America's First Mafia War," American Mafia, http://www. onewal.com/a016/f_nolafeud.html (accessed Feb. 3, 2011).

Jones, Thom. "Get 'The Right Man': How the FBN Nailed Vito Genovese," Gangsters Inc., http://gangstersinc.ning.com/profiles/blogs/get-the-right-man-how-the-fbn (accessed April 20, 2011).

_____. "Lucky's Luck." Mob Corner, http://realdealmafia.com/luciano.html (accessed March 19, 2011).

La Sorte, Mike. "Attendee Profiles at the 1957 Apalachin Mob Confab," American Mafia, http://www.americanmafia.com/Feature_Articles_415.html (accessed Jan. 9, 2011).

_____. "The Mob on the Nob," American Mafia, http://www.americanmafia.com/Feature_Ar ticles_259.html (accessed Jan. 9, 2011).

Mafia Wiki (various articles), http://mafia.wikia.com/wiki/Mafia_Wiki.

"Mob Meeting at Apalachin: The Big Barbeque," Gangsters Inc., http://gangstersinc.ning. com/profiles/blogs/mob-meeting-at-apalachin-the (accessed Jan. 19, 2011).

"Mobsters at the Apalachin Mob Meeting," The Chicago Syndicate, http://www.thechicagosyn-dicate.com/2007/11/mobsters-at-apalachin-mob-meeting.html (accessed Jan. 19, 2011).

Tuohy, John. "New York Stories," American Mafia, http://www.americanmafia.com/Feature_Ar ticles_185.html (accessed July 9, 2011).

_____. "The Raid at Apalachin," American Mafia, http://www.americanmafia.com/Feature_Ar ticles_174.html (accessed Jan. 9, 2011).

Wikipedia (various articles), http://www.wikipedia.org.

Index